FROM THE BLACK BAR

From the Black Bar

VOICES FOR EQUAL JUSTICE

Gilbert Ware

New Perspectives on Black America
Herbert Hill, *General Editor*

Capricorn Books

G. P. PUTNAM'S SONS, NEW YORK

*For my mother, Evelyn Brightful, and my aunt,
Jessie Manuel*

Contributors

Further notes on contributors and acknowledgments:

Grateful acknowledgment is made to the following publishers and individuals for permission to reprint material which is in copyright or of which they are the authorized publishers:

Langston Hughes, *The Panther and the Lash: Poems of Our Times*, New York: Alfred A. Knopf, 1969, p. 45.

Haywood Burns, "Black People and the Tyranny of American Law," *The Annals of the American Academy of Political and Social Science*, CCCCVII (May, 1973), p. 161.

Bruce McM. Wright, "The Black Judicial Officer and the Black Bar," a paper read at the meeting of the Judicial Council, National Bar Association, in Miami Beach, Florida, August 2, 1972.

Harry T. Alexander, quoted by Michele Washington, "Black Judges in White America," *The Black Law Journal*, Vol. 1, No. 3 (Winter, 1971), p. 245.

Milton B. Allen, Coppin State College; LLB, University of Maryland; JD, Univeristy of Maryland; state's attorney of Baltimore City, Maryland.

D'Army Bailey, AB, Clark University; LLB, Yale University; former city councilman, Berkeley, California, and now with Bailey & Bailey, Memphis, Tennessee; "Inequities of the Parole System in California," reprinted with permission of the author and the *Howard Law Journal* of Howard University.

Solomon Baylor, Coppin State College; LLB, University of Maryland; judge, District Court of Maryland (Baltimore).

Derrick A. Bell, Jr., AB, Duquesne University; LLB, University of Pittsburgh; professor of law, Harvard University; "Black Faith in a Racist Land," reprinted with permission of the author, the *Journal of Public Law* of Emory University, the *University of Toledo Law Review*, and the *Wisconsin Law Review* (copyright held by the *Wisconsin Law Review*).

Howard E. Bell, AB, Virginia Union University; LLB, and JD, Brooklyn Law School; judge, the Civil Court of the City of New York.

William H. Brown III, BS, Temple University; JD, University of Pennsylvania; former chairman, Equal Employment Opportunity Commission; partner, law firm of Schnader, Harrison, Segal and Lewis, Philadelphia, Pennsylvania.

Haywood Burns, AB, Harvard University; LLB, Yale University; former national director of the National Conference of Black Lawyers; professor, University of Buffalo Law School; "Political Uses of the Law," reprinted with permission of the author and the *Howard Law Journal* of Howard University.

George W. Crockett, Jr., AB, Morehouse College; LLB, Detroit College of Law; former chairman, Judicial Council, National Bar Association; presiding judge, Recorder's Court, Detroit, Michigan; "Racism in the Courts," reprinted with permission of the author and the *Journal of Public Law* of Emory University.

William H. Hastie, AB, Amherst College; LLB, Harvard University; SJD, Harvard University; senior United States circuit judge, U.S. Court of Appeals for the Third District.

A. Leon Higginbotham, Jr., AB, Antioch College; LLB, Yale University; judge, U.S. District Court for the Eastern District of Pennsylvania.

Joseph C. Howard, BS, University of Iowa; JD, University of Washington and Drake University; MS, Drake University; former chairman, Judicial Council of the National Bar Association; associate judge, Supreme Bench of Baltimore City, Maryland.

Mark E. Jones, AB, Roosevelt University; JD, Loyola University; treasurer, Judicial Council, National Bar Association; judge, Circuit Court of Cook County (Chicago, Illinois); "Racism in Special Courts," reprinted with permission of the author and the *Journal of Public Law* of Emory University.

CONTRIBUTORS

Damon J. Keith, AB, West Virginia State College; LLB, Howard University Law School; LLM, Wayne State University; judge, U.S. District Court for the Eastern District of Michigan.

Joyce I. London, AB, Howard University; JD, New England Law School; Reginald Heber Smith Community Lawyer Fellowship assigned to the Boston Legal Assistance Project.

Thurgood Marshall, AB, Lincoln University; LLB, Howard University Law School; Associate Justice, U.S. Supreme Court.

Robert L. Millender, Sr., AB, Detroit Institute of Technology; LLB, Detroit College of Law; senior partner in the law firm of Goodman, Eden, Millender, Goodman and Bedrosian, Detroit, Michigan.

Howard Moore, Jr., AB, Morehouse College; LLB, Boston University; partner in the law firm of Moore, Alexander and Rindskopf, Atlanta, Georgia, and Jane Bond Moore, AB, Spelman College; class of 1975, School of Law, University of California, Berkeley, California; founder and director, Research Center for Prison Movement Information, Berkeley, California; "Some Reflections: On the Criminal Justice System, Prisons, and Repressions," reprinted with permission of the author and the *Howard Law Journal* of Howard University.

Constance Baker Motley, AB, New York University; LLB, Columbia University; judge, U.S. District Court for the Southern District of New York.

Basil A. Paterson, BS, St. John's College; JD, St. John's Law School; vice-chairman, Democratic National Committee; partner in the law firm of Paterson, Michael, Dinkins and Jones, New York City.

Sherman W. Smith, AB, West Virginia State College; LLB, Howard University Law School; judge, Superior Court of Los Angeles, California.

Bruce McM. Wright, AB, Lincoln University; LLB, New York University; judge, Criminal Court of the City of New York now sitting on the Civil Court of the City of New York.

Contents

Preface

WHAT are black lawyers and judges thinking, saying, and doing about law, order, and justice? That is the central question in this book, which seeks to answer it through essays, interviews, and decisions that explain the administration of justice as it is and as it should be—according to black jurists. The book deals with the effect of race and class—not one, but both—on the administration of justice, which is considered a political process. Its rationale is that their dual experience as blacks and jurists makes these people particularly qualified to point the way toward fulfillment of America's promise of equal justice for all, even those whose race or class has made them politically powerless and therefore judicially abused. In this multifaceted treatment of race, class, law, and politics, the contributors are vigorously but constructively critical of the order of things. Their commentary is practical rather than theoretical, comprehensive rather than narrow.

This book grows out of my service as executive director of the Judicial Council of the National Bar Association since its inception in August, 1971. I am indebted to its members, especially JudGe Joseph C. Howard, for the opportunity to improve my understandiNg of our system of justice through my association with them. My work with the Judicial Council in its early months was facilitated by a research grant from Drexel University and a fellowship from the Metropolitan Applied Research Center whose staff, Ms. Dixie Moon and Ms. Ethel Woodson, were of immeasurable assistance to me. Similarly indispensable has been the research assistance I

A Cry For Equal Justice

GILBERT WARE

. . . The truth that blacks and whites must recognize is that whites, however sympathetic and concerned, are beneficiaries of a system and structure that grinds [*sic*] black people down. Blacks want a total change, and while sympathetic whites see the need for reform because the pinch is one of conscience or of a specific felt need, most have reservations about going as far as blacks deem necessary, or have far greater patience in waiting for needed change. All this means is that Negroes and whites can work together to the point where interest and understanding diverge. At that point, blacks had better be ready and prepared to protect their own interests. It is in the interest of white Americans as much as of blacks that the effort to obtain a truly democratic society here succeed, but the white man's interest seems more remote, more theoretical and less urgent. He seems under less immediate threat, and therefore can postpone dealing with the problem.[1]

—JUDGE ROBERT L. CARTER

IN New York City the lawyer asked the judge to put the defendant on probation to facilitate his rehabilitation. All three were white. Scanning the probation report about the defendant, the judge muttered bitterly three times, "How can he be rehabilitated? He's living with a colored woman." Hearing that, a black lawyer stepped forward to offer "some expert testimony on the question of living with a colored woman," but the judge hurried away when the lawyer announced his purpose. Charges were preferred, but the judge was exonerated. Later he became a Supreme Court justice.[2]

This anecdote illustrates the truism that lies at the heart of this book, which is that white judicial racism runs rampant in

America, systematically nourished by white judges and lawyers and steadfastly resisted by black judges and lawyers. Classism also poisons justice in America, but the emphasis here is on color rather than on class, primarily because the historic victims and opponents of American injustice, whatever its rationale, are black people. Many of these blacks have been, and are, lawyers and judges whose words and deeds constitute a powerful brief against blind justice. These jurists believe that the goddess Justice is not so much blindfolded as she is blind—blind to the imperative of ensuring equity in law enforcement. Their advocacy of judicial reform is rooted in their professional and personal experiences, and it brings to mind an assertion by John Oliver Killens.

"There are glaring exceptions to every rule, but it is a truism that American Negroes are the only people in America who, as a people, are for change," Killens writes. "This is true, again, not innately because of our color, but because of what America made of our color. The status quo has ever been the bane of black existence."[3]

Many black jurists are crying out for equal justice for people who suffer because they usually are deprived of it. The sufferers are people who are black or poor—or both. The criers are "the other blacks" in the system—that is, not the highly publicized arrested, accused, convicted, incarcerated blacks, but the highly unpublicized judges and lawyers who are themselves ensnared by the racism and classism that run through the system. By their words and action, many of these jurists are dramatizing both the difficulty and the possibility of changing the system to ensure equal justice under law regardless of class or color. To put their cry for equal justice in perspective, we must consider briefly the judicial process, the issue of racism and classism in the law, and the evolution of the black bar and bench. This will bring us to the core of this volume—namely, the readings that provide a firsthand account of the administration of justice as experienced and examined by black judges and lawyers.

The Judicial Process [4]

The distinctive characteristics of judicial power in America and other nations, Alexis de Tocqueville wrote in 1835, are its use to arbitrate disputes, its application to particular cases rather than to general principles, and its non-initiative quality. Additionally in America, judicial power is politically important because judges are authorized to base their decisions on the Constitution instead of the law. The moral sanction of laws is affected by judges' decisions to apply or not to apply them. It is not that law and morality are indistinguishable one from the other, Oliver Wendell Holmes noted in 1897, but that for purposes of learning and understanding the law, we must remember that law and morals differ. Bad and good people alike want to spare themselves the risk of contesting the state power that backs up the law. For other purposes, however, the distinction between law and morals may be of little, if any, significance.

Failure to differentiate between law and morals is the first of two fallacies Holmes mentioned. The second is the idea that logic alone determines the development of the law. Practitioners and professors of law often (and dangerously) think that the legal system "can be worked out like mathematics from some general axioms of conduct." Judicial decisions, like law school instruction, usually are couched in the language of logic. But any conclusion can be so stated. "You can always imply a condition in a contract," Holmes explained. "But why do you imply it? It is because of some belief as to the practice of the community or of a class, or because of some opinion as to policy, or, in short, because of some attitude of yours upon a matter not capable of founding exact logical conclusions."

As Holmes saw it, law lives not on logic, but on experience, on the demands of the time, the dominant moral and political thought, "intuitions of public policy, avowed or unconscious, even the prejudices which judges share with their fellowmen," and considerations of what is advantageous to given communities. Judges make decisions in accordance with their personal predilections, ethics, and comprehension of political realities, Holmes maintained, although they are also affected by the ethos and traditions of their profession. Adding to the complexity of the legal system suggested by Holmes' observations is what another eminent jurist, Felix Frankfurter, called "the core of the difficulties and misunderstandings about the judicial process." That core is the resolution of conflict involving contending principles. Single-principle questions are easy to resolve, but they are also very rare.

The resolution of conflict by judges and other lawmakers is likely to unsettle people who want rapid and sweeping change in the legal or larger order. Judges and lawyers, who have made the law their domain, belong to a conservative profession. It is conservative because lawyers have a vested interest in preserving the rules and procedures that undergird their claim to control of the legal system, because they are closely affiliated with big corporations, and because they work with the common law, which historically has handled new developments with old rules for as long as possible. Their social background and income help account for the conservatism of lawyers. As De Tocqueville wrote, however, not *all* members of their profession *always* favor order and oppose change, but most of them usually do. This helps account for their having won high social, economic, and political rewards, on the one hand, and having drawn serious distrust and resentment, on the other.

In conducting the legal business of the community, judges and lawyers are not immune to pressures. The canons of professional ethics, interest group activity, administrative and legislative action, trial by jury, the right to appeal, public opinion, mass media publicity, and their own conscience generate pressure. Of concern here is the response of judges whom Americans greatly respect, if not quite revere. Some judges are more concerned about the proper results than about meticulous respect for the technicalities of a case, while others value procedure more highly than outcome. Generally, they have leaned more toward restraining than toward inciting themselves in using the law to shape public policy. Attempt by anyone inside or outside their ranks to foster activism must be considered in this light, which is largely provided by the fire of politics.

Racism and Classism in the Law

Conflicts coming before the courts involve a varied set of contestants: individual versus individual, individual or group versus the state, executive officers versus legislative officers, or officials of one level of government against those of another level. The range and nature of both issues and litigants were suggested by De Tocqueville: "Hardly any question arises in the United States that is not resolved sooner or later into a judicial question."[5] In both general and special (or legal) politics, society provides for representation and other features of democracy. Perfect provision would result in legislative prescription of conflict resolution and redress, executive enforcement of the formula, and judicial interpretation of it in individual cases—all on an equal basis. But the ideal has eluded us; people with little economic organizational means have had minimal power to shape legislative or executive action. For redress of grievances, therefore, they have had to turn to the courts.[6]

On their behalf mainly has been raised what Frederick Douglass designated "the all-commanding question"—namely, whether "American justice, American liberty, American civilization, American law, and American Christianity could be made to include and protect alike and forever all American citizens in the rights which have been guaranteed to them by the organic and fundamental laws of the land."[7] Including black citizens, the historic victims of white racism, which is the attitudes, actions, and institutional arrangements that subordinate blacks by reason of their color.[8] And including poor citizens, not all of whom but many of whom are black and thus, by class and color, are battened down deep in powerlessness and the injustice born of it. It is possible for the law to be racist without being classist, but not the reverse, not just because blacks are a disproportionate segment of the poor but also because the law perpetuates the foul treatment that plunged them into impoverishment to begin with. "Systems which place or keep nonwhites in positions of inferiority or disadvantage, using not race itself as the subordinating mechanism, but instead other mechanisms indirectly related to race, are properly designated 'institutionally racist,' " Haywood Burns goes on to say. "This species of racism abounds in our law."[9]

Part of modern America's horrible heritage is this pervasive antiblack sentiment in the law. It was evident from colonial days to the Civil War, when blacks typically were pawns in litigation initiated to settle disputes among white interests. According to Donald M. Roper, under Chief Justice John Marshall, the United States Supreme Court sacrificed the slave's human interests to protect the slaveowner's property rights and the court's position in the political system. And under Roger B. Taney, adds Derrick A. Bell, Jr., it denied the rights of citizenship even to blacks in free states. After the Civil War and until 1877, citizenship rights for blacks were placed on legal foundations, but economic and political rights were not. "Without the latter, the former proved, then as so often today, all but worthless," Bell concludes.[10]

It has always been so. Even before Taney's dictum in *Dred Scott* v. *Sandford* (1857) that the Constitution gave the black man "no rights which the white man was bound to respect," America in its hypocrisy functioned according to that proposition. The equally racist Supreme Court decision in *Plessy* v. *Ferguson* about half a century later further ensured the separation of blacks and whites to the continuing disadvantage of the former. Between 1896 and 1946 no branch of government fostered meaningful change that was advantageous to blacks. Nor did the legal profession through the American Bar Association strike a blow for their full freedom. No sacrifice was too great for blacks to make: They served to death, for example, in war to secure life and liberty for others against the threat called Hitler. And yet no sacrifice was sufficient to secure their life and liberty in America.[11]

But that was as intended by the architects of the nation whose Constitution was drawn to protect the barbaric institution that it did not mention explicitly until 1865, when, by name, slavery was abolished—at least on paper. Between 1789 and 1865 a majority of the Supreme Court Justices owned slaves; when given options on the question of enslavement or liberty for blacks, the Court chose enslavement. And the lawmakers and the law enforcers (Presidents) joined the law interpreters in their hideous choice. Situated in the highest offices in the land, charged with the sacred duty of enforcing the law that freed the slaves and guaranteed to them the blessings of freedom, those officials—not in totality, to be sure, but in the main—used state power to perpetuate (in Thomas Jefferson's words) the masters' "unremitting despotism" and the slaves' "degrading submission." They embraced the separate but (un)equal doctrine in *Plessy* v. *Ferguson* rather than the principle that Justice John M. Harlan expressed in dissent: "The destinies of the two races, in this country, are indissolubly linked together, and the interests of both require that the common government of all shall not permit the seeds of race hate to be planted under the sanction of law."[12]

Individually and collectively, black and nonblack, men and women and children, we reap today the tragic fruits of the failure of the legal system thoroughly to execute the Thirteenth, Fourteenth, and Fifteenth Amendments to the Constitution. There is no denying that noteworthy progress has been made toward the goal of equality for blacks, but the goal remains demonstrably distant, not entirely but significantly as a result of the pall of racism over the legal system. There is no dearth of commentary on this topic. But we desperately need commentary that is both sensitive to the prerequisites of equal justice and informed about their satisfaction in the actual administration of justice. From the men and women who are in the judicial arena we need more than explanations: We need examples of judicial activism against racism and classism so that people who possess or obtain judicial power will have models to emulate. For both explanation and example we can look to part of the black bar and bench.

The Black Bar and Bench

For understandable reasons but with unfortunate consequences, black jurists have been hard pressed collectively to combat racism. The reasons include the restricted opportunities for blacks to become lawyers, the contradiction between black lawyers' need to handle many cases quickly to earn a living and the extended involvement civil rights cases require, the unavoidable shift of emphasis from offensive to defensive litigation in the late 1950s and early 1960s, and the gross misconception that court victories in the South would ruin racism. Moreover, in charge of the legal battle, whose organizational base has always been the National Association for the Advancement of Colored People (NAACP), were brilliant black lawyers—the late Charles Hamilton Houston, William H. Hastie, and Thurgood Marshall—who had remarkable assistance from the Howard University Law School.[13]

The consequences include assumption of leadership by whites now that Houston, Hastie, and Marshall are out of the battle. And this, in the opinion of a man whose name belongs with theirs, Judge Robert L. Carter, bodes ill for blacks because "Today's typical civil rights lawyer is white by race and values." A relative newcomer to the battle, he is marginally—if at all—linked to the black community, serves part time and according to his priorities, and leaves open to question his commitment to or understanding of the removal of "all vestiges of discrimination" and not only flagrant discrimination.[14]

These consequences are not the only reason for black lawyers to lead the legal fight against racism. Blacks should not rely on white lawyers or white legal institutions to press the fight energetically and adequately. Rooted in their blackness is their personal obligation to take up the sword and shield on behalf of their people. To be most faithful to that duty, Carter believes, they must discharge it collectively. No longer will the efforts of a few or the initiation of a few test cases suffice. The entire black legal community must provide the talent required for implementation litigation. This does not preclude participation by white lawyers. It "merely assumes" that *blacks should direct their struggle for freedom,* Carter concluded, as have Charles Hamilton Houston and Bruce McM. Wright.[15]

"The social justification for the Negro lawyer as such in the United States today is the service he can render the race as an interpreter and proponent of its rights and aspirations," Houston wrote in 1935. White lawyers were unreliable allies, he added, because they usually benefited from the exploitation of blacks which, as allies, they would be asked to destroy. As that exploitation engulfs blacks, Puerto Ricans, and other poor people, Wright says, black jurists have to do more than watch in "a rage of black silence." "We should never abdicate an activist role in the law and permit the dictates of the American Bar Association [ABA] to beatify and then give us its readymade articles of separate-but-unequal faith," he declares. "Too long have the black legal professionals been no more than an audience for the ABA's glittering pageant, while sitting quietly in some distant balcony."

Who are these men and women whom Houston, Carter, and Wright have beseeched to form a phalanx and enter the battle against racism and classism? They are the black bar and bench, whose story, given the scarcity of black jurists and of information about them, must be told as the story of individuals and not that of a group effort. It began in 1844, when three blacks became lawyers: John Mercer Langston in Ohio, Robert Morris in Massachusetts, and Garrison Draper in Maryland. Jonathan J. Wright joined the bar in Pennsylvania before the Civil War.[16] Other blacks who were pre-

Civil War lawyers were Aaron A. Bardley in Massachusetts and Georgia, Edward G. Draper in Baltimore, and Robert B. Elliott in South Carolina. Elliot, who studied law in London, was a partner in America's first black law firm, which was established in Charleston, South Carolina, and had Macon B. Allen as a partner. It is possible that Dr. John S. Rock was admitted to some bar prior to the Civil War. physician and dentist, Rock was the first black lawyer authorized (in 1865) to practice before the United States Supreme Court.[17]

Frederick Douglass, the great black abolitionist, called Elliott "a marvel."[18] There were other marvels. George Lewis Ruffin, the first black graduate (1869) of Harvard Law School, became a state legislator in Massachusetts and the first black judge in the North by virtue of appointment to the municipal court in Charlestown, Massachusetts. Charlotte E. Ray is said to have been the first woman to have been graduated from Howard Law School (1872), to have been trained at a law school, and to have been admitted to practice before the Supreme Court of the District of Colombia. Josiah T. Settle, another graduate of the Howard University Law School (1875), who was also admitted to the Supreme Court of the District of Columbia, opened his office in Memphis, Tennessee, and in 1885 became an assistant attorney general of the Criminal Court of Shelby County.[19]

The emergence of these and other able black lawyers was one of several developments that brightened the Reconstruction period. A related phenomenon was service by some of them in state legislatures and in Congress where, for example, Ruffin and two other blacks were South Carolina's full delegation in 1872.[20] The general shift in the principal source of legal training from law offices (where apprenticeship tutoring was provided) to law schools seemed to be a good omen for blacks with the opening of the law department at Howard University in 1869. From 1869 to 1876 the department was headed by John Mercer Langston, an Oberlin graduate who was an attorney in Ohio and former inspector general of the

Freedmen's Bureau. The department's 238 graduates comprised almost the entire cadre of black lawyers who were trained academically between 1871 and 1900.[21]

But the glow of potential progress for blacks in the legal profession was short-lived in Reconstruction America. Technical and agricultural training was considered appropriate for them, and the limited number of black lawyers is partially attributable to the prevalence of this opinion among whites in all sections of the country. A graphic account of these results is given by Professor Kenneth S. Tollett whose research is the basis for the table below.

Number of Black Lawyers, 1910-1970

	In the Nation	*In the South*
1910	779 or 798	361
1920	950	366
1930	1,175	330
1940	1,023	
1950	1,450	232
1960	2,200	400
1970	4,200	600

As Tollett reports, black women have been pursuing legal careers since 1872, barriers of race and sex notwithstanding. Since that year, when Charlotte G. Ray was the first of Howard University Law School's female graduates, their representation among women lawyers has been favorably comparable to blacks' representation among male lawyers. In three of five relevant decennial census reports since 1900, the black percentage on the distaff side matched or exceeded that on the male side. In 1900 among female lawyers blacks were 1.9 percent; among male lawyers, 0.6 percent. In 1960 the percentages were 2.0 and 1.0 respectively. At the time 200 of the 2,200 black lawyers in America were women. Between 1939 and 1974, 28 black women became judges.[22]

Although important, the shortage of black lawyers is not the total problem of their underrepresentation in their profession. This problem has qualitative as well as quantitative dimensions, because social justice cannot be won at the bar alone and because the underrepresentation of blacks extends to the real power pockets in America—namely, banks, corporations, brokerage houses, government, and established law firms. If black lawyers are to become a more influential force, Harry T. Edwards writes, they must gain meaningful participation in such societal decision-making centers. The predicament of blacks in America will not ease as they gain proportional representation unless this puts "Black-thinking Black lawyers" in those centers, opens to blacks all areas of the practice of law, and improves the opportunities blacks have to enter the profession.[23]

Among the key governmental positions are those of prosecutor and judge. In 1974 there were 58 blacks among 1,554 prosecutors in twelve major cities containing 24 percent of the nation's black population.[24] Black judges are also scarce: In 1971-72, they numbered 255 among 21,294 judges at the state and local levels and 31 among 475 judges at the federal level. Two were on state supreme courts, and seven were on intermediate state appellate courts. Of the respondents in a survey of black judges conducted by the Judicial Council of the National Bar Association and the American Judicature Society, 78 percent held both a bachelor's and a law degree. More than a third (37 percent) had held political office before taking the bench, and about a third (33 percent) indicated that they had remained active in politics after having become judges.[25]

More than half the black judges in America are in six cities—namely, New York City, Philadelphia, Washington, Chicago, Detroit, and Los Angeles.[26] Beverly Blair Cook has fully documented their presence—and absence—throughout the country.[27] Concern about their absence from the federal bench in the South[28] was underscored in 1972, when former President Richard M. Nixon was asked to appoint at least one or two blacks to vacancies that existed at the time. The request was made by the Judicial Council of the National Bar Association. It drew praise from the Senate Minority Leader, Hugh Scott, and from such other Congressional leaders as Gerald R. Ford, Minority Leader in the House of Representatives, and his colleagues, Speaker Carl Albert and Majority Leader Hale M. Boggs. But the Judicial Council never received the "detailed response" promised by Nixon's specilassistant, Robert T. Brown.[29]

An organization of judicial and quasi-judicial officials, the Judicial Council represents the latest attempt by some members of the black bar and bench to make a collective assault on racism and classism. At its founding convention in Atlanta, Georgia, in 1971, Judge George W. Crockett, Jr., its first chairman, urged its members to work against this "cancerous effect."[30] He expressed the hope that the Judicial Council would provide means by which its members could exchange information, encourage each other, and prod their profession to rid the legal system of racism and classism.[31] Interviewed at the convention, Judge Edward F. Bell, who as president of the National Bar Association had appointed Crockett chairman of the committee that laid the foundation for the Judicial Council, added, "We want to administer justice in our courtrooms so that the sword begins to cut more evenly, and black people and poor people can come to court without feeling that the only thing that separates them from an adverse judgment is the time it takes to try the lawsuit." Since then I have often thought of other remarks he made that year at a symposium at Harvard Law School. Those comments made it clear that black bench power would remain an elusive goal. "Whenever the white man surrenders to you one of his benches, he has given up one of his most powerful tools," Bell observed. "He has given up the tool that normally keeps his oppressive boot on the black man's neck."[32]

But even when they possess that tool, black judges can go only so far in flailing racism and classism. They must restrain themselves for fear of running afoul of judicial disability commissions, newspapers, and police officers' associations. They must avoid alienating colleagues whom they need to persuade to a different way of thinking and acting. And they cannot start lawsuits, defend litigants, or engage openly in the rough-and-tumble politics that, directly or indirectly, determines whether justice will be done or done in. But lawyers are freer to take such action, and some of those who want to do so, pooling their talent and time for that purpose, established the National Conference of Black Lawyers two years before the Judicial Council's birth.

The National Conference of Black Lawyers (NCBL) was formed in May, 1969,[33] before Robert L. Carter became a judge. His service as its co-chairman was harmonious with his call for collective and comprehensive action by black lawyers to promote the interests of their people. "We are not interested in forming a bar association in the original sense," his letter of April 24, 1969, informed Charles M. Waugh, president of the National Bar Association. Rather, NCBL wanted to give black lawyers a means of helping their people and themselves by fighting racism, including that within the legal profession.[34] NCBL also gives black law students an opportunity to take part in the fight. That it is properly theirs, too, is suggested by the paucity of black law students (4,817 of the 106,102 students in 1973-74 in schools approved by the American Bar Association),[35] the "reverse discrimination" controversy that threatens to curtail or cut out affirmative action programs designed to increase their proportion in school and in the profession,[36] and the shockingly adverse impact that bar examinations have on them (with three out of four failing, the NBA claimed in 1973).[37] It is fitting that the NCBL and the Black American Law Students Association (BALSA), which was founded at New York University in

1967, cooperate because BALSA also encourages service to the black community by students and lawyers.[38]

"Where are you black lawyers?"

That question from black inmates at Attica Correctional Facility in New York sparked NCBL's involvement in the litigation resulting from the rebellion of prisoners at that institution and the retaking of the prison by the state police between September 9 and 13, 1971. Lennox S. Hinds, who succeeded Haywood Burns as national director of NCBL, says that the organization is defending the sixty inmates who were indicted in December, 1972, on charges associated with the uprising.[39] Also illustrative of NCBL's activism are its organization of the successful defense of Angela Y. Davis; the law suit against Judge Julius Hoffman, who had had Bobby Seale, chairman of the Black Panther Party, chained, bound, and gagged during the Chicago Seven trial in 1969; opposition to President Nixon's nomination of Clement F. Haynesworth, Jr., and G. Harrold Carswell to the Supreme Court; representation of Cornell University black students who took up arms in self-defense; assistance to black men and women who complained about racism in the military service; support of Martin Sostre by challenging New York State prison policies; opposition to the American Bar Association's practices; challenge to law enforcement officers who arrest and even murder Black Panthers; and, Burns points out, daily service "to many of the more anonymous victims of the law—persons who do not have media following, political backing or an organized, developed defense apparatus, but who are representative of millions of those victimized by reason of race and/or economic status."[40]

Responding to Carter's letter concerning the formation of NCBL, Waugh took umbrage at the statement that no legal institution was addressing itself to "the problem of white racism as it affects substantial justice for the Black Americans of this Country." The National Bar Association (NBA), Waugh wrote, had been doing so for forty-four years. The

NBA saw no need for a new organization, he added, but it wished the NCBL well.[41] It was in 1925 that the NBA was founded "to strengthen and elevate the Negro lawyer in his profession and in his relationship to his people; to strengthen his standing at the bar . . . and to create a bond of true fellowship among the colored members of the Bar of America for their general uplift and advancement and for the encouragement of the Negro youth of America who will follow their choice of this profession."[42] The first step toward formal organization of the 1,200 black lawyers in America had been taken the year before, when a small group of them met in Chicago. At that summer meeting George H. Woodson from Des Moines, Iowa, and members of the Cook County (Chicago) Bar Association[43] agreed to create a national organization to supplement and spawn local bar associations. At neither the national nor the local level were blacks admitted to white bar associations. For the first thirty-four years of its existence, the American Bar Association (ABA) barred blacks, and in 1912, when it admitted the first blacks (three in all), it adopted a resolution requiring black applicants for membership to identify themselves racially. It was not until 1943 that the ABA announced its policy of granting membership without regard to race, creed, or color.

In December, 1924, on Woodson's motion, the eight members of the Iowa Bar Association, which he had organized in 1902, agreed to invite black lawyers to Des Moines to establish the National Bar Association. Twelve lawyers assembled at the Polk County Court House on August 1, 1925, and, with Woodson as president, organized the NBA.[44] On July 29, 1926, Woodson, S. Joe Brown, and Charles P. Howard signed and filed the articles of incorporation in Polk County, Iowa, paid the sixty-cent filing fee, and officially launched the National Bar Association.[45]

Although denied membership in the white bar association, black lawyers have not been of one mind regarding the formation of an association of their own. That denial was reason enough to establish the NBA. Of greater importance, however, was the NBA's representation of the black lawyer's belief in his individual and collective capacity to develop and use the law to advance the cause of equal justice for his people.[46] The NBA can no more dissolve in good conscience now[47] than it could in its early years when black people were in dire need of legal aid to secure their rights. To that need, the NBA responded with lawsuits in courts throughout the land. NBA members were chief and exclusive counsel in twenty cases before the U.S. Supreme Court between 1923 and 1941.[48] The relentless endeavor was made in the face of tremendous odds. As it proceeded, a shift from white to black legal leadership occurred, reflecting a growing realization that blacks must fight their own battles. "Those who suffer the wrong must surely bring the action and prosecute it vigorously," wrote Sidney R. Redmond. "You may make [*sic*] certain that those who cease to prepare, who fail to be vigilant, who are too proud or too afraid to fight, will not be accorded the rights of men."[49]

From the outset, the NBA stressed the necessity of black lawyers' mounting a united, vigorous, and sustained assault on inequality to ensure to all blacks "the blessings of civilized society." NBA leaders such as Charles W. Anderson, Jr., have urged black lawyers to accept the challenge of solving problems that beset blacks. To do this, Anderson said, these lawyers should fight racism as a bar association, not only as individual attorneys.[50] In a similar vein, Earl B. Dickerson told NBA members that the fight involves more than "mere speech-making at annual meetings."[51] It involves hard work, organized resistance, and risks. "The road ahead is tortuous . . . reaction is riding high everywhere," he observed. "But the lawyers of our Association must not falter in this struggle."[52]

Concerted action must be their primary goal. Justice Robert N. C. Nix, Jr., the black member of the Pennsylvania Supreme Court, told them that at the NBA's fiftieth anniversary in Chicago on July 26, 1974. "In the past, most of our significant accomplishments represented the efforts of single individuals," he said in the keynote speech, "and while those who expended that effort are most deserving of acclaim, we nevertheless must recognize that such a contribution fails to provide the impact that can be engendered if we are able to collect our forces and proceed as a cohesive group." Nix's remarks were part of a continuous stream of exhortation intended to spur to action the organization that Revius O. Ortique, Jr., calls "a symbol of emancipation."[53] The NBA does have symbolic value, as have the NCBL and the Judicial Council. But that is not nearly enough armament for the war on injustice. It falls far short of the resources required for a collective attack on the lions of the judicial jungle, racism and classism, whose predatoriness threatens everyone and whose demise would benefit all of us in the future as legal precedents won by blacks have benefited other minorities and even whites.[54] No one knows this better than black jurists.

To some it may seem that the call for black solidarity smacks of support for separation from the general legal community. Nothing could be further from the truth. Rather, the purpose of the mobilization of black jurists, as Judge William H. Hastie said at the NBA convention in Atlanta, Georgia, on August 5, 1971, is to devise more effective means of fighting racism. "It is no contradiction to say that we band together as blacks in order to speed the day that this will not be necessary," he explained. But the responsibility for sweeping racism and classism out of the judicial system is, as Judge Joseph C. Howard sees it "peculiarly ours because our people bear the brunt of the injustices visited upon the socially, economically, and politically disadvantaged."[55] The responsibility is properly that of the entire legal profession, Judge Crockett maintains, but the profession will shirk it "unless and until its black component pushes it in that direction."[56] Numerically and organizationally, the black bar and bench are thin and frail—like spider webs. But according to the Ethiopian proverb, "When spider webs unite, they can tie up a lion."[57]

Auction Block Justice

Black jurists lack luster as a group unified in pursuit of equal justice, but their individual splendor is often impressive[58] as they assail injustices that are almost tantamount to those symbolized by the auction block. Insofar as it represented the use of law by whites to subjugate and terrorize blacks, the auction block is a suitable symbol for the judicial system today. When they see, read, hear about, or spend time in courts, police stations, jails, prisons, or juvenile training institutions, many blacks—regardless of their roles inside or outside the system—feel as Frances W. Harper felt about the slave market:

> And men, whose sole crime was their hue,
>   The impress of their Maker's hand,
> And frail and shrinking children, too,
>   Were gathered in that mournful hand.[59]

Many black jurists who are reasonable and rational and therefore are not about to romanticize criminal behavior are striving to explain to others, including some of their brothers and sisters in their profession, the evil and danger inherent in auction block justice. Why evoke the auction block? Can we deny that justice for blacks has improved since the days of formal slavery? Or since *Plessy* v. *Ferguson*? No such denial would be tenable. But frequent glances down "the corridor of history," Judge A. Leon Higginbotham, Jr., advises us, might make us aware of the law's role as handmaiden to racism and strengthen our resolve to make racism, hatred, and violence "solely memories of our tragic past." Achievement of these goals is an appropriate job for all of us—black and white, rich and poor, powerful and weak,[60] leaders and followers, lawyers and laymen, wherever we are in America. "For in the 1970's we must not act as if we believe in the folly of the lines from Gilbert and Sullivan: 'The law is the true embodiment of everything that's excellent. It has no kind of fault or flaw, and I, my Lords, embody the Law.' "[61]

From the black bar and bench emanates an insistent cry for equal justice for people who, with horrifying and often unconstitutional regularity, are denied fair treatment in the area of activity—law enforcement—in which the warranty of citizenship should be most respected. The cry is made on behalf of all such people. If it reflects a more explicit concern about legalized brutalization of blacks, attribute that to these hard facts of life: Blacks are the prime victims of such auction block justice; and black jurists have a personal as well as group interest in its eradication, for they themselves have not fully escaped the mistreatment heaped upon people of their color, if not their class. Their angry, plaintive, hopeful cry is recorded in this book in the words of some from whose lips and pens it is emitted. Its essence is that freedom will not flourish in America until blacks can sing in truth rather than in tragedy their ancestors' spiritual:

> No more auction block for me,
> No more, no more,
> No more auction block for me,
> Many thousand gone.[62]

FROM THE BLACK BAR

I.

RACE, JUSTICE, AND POLITICS

"SINCE SLAVERY DAYS, blacks have received the butt end of justice," declares Sherman W. Smith, a black judge in Los Angeles.[1]

Why? Because they have been and still are politically powerless, and justice is a political commodity. It is awarded or denied according to the political clout that the target of law enforcement can muster. Whether a person or a group, that target's vulnerability to abuse by law enforcement officials is determined by its position on the totem pole of political power. And blacks are the historic occupants of the lowest rung. They still are abused lawfully because they are largely without political power, and they are largely without political power because they still are abused lawfully.

Blacks are trapped in the politics of race and justice. An element of class is also involved, because many nonblacks are caught in the same vicious circle of injustice. Men who enjoy a favored position over other men use law and politics to maintain that edge. That disposition becomes evident as we examine the formulation and administration of criminal law. The people who are responsible for designing and executing the law—legislators, police, prosecutors, and judges—function in "a politically organized society." They discharge their responsibility in such a way as to protect the interests of the most powerful segments of society whom they represent.

1

"Those whose interests conflict with the interests represented in the law must either change their behavior or possibly find it defined as 'criminal,' " Richard Quinney writes.[2]

Quinney's comments apply to civil justice as well as to criminal justice because the legal system is a means by which values or advantages are allocated among persons and groups. It is, therefore, a political system or, to be more precise, an integral part of the overall political system whose purpose is to provide for such an authoritative allocation.[3] And if politics is a matter of who gets what, when, and how,[4] it is also a matter of who does not. Either way, the explanation lies largely in the politics of the judiciary.

Assertions that courts, the nucleus of the justice system, are or should be kept out of politics abound, but the undeniable truth is that they are deeply involved in politics. It could not be otherwise, because courts are called on to resolve personal and group conflicts over available values, material and otherwise. The party that wins their approval gains the advantage of having its cause backed up by the power of the state.[5] Because the state is a powerful ally (or opponent), the contest for its support is fought as vigorously in the so-called third branch of government as in the other two branches. Furthermore, public officials are just as much caught up in the allocation of values—"money, honor, or freedom"—through the courts as through the legislature or the office of the mayor, governor, or President. It is as Herbert Jacob says:

> Thus, the quest for justice resembles the quest for many other government services. It engenders conflict in which the benefit of one person is often obtained at the cost of another. Everyone seeks to be a winner, and no one wants to be among the losers. . . . The conflict over justice and the power employed to execute judgments combine to anchor the administration of justice firmly in the center of the political arena.[6]

Justice and politics commingle for many reasons, one of which is that the ranks of court personnel are replete with politicos. This is pointedly true about judges, who, after all, are elected or are appointed by chief executives who hold elective office. Prosecutors are highly politicized officials. And the police, who are controlled by the mayor, to a considerable extent determine the nature of court activity. Legislators influence the distribution of advantages and disadvantages through the laws they produce.[7] Into courts are brought the issues that whip up political sentiment—crime, corruption, civil rights, crises of all kinds—the issues that whet the appetite of politicians, stir the interest of the mass media, and quicken the pulse of the public. Judicial politics, as Jacob asserts, differs from executive and legislative politics by virtue of the legal culture consisting of rules and rituals peculiar to courts. Still, the judicial process is a political process.[8]

The political nature of the court system is illustrated by the periodic campaigns of reformers whose announced goals are to simplify and unify it, to improve court administration, to insulate courts from politics, and to replace amateur judges with professional judges.[9] Some observers suggest that an additional motive of "reformers" is a desire to curtail the slowly increasing influence of blacks in judicial politics,[10] particularly but not exclusively as judges.[11] The judicial selection process highlights black political powerlessness. That the process is thoroughly political is made clear by mere mention of the methods of selection and the people involved in choosing judges. At the state and local levels, the methods used are appointment (executive and legislative), popular election (on partisan and nonpartisan tickets), and the nonpartisan court plan (the Missouri or Merit Plan). Touted as the best guarantee of placing qualified persons on the bench, the Missouri Plan provides for initial selection by the governor from a list of candidates provided by a commission consisting of lawyers and laymen. The appointee serves for a year or until the next election and then is subject to public approval or rejection. If approved by a majority of the voters, the judge remains in office and subsequently comes up for "reelection." If rejected at the polls, the judge is replaced by appointment as described above. The plan has made judgeships less political and bar associations more political.[12] The associations, in fact, perform as political parties in the states that use the plan.[13]

The cast of characters in this drama includes party leaders, governors, voters, pressure groups, and bar associations. At the federal level, it includes the President, Attorney General, Senators, Congressmen, and judges themselves. Joel B. Grossman's explanation of the way in which federal judges are chosen clarifies the linkage between the judiciary and politics.[14] The President, acting on his Attorney General's recommendation, appoints federal judges subject to the Senate's concurrence. Among the variables that figure in a candidate's success in ascending to the bench are personal friendships; service to the party, individual Senators, or the President; geography; ideology; religion; interest group activity; ethnicity; and Senatorial courtesy, the practice that gives Senators virtual veto power over Presidential nominations. Approval of the American Bar Association (but not its black counterpart, the National Bar Association) is also prerequisite to nomination. Two less publicized practices that are built into the selection process are the President's solicitation of sitting judges' views about candidates and the vigorous, though discreet, politics played by candidates themselves to win the backing of the Senator(s) of their state who belong to the President's party, state party leaders, public figures (including judges), and even the Attorney General.

The prominent role of the American Bar Association stands in striking contrast with the nonparticipation of the National Bar Association. For example, the NBA was not asked for its views about Lewis F. Powell, Jr., and William H. Rehnquist when President Nixon nominated and the Senate confirmed them for appointment to the U.S. Supreme Court. Nor was its opinion about other nominees solicited. "We, of course, consider this an insult to the integrity and interests of a people most affected and concerned with the business of this court," NBA President James B. Cobb declared.[15]

President Nixon paid attention neither to the NBA's complaint nor to the Judicial Council's subsequent plea for the appointment of blacks to the federal bench.[16] These organizations made no headway against Nixon's insensitivity because they posed no political threat to him. What power could they summon to influence or coerce him? Even if they could have applied the totality of black political power, their impact on Nixon would have been negligible. Such is the impressiveness of that power that as late as April, 1974, blacks held only 2,991 public elective offices in the District of Columbia and forty-five states. Those officials ranged in number from 1 in each of three states (Idaho, Wyoming, and New Hampshire) to 194 in Michigan. There were none in five States (Hawaii, Montana, North Dakota, South Dakota, and Utah). In number of black elected officials, the regional rankings were the South (1,609 or 54 percent), North-Central (691 or 23 percent), Northeast (497 or 17 percent), and West (194 or 6 percent). These rankings in terms of percentage of the nation's black population were the South (53 percent), North-Central (20 percent), Northeast (19 percent), and West (8 percent).[17] By level of government, blacks held 17 federal offices (16 seats in the House of Representatives and 1 in the Senate). State offices were held in forty-one states by 238 legislators (196 representatives and 40 senators), a secretary of state (Richard H. Austin in Michigan), a state superintendent of public instruction (Wilson C. Riles in California), and a state Supreme Court justice (Robert N. C. Nix, Jr., in Pennsylvania). At the county level were 242 black elected officials, the largest group (32) being in Louisiana, the next (28) being in Tennessee, and the next (24) being in Michigan. The 108 black mayors include the chief executives of Atlanta, Cincinnati, Dayton, Detroit, Gary, Los Angeles, Newark, and Raleigh. The President appointed the black mayor of Washington, D.C. Exceeding in number all other groups of black elected officials were the 1,080 who were on municipal governing boards.

About half (172) of the 340 black elected officials in law enforcement were judges, justices, and magistrates. The highest numbers of jurists were in New York (26) and Pennsylvania (25), but the greatest numbers of law enforcement officials were in Alabama (56) and Mississippi (43), with most of them being sheriffs, constables, marshals, and chiefs of police. Blacks served on state and college boards of education in eight states, and on local boards of education in thirty-nine states.

That blacks exert minimal power in key policy-making institutions is a demonstrable fact in the city in which they have been involved in politics for the longest time, Chicago. About ten years ago, according to the Chicago Urban League, blacks held only 285 (or 2.6 percent) of the 10,997 highest decision-making positions in Cook County. Of the 1,088 posts in federal, state, and local government, they held 58, which was two and a half times as many significant positions as they occupied in the private sector (227 out of 9,909). Blacks held none of the 757 positions in corporate law firms, only 42 of the 6,838 in business corporations, and just 5 of the 380 in the most prestigious universities, which have been rising in the esteem of the other institutions, public and private, and exert "real—not nominal—power" in urban renewal and other policy areas. Even in voluntary associations blacks were underrepresented, holding only 72 of 1,115 posts.

But the emasculation of blacks did not end with their complete or virtually complete exclusion from important positions. Those who held such offices were weakened by placement in positions of less power than those held by whites, by restrictions on the number allowed to seek election to a board or judicial office, by appointment primarily to positions governing largely black clientele, by prevention of their developing an independent power base, by requirement that they share power with a board, and by "processing" that resulted in their placing the institution above their people. "It is therefore safe to estimate that Negroes really hold less than 1 percent of the effective power in the Chicago metropolitan area," Baron and his colleagues concluded. "Realistically, the power structure of Chicago is hardly less white than that of Mississippi."[18]

Much is made of the snail's pace of blacks toward political power positions. Some whites fear and lament a "black takeover" of the cities. "Maybe we should really investigate that mentality which would describe every achievement of a 'minority race' or religion as a take-over," Vernon Jarrett suggests, because there is no basis for assertions that blacks are making such an inroad into the world of meaningful power.[19]

Piven and Cloward remind us that the political impotence of blacks is being assured by new administrative arrangements that transfer power from the city to the metropolis whose controllers promote the combined interests of suburban and inner-city whites. Blacks may win big-city electoral battles, but they will lose the metropolitan political war as the federal government continues to require area-wide programming as a condition of receipt of its funds. Black political power is being nipped in the bud to prevent several things—namely, the possible endangerment of major interests that need the city core, the alienation of whites in the city (all of them cannot afford the exodus to suburbia), and perhaps above all the formation of a national black separatist political bloc. Can blacks prevent the federal subversion of city power? Not readily and probably not at all, because they are not politically unified and disciplined, they do not possess the city clout required to compensate for that deficiency and will not possess it before metropolitan consolidation is well advanced, and their traditional leaders probably will abet metropolitanism in self-interest instead of trying to undermine it in group interest. Will all this result in "creative federalism"? It is more likely to result in "the demise of local government and the submergence of the minority which now stands to gain most from localism—the Negro."[20]

The Negro also stands to gain from the increase in black judicial power, and that accounts largely for the firm white resistance to that acquisition. Appreciating that power as a means of oppressing blacks, the white man is unwilling to share it with them.[21] Whites are afraid that blacks will use it to curb the oppression. Some blacks will not put it to that use. But others will, and when they do, the linkages among race, justice, and politics come rapidly and clearly into view. Take, for example, Judge Crockett's handling of the New Bethel incident in Detroit in the spring of 1969 when a gun battle between blacks and two white policemen left one policeman dead and the other wounded. The blacks were alleged to have taken refuge in the New Bethel Baptist Church where the Republic of New Africa, a black separatist group, was holding its first annual convention. Policemen, notified by their wounded colleague, soon surrounded the church, riddling its front with bullets before arresting the 142 men, women, and children who were inside. It was then about 11 P.M. on a Saturday night. At 6 A.M. the next day the Reverend C. L. Franklin, pastor of New Bethel, and State Representative (now Judge) James Del Rio awakened Crockett and told him that the arrestees were being held incommunicado at the first police district.[22]

Crockett was serving as the presiding judge of the Recorder's Court on that Sunday and was therefore duty bound to act. Grabbing two blank habeas corpus forms, he went to police headquarters and held hearings. By 1 P.M. he had released 130 arrestees on a motion by the prosecutor (whose initiative the news media did not mention). Of the other 12, 1 was released on $1,000 bond (and subsequently appeared in court voluntarily after having been charged with the shooting), 2 were carried over to a subsequent court date on warrants for other offenses, and 9 were released by Crockett because, in violation of state law, the police had performed nitrate tests on them while holding them incommunicado, failing to explain their rights to them, and refusing them an opportunity to obtain counsel.[23]

Crockett broke precedent by holding immediate hearings rather than simply issuing a writ of habeas corpus but allowing the police enough time to show that the arrests had been legal. "Had I inquired into the legality of their arrests, I would have released all of them," he said later. "But had I strictly followed the law, it would have been more favorable to the arrestees and the newspapers would really have been yelling."[24] The newspapers yelled anyway, and so did the police. They were upset, Crockett believes, because a black judge had used his power to protect black people. Would the police have invaded a white church and made a mass arrest? Would they have locked up white men, women, and children all night without any evidence at all about their involvement in a crime? No. "But you see these were 142 black people and the police have been doing all these things to black people all the time, and judges have been letting them get away with it. Well, they aren't going to get away with it as long as I'm around."[25]

He would not have been around for long if they had had their way. Heeding demands for an investigation, the State Judicial Tenure Commission conducted one—and found no cause for action. The state legislature passed a resolution criticizing Crockett. The Detroit Police Officers' Association picketed his court (black officers counterpicketed) and twice castigated him in a full-page advertisement in the Detroit *News*. The media was consistent in its distorted coverage, never even requesting to see the report that, by law, Crockett had to file immediately after the hearing. No local judge, black or white, defended Crockett in public or in private. But the black community sprang to his defense, sensing the true nature of Crockett's offense: He had bucked the Establishment's "arrangement" for dispensing justice to people who are poor, black, or both.[26]

The "arrangement" had been shaken, and it would be more difficult for judges to allow the police to hold people as long as seventy-two hours "for investigation" and to grant prosecutors' requests for long adjournments to complete their investigations. Some people did not appreciate Crockett's courage. But others like the Black United Front, a coalition of fifty groups, and New Detroit, Inc., a civic group, did appreciate it.[27] New Detroit's legal subcommittee confirmed Crockett's correctness. So did the deans of the four law schools in Detroit. The prosecutor might not have approved

Crockett's action, but he did not appeal it. About two weeks after the incident, the U.S. Supreme Court, in a case concerning mass arrests (*Davis* vs. *Mississippi*), confirmed Crockett's decision.[28]

The lessons of New Bethel, Crockett said later, are several. The first is that we have so complacently and for so long witnessed the abuse of basic freedoms that "to most of us, the violation of the law is the law." This has bruised faith in our judicial system to the point that many of us simply do not believe that we do or will receive our fair share of justice. The second lesson is that the prompt and fair administration of justice can avert urban race riots. A third lesson is that black judges have special roles to play—namely, using the law to do justice, promoting reform, and symbolizing American democracy. Of these several roles, perhaps the last is the highest: "being a symbol of law and order with justice insofar as the poor and underprivileged in our society is [*sic*] concerned."[29]

Another lesson of New Bethel is that the selection of black judicial officers will remain a hot political issue. Whites want to keep their monopoly on power, but blacks have begun to realize that the power of judges and prosecutors matches and even exceeds that of mayors and legislators. Belatedly, but assuredly, they are placing the acquisition and utilization of judicial power higher on their list of priority. And of all the linkages among race, justice, and politics, that could be the most beneficial for blacks and nonblacks alike.

Law has figured importantly in the subjugation of blacks from slavery to the present time. Its duplicity, which has been exposed all along the way, is never clearer than at moments of crisis when powerful whites disguise attempts to help themselves as efforts to assist blacks and conceal their determination to preserve black powerlessness behind such semantic sagebrush as calls for law and order. For example, the Emancipation Proclamation and repression of the civil rights movement in the North and South were put in this perspective by Derrick A. Bell, Jr., in an address at the National Bar Association's convention in Atlanta, Georgia, on August 4, 1971. His article is reprinted with the permission of the author and the *Journal of Public Law* of Emory University, *University of Toledo Law Review,* and *Wisconsin Law Review* (which holds the copyright). An alumnus of Duquesne University and the University of Pittsburgh Law School, Professor Bell teaches at Harvard Law School.

BLACK FAITH IN A RACIST LAND

A Summary Review of Racism in American Law

Derrick A. Bell, Jr.

... FROM the beginning, this nation has taken pride in its dedication to the rule of law and the protection of individual rights. But black people, by their status as slaves in the South, and freemen without the rights or privileges of freedom in the North, understood that those who urged respect for and compliance with the law, relied themselves on force, wealth, and power. And black people, having none of these, had to place their faith in the law, and from the first, they placed a quality of reliance on the law to gain their freedom that amazed white America and finally helped achieve the partial measure of dignity which we enjoy today.

The history of black people's reliance on the law in their centuries-long struggle for freedom and equality is a story little known because seldom told. There is some exposure to the highlights of history, the major moments of our slow, painful ascent from slavery; but little is said about the duality of motive with which even minor steps on our behalf were taken, and virtually no attention is given to just how little even some of the major events changed or improved our status.

. . . They didn't tell us how many slaves were freed as a matter of law by the Emancipation Proclamation. The answer is, of course, NONE. The order could have no legal effect in areas not then under control of the Union forces, and it specifically excluded slave-holding areas in Virginia and West Virginia which had not joined the rebellion.

. . . It is true that adoption of the Civil War Amendments had the effect of voiding the decision in *Dred Scott* as legal doctrine, but we learned the bitter truth during Reconstruction that the North had pressured through enactment of the thirteenth, fourteenth, and fifteenth amendments as much to punish the South as to liberate the Negro.

And as the gains made by blacks—political, legal, and social—were erased in the 1870's, the Supreme Court and the lower courts confirmed in their decisions what blacks had feared, that the citizenship they had been granted, which indeed they believed they had earned through the blood of thousands of blacks who had died fighting on the Union side during the War, was citizenship in name only. It was the Emancipation Proclamation all over again.

. . . The decision in *Brown* v. *Board of Education* is usually cited as the beginning of the modern era in American race relations. But as former NAACP attorney Lewis Steel pointed out in his famous "New York Times" article about the Supreme Court, *Nine Men in Black Who Think White*, it was World War II, the ending of classical colonialism, and the desire by America (which had emerged from the war as a world leader) to compete with the Communist nations for the allegiance of the emerging non-white nations of Africa and Asia that made it imperative that we put our racial house in order, and end the blatant credibility gap between our democratic precepts and our racist practices. And as was the case at the end of the Civil War, where better should the nation set the example than in the South where racial bigotry was so open, obvious, and damaging to our foreign image? The men who decided *Brown* were probably sincere, and even courageous, but with hindsight it becomes clear that the decision was as predictable as was the thirteenth amendment, and (as we should have known) as unlikely to be enforced. And, for a long time, it wasn't enforced. The first *Brown* decision in 1954 delayed relief for a year and the second decision in 1955 permitted the granting of relief by the unmeasurable standard of "all deliberate speed." Thus, white America had succeeded in cleaning up its legal image, and black folk had received, as they so often do in civil rights "victories," the equitable remedy of beautiful language and the promise of more substantial relief further down the line. There was indeed some school desegregation in border areas during those early years, and a whole series of orders applying *Brown* to publicly-owned facilities, some of which actually desegregated.

But by this time, blacks had learned that faith is fine, but the Lord helps he who helps himself. And so, beginning with Mrs. Rosa Parks in Montgomery, they began combining religion and action based on the rights they were supposed to have, and found the formula produced marvelous results. Later the freedom rides, sit-ins, and other direct action peaceful protests utilized similar methods, and blacks succeeded in effectively exposing to the nation and the world that the rights of citizenship which had been granted at least twice in less than a century remained unredeemed and, seemingly, unredeemable. For a while it worked. The nation's racial duplicity was exposed, and Southern bigots reacted as they always had, except this time television was watching. National embarrassment grew, and the nation, first through the Supreme Court, and then through the Congress, decided to teach those Southerners a lesson. It was like the 1860's all over again, and like the 1860's, the commitment, which was more to racial image than to racial equality, didn't last.

When, having seen on television the gains the Southern

brothers seemed to be making by their willingness to face up to policemen's dogs and firemen's hoses, Northern ghetto residents tried a few protests of their own, the country stopped being sympathetic. Not only did the Northern protesters feel the righteous indignation of the white backlash, but those in the South whose convictions for protesting had been regularly overturned by the Supreme Court found that for activities which earlier they were being hailed as civil rights warriors, they were now receiving fines and jail terms that were not reversed on appeal.

Justice Black issued a warning while dissenting in *Cox v. Louisiana.* "Those who encourage minority groups to believe that the United States Constitution and federal laws give them a right to patrol and picket in the streets whenever they choose, in order to advance what they think to be a just and noble end," the Justice said, "do no service to those minority groups, their cause, or their country."

There have been a number of adverse decisions since, but also a continuing number of favorable ones. It is not likely this ratio will change a great deal because the world is, after all, a different place than it was in 1871. The political pressures that helped give birth to *Brown* are still present, and blacks whose faith has been rewarded with a measure of knowledge and the beginnings of power are far more adept at maintaining these pressures. Our reliance on the law remains strong, and I think appropriately so. But we in the law recognize, and more importantly, black leaders recognize, the truth in Judge A. Leon Higginbotham's statement:

> Recent advances in the field of civil rights have not come about and could never have come about solely through judicial tests made "by one individual" while all others in the silent black majority waited for the ultimate constitutional determination.
>
> Rather, the major impetus for the Civil Rights Acts of 1957, 1960, 1964, and 1965, which promised more equal access to the opportunities of our society, resulted from the determination, the spirit and the nonviolent commitment

of the many who continually challenged the constitutionality of racial discrimination and awakened the national
conscience.

. . . In the main, decisions on racial issues today do not
contain the overt racism of earlier years. Rather, they reflect
"institutional racism" which Anthony Downs defines as
"placing or keeping persons in a position or status of inferiority by meeans of attitudes, actions, or institutional structures
which do not use color itself as the subordinating mechanism,
but instead use other mechanisms indirectly related to color."
The technique is different. The result is the same.

Racism, often in this neutral guise, is present in every aspect
of the Administration of the American judicial system. But
because the Jim Crow signs are down, there is a tendency to
ignore the problem or to categorize it for solution under the
general heading of fairness. Such was the case with a new
Criminal Justice Plan, evolved in New York by a special Council after much work and effort. Commenting on the plan, one
of the outstanding attorneys of the civil rights era, Robert L.
Carter, noted the omission of any reference to racism which
he deemed a root cause of the present crisis in the administration of criminal justice. Carter continued:

> It is stated that a primary need is fairness, but general
> fairness is not a cure for racism. Racism and race discrimi-
> nation in the administration of criminal justice is a sepa-
> rate, distinct question that must be faced and dealt with
> apart from efforts at improved efficiency, crime preven-
> tion or rehabilitation in general. Anyone with any practical
> experience in race relations knows this although far too
> many whites want to submerge this troublesome problem
> as the Council apparently seeks to do, under some more
> generalized social issue.
> Racism pervades the criminal justice system, and it is not
> going to be eliminated without a conscious effort.

. . . Haywood Burns, Executive Director, National Conference of Black Lawyers, points out that although many deci-

sions may seem neutral on their face, their failure to consider the history of racism that has infested all of our institutions, can give a racist impact to actions and decisions that were not motivated by a desire to discriminate. But, says Burns:

> the very failure to take this legacy into account must itself be regarded as racist, for to act as if the overt racism of the past never occurred, and to design systems of law without taking it into account is to perpetuate the historical effect of racism.

Decisions of this character have been handed down by courts at every level including the highest. Thus, during the past term, while an unanimous Court furthered school de-segregation in the South with a series of decisions adopting arguments about busing, neighborhood schools, and pupil percentages that civil rights lawyers have been making for years, the Court continues its refusal to invalidate so-called de facto school segregation in the North, thereby contributing to the present situation in which the percentage of black children attending segregated schools is greater in the North than in the South. It is likely that this gap will grow appreciably as a result of the Court's surprising decision in *James v. Valtierra*, which approves the use of referenda procedures to bar low-income housing projects in suburban communities. Lower courts had been split on the issue, but the majority in *Valtierra* distinguished its earlier rulings which voided referenda-initiated provisions that barred fair housing laws, stating that the record in *Valtierra* "would not support any claim that a law seemingly neutral on its face is in fact aimed at a racial minority." The Court also refused to find that the referendum provision served to deny equal protection to the poor. Mr. Justice Marshall, joined by Justices Brennan and Blackmun, dissented.

Earlier in the Term, the Court had seriously undercut the *Miranda* doctrine in *Harris v. New York* by holding in a five-four decision that while prosecutors could not use information obtained without giving the *Miranda* warnings in direct

testimony, such information could be used to impeach a
defendant who took the stand and made statements in conflict

> with his earlier illegally obtained utterances. In effect, this
> means that the defendant who takes the stand waives his
> *Miranda* protections, a loss that will fall heavily on those few
> criminal defendants (guilty or innocent) who dare go to
> trial, rather than accept the best guilty plea they can get.
> Mr. Justice Marshall joined the dissenters. The decision is
> neutral as to race, but its impact on blacks is obvious, as is
> the decision this last Term in *Wyman v. James*, upholding
> the validity of New York statutes requiring entry into wel-
> fare recipients' homes on pain of termination of bene-
> fits. . . .

These citations should suffice to show a hardening of
attitudes toward the poor. A hardening of attitudes toward
the poor equals a more difficult time for blacks, even though
race is never mentioned. It thus behooves all of us to be
sensitive to these unannounced dangers and ready to expose
the racial significance of cases and decisions that are silent on
the racial question.

I have spoken much about the role of religion in the black
past, and this is appropriate whether or not we as individuals
remain bound to the faith of our fathers. I have also referred
to the pressing need for an accurate presentation of American
history, for it is crucial that the depth of the continuing racial
hostility in which black people must function be made clear,
both to us and to those who come after us.

Haywood Burns, former national director of the National Conference of Black Lawyers, is convinced that law enforcement officials have perverted the fundamental notion of equal justice by making the law an extension of their politics of oppression. Their arsenal includes repressive legislation, preventive detention, disparate sentencing, exorbitant bail, and agents provocateurs. Our success in stemming the tide of their lawlessness will be determined by the extent to which the general community supports efforts to that end. Professor Burns was educated at Harvard University and Yale Law School. He teaches at the University of Buffalo Law School. This selection appeared in the *Howard Law Journal*, Vol. XVII, No. 4 (1973).

POLITICAL USES OF THE LAW

Haywood Burns

I AM GOING to be talking about political uses of the law as it relates to our overall subject of crime and punishment in minority communities. Professor Madison has already alluded to the quote from Samuel Yette that "in 1970 the police state not only became fact, it became legal." Professor Henry Steele Commager, who looked at the same problem from an historical perspective, has also commented recently that "if repression is not yet as blatant or as flamboyant as it was during the McCarthy years, it is in many respects more pervasive and formidable, for it comes to us now with official sanctions and is imposed upon us by officials sworn to uphold the law—the Attorney General, the FBI, state and local officials, the police and even judges. . . ."

I'd like to second the remarks both of Brother Samuel Yette and Professor Commager with respect to the overall problem of political uses of the law. There is a special dimension to that problem when we address it in the context of the experience of persons in the black and other minority communities who are attempting to challenge things as they are—for increasingly the law has been systematically used in recent years to repress this kind of activity. . . .

Repressive Legislation

The contemporary manifestation of this historical problem, a brief survey of which follows, can be seen in the kinds of legislation recently passed.

Preventive Detention

I point, as signpost number one, to preventive detention, both here in the District of Columbia and as proposed in other parts of this country. The idea that you do away with the presumption of innocence in some cases and that you ignore the Eighth Amendment, or that you put some people behind bars prior to having been convicted of a crime, is, to me, a very dangerous development, particularly because I know who will be especial victims of this preventive detention legislation. However, I do not feel that much of the excitement that has been generated by this kind of repressive legislation fully takes into account that in a very real sense we already have preventive detention in this country. We have had preventive detention in this country for a very long time because the operation of the money bail system is such that in particular cases you are going to have preventive detention. The moment that you set a $250,000 bail for H. Rap Brown, who is not making $250 a year, that is preventive detention. The money bail system, I think, has done for a long time what this new legislation proposes to do. But there is something more sinister about it when you take away the veil that has enveloped the bail system up to now. That system supposedly operated on the presumption that everyone was entitled to bail in noncapital cases, and it reveals the true ugliness of what is being done in certain political quarters.

"Legalized" Invasion of Privacy

Further examples of legislation include the "no-knock" legislation and the way in which it encroaches upon the Fourth Amendment, as well as the provisions in recent federal legislation which relate to wiretap, in particular those which support wiretaps without judicial scrutiny in national security cases.

Grand Jury Immunity

There are other indications of this kind of repression which are not of as high visibility but in some ways are perhaps of even more importance. I wonder how many of you, particularly law students, are aware of some of the changes that have been made in the grand jury through federal legislation, particularly, in the area of the immunity that a witness gets before the grand jury. Traditionally, the idea of immunity has been one in which the person who was given immunity had immunity for the entire transaction—that is, that his immunity was coextensive with his right against self-incrimination. Under recent federal standards, the prosecution, the United States Attorney, can bring you before the grand jury, give you limited immunity, and force you to testify. The immunity is only granted with the limited assurance that the particular testimony will not be used against the witness. The witness still can be indicted for the transaction which was the subject of the testimony. What that means in practical terms is that you can be brought before the grand jury if you are a political activist these days, be questioned about your activities and activities of your group under a grant of limited immunity, and yet be prosecuted, convicted, and jailed for something about which you have, in effect, been forced to testify. This, in my view, operated in derogation of the Fifth Amendment right against self-incrimination.

Interstate Riot Act

In the catalogue of repressive legislation, I think, we should include the Interstate Riot Act which focuses upon what is in one's mind when crossing state lines, rather than what behavior one is engaged in. What one might be thinking when he crosses from Indiana to Illinois thus becomes the subject of criminal prosecution—the so-called H. Rap Brown Statute. It has been suggested that if you take this statute seriously, and accept its assumptions, then a prime candidate for prosecution under this statute is the Vice President of the United States.

Repressive Administration of the Law

In the area of repressive administration of the law, in attempting to delineate those problems which we see in the law as far as political activists are concerned, one of the first areas that concerns me is the street level violence, the administration of law at the end of the policeman's nightstick, and the way in which the new technology is being integrated into the street level violence to make all the more powerful the forces of the state when it deals with the citizen. I am speaking in particular of the black citizen at the street level. We think about the daily police abuse that persons in minority communities experience—both verbal and physical. We think in particular of police riots. I personally witnessed events at Mohammed's Mosque #7 in New York last week, in which police with the butts of their pistols smashed in windows of the mosque, and I watched them fire in the mosque and go in and fight with people on the inside.

This is only the most recent example of a long scenario stretching back through our entire history. We think about the police riot at the 1968 Democratic Convention. We think about the police attack upon the Oakland Panther Office. We think about the police in Brooklyn, New York, who in the halls of a courtroom, in plain clothes, attacked members of the Black Panther Party. We think about the systematic attacks that have been made upon the Black Panther Party and other political organizations around the country. We think about the attack made upon the Republic of New Africa in Jackson,

Mississippi, and of the whole catalogue of official murders.
We think of the death of the forty-three persons in Attica, of
the death of Mark Clark and Fred Hampton, the deaths at
Jackson State, at Orangeburg, at Kent, and perhaps the death
of George Jackson.

"Red Squads" and Surveillance

Street-level violence is only the beginning of problems in
the administration of criminal justice where minorities and
political activists are concerned. We have as well very serious
legal and constitutional problems in the way in which it is a
generalized police practice in this country, usually through
bureaus of special services or "red squads" or whatever they
are called in local communities, to operate and carry out an
intelligence function in the community, particularly directed
at activists' communities. The dossiers that are kept on groups
and individuals who are not engaged in any criminal conduct,
I would submit, are illegal. The fact that there are data banks
in the red squads, in bureaus of special services and special
units of police departments throughout the urban areas of
this country which store and transmit information on individuals who have been involved in no criminal conduct, who
are suspected of no criminal conduct, but whose First Amendment activities have become the subject of police scrutiny,
violates fundamental constitutional principles.

I do not know how many of you have witnessed in your own
experience persons at demonstrations being photographed
either by the police covertly or by the police acting under the
veil or secrecy granted through a press pass, posing as reporters, or, as I know on some occasions, operating cameras from
the roofs of buildings. This kind of surveillance has its impact-
—not only in the form of the "chilling effect" it has on would-
be demonstrators, but also in its consequences for those so
bold as to act notwithstanding surveillance. A special incidence of the problem, and something that should be of special
concern to law students, is the way in which this kind of

intelligence gathering can come up at a later point to affect a person who has been a political activist who wants to function as a lawyer. It has been my experience in a number of instances that this intelligence information gathered by city police forces has been turned over to the character and fitness committee of the bar examiners to act as a barrier for admission to the bar. This was done *not* on the basis that the person was engaged in any kind of criminal conduct, but that the person was engaged in political activity.

Electronic Surveillance

In the whole area of surveillance and political uses of the law, I feel that we must put a great deal of emphasis upon the use of electronic surveillance and wiretap or "bugging," especially the Crime Control Act and the provisions of the Crime Control Act which I mentioned earlier, which remove from judicial control the so-called "national security exception." The Department of Justice records for 1970 indicate that there were 113 bugs authorized under this exception—that is, without judicial scrutiny. The awesome number that this represents can be understood when we realize that in the same period all of the other authorized bugging by the federal judiciary totaled only 183.

Informants

The next signpost in political use of the law is the way in which increasingly the informant is being used against political groups and individuals. Now this is not new. We have always had informants involved in the administration of criminal justice—the so-called squealer. But many of the practices today are much more nefarious than we have generally experienced in the past. There is a special problem today in the black community in the way in which black individuals are being used to infiltrate groups and to act as informants on groups.

... The special problem with informants is that increasingly informants are being used who have very serious criminal charges pending against them or otherwise have the "sword of Damocles" hanging over their heads. The fact that this man or woman, quite often a narcotics addict who has serious charges or even long sentences hanging over his head, is pressed into service as an informant can have dire consequences for fair and effective law enforcement. What you have is the natural situation in which entrapment flourishes. If a person is placed in the position in which he or she is supposed to produce, they are going to produce. And what you get as a result are the worse kinds of police practices where arrests are made pursuant to this kind of information.

Agent Provocateur

The next signpost, the agent provocateur, the person who establishes a certain credibility in the community at the insistence of police by working with aboveground, visible groups and then uses that liaison to work with groups of lower visibility to gain their confidence, himself becomes the initiator of criminal conduct which results in the arrest of the leaders of the group. We have seen this pattern develop in many situations with political groups around the country, in the Black Panther Party and other political groups, where a person comes into the organization and then, in effect, "sets up" the leadership by instigating criminal conduct which results in indictments which are quite often spurious indictments against the leadership of the organization.

We had an experience not too long ago in New York City where Officer Wilbur Thomas joined the Brooklyn branch of the Black Panther Party, and where he convinced Alfred Cain, Ricardo De Leon, and Jerome West, members of the party, that it would be a good idea to carry out an armed robbery; in fact, he said: Let me draw the map, let me provide the car, let me get you some guns. He did all those things, and then these leaders of the Black Panther Party in Brooklyn were arrested for conspiracy to rob and murder. It was only after we discovered his role as agent provocateur that we were able to win an acquittal in that case. But that is not an isolated case. The agent provocateur is among us. If you have been listening to some of the testimony in the peace movement cases, the Camden, New Jersey, case in particular, you know that many times the criminality, if there is any, is criminality which has been instigated by a person who is there as a representative of the state.

Mass Arrests

I will next draw your attention to the problem of mass arrest, without probable cause, in so-called emergency situations. This political administration seems prepared to do away with constitutional guarantees on the theory of "emergency." Mass arrests of hundreds of persons were made here in this city [Washington, D.C.] during the May Day demonstrations which completely ignored the constitutional requirement of probable cause for an arrest and betrayed the small regard that those in power have for the right of the citizen to be free from arbitrary arrest.

Grand Jury Manipulation

In addition, I have already mentioned the immunity problem before the grand jury. However, the whole functioning of the grand jury today is a political problem, a problem for political activists. . . . The problem is that historically, the grand jury was meant to be a shield against the state, while increasingly in these times, particularly in political cases, it is being used as an arm of the state, a rubber stamp of the state. It is the way in which prosecutors are increasingly creating their files on political organizations. Grand jury investigations are conducted in secret, adhering to an essentially ex parte format in which the person testifying is not represented. They compile as much information as possible about a political group. Even though the investigation may not result in an indictment, it does result in significant amounts of intelligence gathering, and it can be a considerable harassment factor as well.

Bail as Ransom

I have mentioned the money-bail system in an institutional sense, in the way in which, institutionally, I think it reflects caste and class bias. But particularly in a political sense the bail system is also a problem because it is used as a political weapon. It is used in a way that gives political activists a "taste of jail" prior to a conviction. It is a way of putting a ransom on political activists: Thus, for example, you have a situation where persons who were charged with the Panther 21 conspiracy in New York City were held in jail for two years under a $100,000 bail. This exorbitant bail is a typical response when a political person is arrested.

The *Stack* v. *Boyle* 342 U.S. 1 (1951) pronouncement that the only legitimate purpose of bail is to ensure the appearance of the defendant at trial. Notwithstanding this judicially acknowledged rule, in political cases, bail is systematically used against persons who are charged with crimes and who have been involved in political activity of a controversial character.

Conspiracy Charge

I would also ask that we look at the nature of some of these charges, in particular the conspiracy charge. Conspiracy has been used since the days of the King of England, when the state felt it had a weak case. When the state did not feel confident about convicting on a substantive charge, it used conspiracy. This is because of the amorphous nature of the conspiracy charge and the elasticity of the rules of evidence under a conspiracy charge. Learned Hand once said, "Conspiracy is the darling of the prosecutor's nursery." And you can see why. *Con-spiro*, the etymology of conspiracy, means "to breathe together," and sometimes that is literally about all you have to do before you will be charged with conspiracy in this country.

Look at the situation of Bobby Seale and Erika Huggins in New Haven, the Panther 21 in New York, the Chicago 8, the Harrisburg defendants, Angela Davis. Time and time again, conspiracy, conspiracy, conspiracy. This charge should be a flag that goes up as an indicator every time that we find it these days and should make us very cautious in appraising what is really occurring.

The fact that the major political cases around the country in the last year or so have in general resulted in major victories for the political activist[s] from the black community who have been attacked, should not in any way give us confidence. . . . I think the more germane issue, rather than the vindication of the system, is why were these charges brought in the first place. Why did the Panther 21 have to spend two years in jail to be acquitted of 156 counts?

Sentencing and Other Discretionary Powers

An additional signpost on the road of the political uses of the law against minority citizens is the whole area of sentencing and the abuse of discretion in this area. In fact, in all areas in which judicial discretion is involved we have a problem with its perversion and distortion in the case of political persons— in parole, probation, sentencing, and commutation. I think a good example of what I am talking about is the experience of a young brother, Lee Otis Johnson, whose alleged crime was the giving of a marijuana joint to an undercover agent, but whose real crime was that he was a SNCC worker, that he was a political activist and a threat to the Texas Establishment. Upon conviction of this charge, this political man was given thirty years in prison. This kind of situation is repeated throughout the country, where a person may be charged with one thing, of which he or she may very well be innocent, and upon conviction be sentenced for another because of who he or she is.

Attorney Persecutions

. . . Increasingly, one of the political uses of the law is not against the activists alone, but against his attorney.

I have seen in recent months a vast quantity of cases in which persons who have been defending political activists have themselves become the subject of contempt proceedings, disciplinary proceedings, or perhaps been charged with a crime. Recent examples include contempt and/or other charges brought against Dan Taylor of Louisville, Kentucky, a very progressive white attorney, who has been representing the poor, black, and the oppressed in that city for some time; Attorney JeRoydx Greene, who will be speaking on the program this afternoon, has had the problem in Richmond, Virginia, along these lines recently, as has Edward Bell of California very recently. These are only a few.

Corrections

The final signpost that I would like to say something about . . . has to do with punishment. That is, the way in which prisons are being run today as it relates to political activity of minority persons. . . .

The experience at Attica is one in which a great deal of focus has been upon the actions of inmates during September 9 through September 13 of 1971. What is often not realized, however, is that in a very political way, persons at the Attica Correctional Facility for a considerable period of time had been organizing and had been attempting in established ways to redress their grievances. They had petitioned the Department of Correctional Services and the superintendent of the prison. Attempts had been made to use the courts. There was a long history of attempts by political persons imprisoned to raise the question of the system that imprisoned them. The point is that the response of the corrections officials was in general mindless and lawless; because not only did they not respond to established grievance procedures followed by the prisoners, but when the prisoners resorted to self-help, the response was one of indiscriminate violence, of wholesale slaughter, of failure to regard the law.

The experience that we had in trying to assist political people in Attica, both during the rebellion and after the rebellion, is instructive as to the way the penal system is functioning in the country today. Lawyers were kept out of Attica;

medical personnel were kept out of Attica despite a federal court order. We went to federal court when we were barred and got a temporary restraining order from the Western District of New York, and still prison officials refused to permit entry. Corrections officials stood in the prison house door the way George Wallace stood in the schoolhouse door. It was interposition and nullification all over again.

The problem of access is a very critical problem, especially for those of us who are trying to address the aspects of political activity in prisons today. It was a problem in the death of George Jackson. I do not exactly know how George Jackson died, but I know he did not die the way they said he died. However, we are not going to be able to find out the answer[s] to these kinds of questions and effectively represent our clients, and effectively get them the full benefits of their rights, if access is going to be controlled by the very persons who are suspect. The problem of Attica and the problem at San Quentin is a problem throughout this country.

One last example that I would give you and that we must begin to address if we are serious about using the law in this area is the way in which interstate compacts are being used to break up positive action on the part of inmates for self-help. These compacts are little known—in fact, I only learned of them last year—but apparently, for some time, there have been agreements existing between states which, under certain conditions, allow corrections officials in one state to remove prisoners from that state and put them in institutions in another state. Now the sinister implications of this are seen by the experience of the brothers in the Afro-American Society at the Adult Correctional Institution (ACI) in Rhode Island, which is a state prison in Rhode Island. They had a very advanced and progressive program of cultural education, of political education in which they had an effective liaison with the outside black community. About the time of Attica last fall, Rhode Island prison officials finally decided that there was going to be trouble there too, and the way to deal with trouble was to have recourse to interstate compacts. So, literally, in the dead of night, they went to the cells of the leaders of the Afro-American Society and took them from their cells and shipped some to Illinois, some to Georgia, some to Kansas. The next morning, one local black woman, who had had two sons in the ACI, found out that one of her sons was in Kansas and the other was in Georgia. She thought all along that they were just a few miles away in the state prison.[7] Her experience and the experience of so many other black people has reinforced the conviction that, in many respects, the legal system —from both the point of view of the administration of criminal justice and the point of view of the operation of the so-called correctional system—poses a real threat to the health and growth of the black community in general, and to the black political activist in particular.

Conclusion

Professor Madison has asked me to say what, if anything, can be suggested by way of strategies, to deal with these particular facts. I have to say at the outset, I know of no simple remedy. Because in the first instance, litigation is, I feel, of only limited benefit since increasingly the idea of the test case has to be reevaluated in the light of the changing composition of the United States Supreme Court. There are certain latitudes we still have, I feel, in using litigation as a tool, but one of our challenges right now in addressing this problem as I see it is to create other tools, to fashion other tools out of our legal experience and expertise. As Professor Madison has already said, law is not a panacea. I do feel, nonetheless, that it is too useful a tool to be abandoned. However, if we are going to deal with this problem, we cannot give over complete reliance on the law to change it, because the political uses of the law relate to the political nature of the society. We cannot expect the law, more than any other single institution of this society, to transcend the society. It is going to reflect the society and answer to the politics of this country.

. . . The law and political uses of it will change fundamentally when the society changes fundamentally. Law and law-yers—particularly minority lawyers—can aid and abet this process through the use of developed and sharpened legal skills. There is a need for *servicing* the general legal require-ments of the people in the community to enable them to carry on their daily lives. There is a need for *test cases* to push the law at its outer limits in attempting to establish precedents that will have a spreading effect and impact on the lives of large num-bers of people. There is a need to create new and *innovative strategies* out of the existing legal arsenal, new approaches to litigation, class action, administrative agencies and legislative solutions. There is a need for the development of in-depth, *long-range policy analysis* of the think tank variety, accom-panied by interdisciplinary attempts at problem solving. There is a need to use the law to *insulate* those who are about the business of challenge and change in other arenas, so that they can continue their political work. . . . Finally, the law and knowledge of it must be used to educate, inform, and *gal-vanize* a wider community into action. A heightened aware-ness of the repressive political uses of the law should provoke a response from its victims. Lawyers are uniquely situated to arm the people with this knowledge and to assist them as they develop their own counterstrategies.

Change is not so much an event as it is a process. The law used in these ways will complement, facilitate, and dovetail with the efforts being made for change in other sectors, con-tributing to the overall process by which the victims of the repressive and political uses of the law may someday bring their victimizers to account and establish a more just social order.

Highlighting the connection between law and politics, the authors of the following article characterize the criminal justice system as an awesome weapon used by the "white racist ruling class" to perpetuate its dominance over poor and powerless people, most of whom are blacks or other minorities, while continuing to deal leniently with elitist lawbreakers. At this time of challenge to the political scheme of things, criminal law takes on increasing utility in controlling the challengers. The article is reprinted with permission from the authors and the *Howard Law Journal* of Howard University. Howard Moore, Jr. (AB, Morehouse College and LL B, Boston University) is a partner in the law firm of Moore, Alexander and Rindskopf in Atlanta, Georgia. Jane Bond Moore is the director and founder of the Research Center for Prison Movement Information in Berkeley, California. She obtained her AB degree from Spelman College and is a member of the class of 1975 at the School of Law, University of California at Berkeley.

SOME REFLECTIONS: ON THE CRIMINAL JUSTICE SYSTEM, PRISONS, AND REPRESSIONS

Howard Moore, Jr., and Jane Bond Moore

ON AUGUST 7, 1970, Jonathan Jackson walked into a virtually empty courtroom in Marin County California, and took command at gunpoint of the proceedings. He liberated three Black inmates, two of whom were killed along with a Superior Court Judge as they attempted to drive away in a rented Hertz Van. That act of courage and total devotion to the liberation of Black people touched off a spark which ignited the prison movement throughout the United States.

Before Jonathan Jackson, killed at age seventeen in the August 7th action, could be memorialized, inmates in the Toombs, [*sic*] a notorious New York City Prison, on August 11, 1970, seized the prison and presented a list of grievances to the Mayor's office and the press. They concluded their grievances with this remarkable statement:

> We are firm in our resolve (for better treatment) and we demand, as human beings, the dignity and justice that is due to us by right of our birth. We not know how the present system of brutality and dehumanization and injustice has been allowed to be perpetuated in this day of enlightment, but we are the living proof of its existence and we cannot allow it to continue.

We will analyze the causes and reasons for the perpetuation of the horrendous conditions which caused the Toombs [*sic*] Revolt. We will also examine the matrix of oppression and repression which reflects itself in the continued revolts of our brothers and sisters on the inside—from Angola to San Quentin to Attica.

Description of the Criminal Justice System

The criminal justice system is the formal apparatus through which the state organizes and rationalizes the identification and control of deviants. Through an interlocking maze of juvenile courts, reform schools, jails, prisons, parole and probation officers, and courts, control over deviants may be imposed from early childhood to the grave. The administrative, managerial, and custodial staffs within this system constitute a vast bureaucracy virtually immune to the imposition of any endurable sanctions and close public scrutiny.

In the Anglo-Saxon tradition, those who broke the law were once punished by physical means—maiming or death. Over the centuries an overtly stated "humane" tradition has evolved. Presently, if one were to ask people knowledgeable about the functions and operation of the criminal justice system, what its objectives are one would find agreement with this broad statement of principle:

> . . . the protection of society from crime and the treatment

of the offender, not the exaction of revenge and the criminal's punishment.

Despite strong empirical evidence that punishment for punishment sake is still the predominant aspect of the system,
rehabilitation and preventive detention, along with the
restraint of the potentially dangerous, are most often stated
by administrators and penologists as the ultimate aims of
prisons and the apparatus surrounding them.

As with any other function of society, criminal justice is
interwoven and intertwined with the whole. The values, judgments, and fears of those in power are expressed in its con-
structs, however obtusely; they become opaque whenever the
system itself is subjected to close scrutiny. Through firm control of the legislative, law enforcement, and the criminal labell-
ing processes, the white racist ruling class defines what acts
are criminal and fixes penalties. Thus criminal law, in both
content and administration, is a political instrument, written
and enforced by the powerful against the poor and powerless,
who are for the most part Blacks or other ethnic minorities.

What sort of crimes do those in power fear? What do they
need to be protected from? [A brief look at the history of the
treatment oriented criminal justice system will suggest answers.]

The post-Civil War racial conflict, growing industry, and
immigration combined to influence the present system. To
the capitalist elite, the most serious threats were in non-
adherence to Puritan values of industry, savings and accumulation.

To control newly freed Blacks and non-WASP immigrant
groups, the elite needed to develop a rationale of criminal
justice that would differentiate between the criminal who
threatened the whole social order by his refusal to abide by
even the most basic norms (i.e. Protestant ethic) and those who
did not, while still maintaining a facade of liberalism and
humanitarianism so as to obscure the breach between theory
and practice. To those who were growing powerful from

industry and what they conceived of as self-discipline, the significance of conventional street crime—theft, pickpocketing, rape—was not so much the violence of the act itself but in its challenge to their was of life.

It becomes a political and practical necessity to differentiate between types of criminals. As the Quakers say in *Struggle for Justice: A Report on Crime and Punishment in America,*

> . . . upper and middle-class criminals, whether [murderers] or embezzlers, have slipped in practice but . . . [retain] as ideals the conventional values . . . they may be morally weak or psychologically deviant, but they are not revolutionary.

When criminal behavior indicates the "criminal" does not share the same core values as the ruling class in society, the criminal is a threat and must be dealt with more severely than one who is of "our kind" but just so inefficient as to be caught. Crime in the streets represents at even an unconscious level a potentially revolutionary impulse. Its rejection of private property, industry, saving and accumulation must be curbed.

The individualized treatment model—with its vagueness, surrounding length of incarceration, and the emphasis on demonstrable rehabilitation—is the ideal model. The underlying rationale, to quote the Friends again,

> . . . is deceptively simple . . . it would serve the offender through constructive measures of reformation, protect society by keeping the offender locked up until that reformation is accomplished and reduce the crime rate not only by using cure-or-detention . . . also by identification of potential criminals in advance . . .

The indeterminate sentence (which pervades the whole criminal justice system—not merely California)—in which a prisoner is kept in a cage until his behavior, attitudes, and ideas please the cager—in turn was the fulcrum for two chief characteristics of the present criminal justice system. One, its wide discretionary powers based on the rationale that treatment should be matched to the criminal's individual needs, and two, centering the power to help the criminal reform in the same agencies charged with protecting society from his deviant acts.

The typical employee of this system is the parole officer who has the ambiguous task of simultaneously helping the parolee, while also constantly checking him out to make sure he has not lapsed into his old criminal ways.

Now where do we as a race stand in this confusing philosophy? The subordinate and powerless position of Blacks within the criminal justice system has remained practically unchanged since slavery. At that time we were legal *nothings* with perhaps the status of real estate or livestock—systematically excluded from jury service, holding judgeships, acting in our own defense and all other criminal law proceedings protecting whites. After the Civil War, the Black Codes, were enacted, containing the same restrictions. Despite 100 years of struggle, what do we have? Police brutality and summary violence are still common within our community, jury service is by and large limited to whites—are we being judged by our peers? The personnel of the justice system is pervasively white from police through wardens, judges, district attorneys all the way to parole board members.

It should be clear that any changes in the structure of the criminal justice system will affect only the administration of justice. They can never eliminate the powerless, null position Blacks, native Americans, Spanish speaking people are forced to assume in any encounter with the justice system—in arrest, trial or imprisonment. Any search for justice in such a system will be meaningless since criminal justice is always dependent upon the justice of the larger society.

Problems of Prisons

Prisons are the ultimate threat of the criminal justice system. Prisons have come to the forefront of the liberal conscience within the last two or three years. Historically prisons developed out of two needs—the need of the Industrial Revolution for cheap labor (i.e. the convict labor or poor whites that help populate colonies such as U.S.A. and Australia) and the growing thought that deviants should be assimilated into dominant cultures (the French philosophers and the rights of man via the English utilitarians). At the present historical stage, prisons are reservoirs for those with black skins, little money and non-middle-class life styles.

What are the functions of prisons? There are the stated functions, the roles the public would respond to, in a Gallup poll for instance. Prisons provide protection from anti-social acts such as murder, rape, assault and theft and by their mere existence deter unknown quantities of potential criminals. (This rests on the belief that *all* crime is a rational act.) Prisons serve to punish (despite all protestations to the contrary of wardens). To most people the state has replaced religion as the ultimate source of authority and to them the state not only has the ability but also the right and duty to punish. In a Law Day speech before the City Common Club, Warden Louis S. Nelson of San Quentin, summarized the prison system by noting, "[n]o one believes prisons will fade away. They will remain as the visible symbol of the wages of sin." Through punishment prison prevents anarchy and in some way improves the criminal, as much as spanking "improves" a child. And finally we have rehabilitation—back to the individual treatment model.

There are also the other functions. Prisons aid us in our ". . . mental acting out of . . . anti-social behavior and transference of guilt to others, i.e. criminals." Prisons are important laboratories for social control—governments can experiment in population management techniques—look at the new MPDU in California where "troublemakers" receive group therapy, lobotomies and other forms of brain surgery, and drugs. Finally, prisons are good places to put problems—what else to do with young Blacks who are too old and/or bored in school and not docile enough for the army? There are certainly no jobs for them.

The actual prison population is an index of what the society really views as crimes. Any study of prison populations in the U.S. indicates the determining factors in incarceration are always racial, social and economic. Dr. DuBois observed:

> What turns me cold in all this experience is the certainty that thousands of innocent victims are in jail today because they had neither money, experience nor friends to help them. . . . They daily stagger out of prisons embittered, vengeful, hopeless, ruined. And of this army of the wronged, the proportion of Negroes is frightful. We protect and defend sensational cases where Negroes are involved. But the great mass of arrested or accused black folk have no defense. There is desperate need . . . to oppose this national racket of railroading to jails and chain gangs the poor, friendless and black.

For instance although the income tax code is the most frequently violated federal law, and though throughout our life the importance of honest monetary transactions are held out as an ideal, delinquent taxpayers are a minute percentage of the prison population. The usual procedure in those cases is to pay back taxes, interests and fines. Compare this to car thieves (even the language is harsher—delinquent as opposed to thief). It is clear that the all encompassing class nature of this society results in a criminal justice system in which burglary and robbery are such serious crimes that they carry maximums of twenty years to life, and in some states the death penalty. On the other hand malfunctioning automobiles that kill or injure three to four times as many persons annually as all violent crimes combined involve no criminal sanctions and even no civil liability in many situations. Any rational person would concede that even the crimes and murders of a Charles Manson are far less damaging to the society than acts against life and health daily perpetuated by the powerful. By this we mean that napalm from Dow Chemical Company has killed many more people than Charles Manson and his weird family. More babies are dead and maimed from eating lead contaminated paint in ancient slums than from parental abuse.

Within the prison the powerless position of blacks is omnipresent. There are always unequal job assignments with blacks receiving the worse—hardest least interesting. We are given fewer chances at meaningful vocational training (if any exists) and severely punished if we decline to take part in the farce the prison administrators denote as meaningful work— *e.g.* Huey Newton.

Black nationalist and Black Muslim literature are banned, even at the risk of letting through Communist materials. (Angela, Mao, Marx and Che).

Prisoners who show signs of becoming leaders or who challenge the institutional way of doing things through law suits, or by personal example are at the mercy of administrative punishment and the wrath of the guards (*e.g.* George Jackson).

> More judges and "more" experts for the courts, improved education and therapeutic programs in penal institutions, more and better trained personnel at higher salaries, preventive surveillance of predelinquent children, greater use of probation, careful classification of inmates, preventive detention through indeterminate sentences, small "cottage" institutions, halfway houses, removal of broad classes of criminals (such as juveniles) from criminal to "nonpunitive" processes, the use of law personnel in treatment—all this paraphernalia of the "new criminology" appears over and over in 19th century reformist literature. After more than a century of persistent failure, this reformist prescription is bankrupt.

The reformers and prison administrators play and re-play the same old theme; the critic attacks; the system co-opts and then reworks the idea for its own use and benefit. The whole drama takes place within a framework that legitimizes this society's right to call others "criminals". Abolition of prisons is a far more rational act than reform. Prisons do not prevent crime—there are more prisons and, according to the F.B.I., more crime than ever before. Prisons assuredly do not aid in any conceivable way to rehabilitate the inmates. ". . . the evils of imprisonment are that regardless of reforms they are still there—whether or not the buildings are antiseptic or dirty, the aroma that of fresh bread, or stale urine . . ."

Repressive Functions of the Criminal Justice System

Under the publicly stated purpose of protecting the public at large from crime and rehabilitating the criminal are the repressive functions of the criminal justice system. By repressive we mean those functions that are unstated, unacknowledged and illicit.

How do we know they exist? By looking at the facts of life—particularly in the Black community—of the impact of the justice system. In *Struggle for Justice*, it is summarized,

> Hundreds of citizens are killed by the police each year, often under circumstances that suggest gross neglect or summary execution. There is indiscriminate paramilitary police brutality on the streets. No effective redress for police victims or civilian controls over the police has been developed. The use of arrest rather than summonses is grossly disproportionate. There is excessive and discriminatory use of pretrial detention. Through confession processes that make a mockery of the adversary system there is usually conviction without trial. Prosecutors have excessive discretionary power, often exercised on the basis of favoritism, political influence, class bias, or caprice. Sentencing is grossly disparate, illogical, and unprincipled, with even such an elementary reform as appellate review of sentencing largely ignored.

Why, despite the facade of humanitarianism and liberalism is it necessary for the criminal justice system to maintain these abuses of civil rights and liberties? Because this is a time when challenge after challenge to the legitimacy of the country's power is being mounted. Blacks and other minorities—including some of the white poor and young—are becoming more and more aware and increasingly vocal concerning their voicelessness in society.

Theodore Sarbin, in his pamphlet, *The Myth of the Criminal Type*, explains,

> Those persons or groups that threaten the existing power structure are dangerous. In any historical period, to identify an individual whose status is that of a member of the "dangerous classes" . . . the label "criminal" has been handy . . . [The] construct, criminal, is not used to classify the performers of all legally defined delicts—offenses against the law—only those whose position in the social structure qualifies them for membership in the dangerous classes.

An illustration of this is the earlier reference to the number of federal prisoners convicted of car theft as opposed to those convicted of income tax offenses. Car "theft" with its flaunting of private property and hard work is clearly a greater danger to the society than stealing money through falsifying government forms.

Parole and probation are another good example of how identification and surveillance of "dangerous classes" is masked by the surface, helpful functions. At best, parole and probation have become a ritual but its common function is as an auxiliary policing device. A parole hearing is a good example of the fallacies inherent in the criminal justice system. No relevant scientific knowledge is available, despite thousands of dollars spent on research, to indicate who is and who is not a good parole candidate. Parole decisions are ultimately based on the bias, prejudices and hunches of the board members.

The absolute power of the administrators of the criminal justice system is necessary to continue its repressive functions.

Indeed, the best antidote . . . to . . . the claims made for the
necessity and importance of the [absolute and unchecked]
discretion that permeates criminal justice administration is
to engage in a comparative examination of criminal law
and the laws governing taxation, corporations, and commercial transactions. [W]hen it comes to matters concerning their vested interests, the men . . . who write the law . . .
give short shrift to discretion. If discretion is written into a
major law it is because legislators are confident . . . they will
be able to control its exercise.

The manipulation of the criminal justice system by the
powerful is perhaps most evident in the economic sphere.
Quoting not a Communist party pamphlet, but the American
Friends Service Committee, this religious and God-fearing
group makes the following analysis:

Tax laws are another means whereby the powerful increase
their economic dominance. Efforts to plug scandalous tax
loopholes have been unsuccessful . . . there are dozens of
millionaires who pay no income tax . . . Taxes are extracted
from salaried workers every payday by means of withhold-
ing; those in the upper brackets have considerably more
opportunity to avoid taxes, legally, semi-legally, or illegally.
When violations are detected, the government rarely
invokes the criminal process. The tax cheater can usually
get off by paying a fine. [T]he government has been
extremely reluctant to prosecute business leaders for such
widespread and socially harmful crimes as deceptive advertising, pollution, selling dangerous merchandise, and
violating anti-trust laws. . . . When the government acts at
all in such cases, it usually prefers administrative rather
than criminal proceedings."

What better example of the racial and class nature of the
entire criminal justice system?

To maintain the repressive functions of the criminal justice
system, an enormous paramilitary system has developed. The
overt repression of numerous political trials—Angela Davis,

"Rap" Brown, the various Panther trials, Lee Otis Johnson, Donald Stone, Pentagon Papers, etc.—is reinforced by the expansion of police power. Beginning with the disorders connected with the civil rights movement and the beginning of anti-war protests, according to the National Action/Research on the Military Industrial Complex, ". . . Police forces . . . have become paramilitary. They have received training from the Department of Defense and are adapting to domestic use weapons developed for Vietnam . . . [this trend] has led to the emergence of a police-industrial-educational complex spawned by the Pentagon." The Law Enforcement Assistance Administration (LEAA), a federal agency created in 1968, is budgeted for $1,750,000,000 in 1973 and is slated to continue to expand. LEAA funds police training programs in 880 colleges and universities. It also includes work on counterinsurgency techniques and the development of new weapons and equipment. According to *Justice*, a magazine that seems to support the viewpoint of the administrators in the criminal justice system, federal funds through LEAA can be spent on technically oriented purchases for ". . . computerized game theory, mathematical environment, command and control systems for jet aircraft, digital communications and the like." Secret police have proliferated. The FBI, the CIA and the intelligence branches of the various armed forces, national and local are spying on us. The most sophisticated electronic surveillance equipment is theirs. Congress aids the creeping facism [*sic*] by passing bills that:

> . . . allow municipal, state and federal law enforcement officials, with court approval to tap and bug anyone who had committed, seemed to be in the act of committing, or was believed to be about to commit a crime punishable by a year or more in prison.

What can we conclude from all this? The criminal justice system is bankrupt—it is certainly more criminal itself than those over whose life it holds complete dominance. There is no possibility of justice or equality of treatment within a society where powers and opportunity are unequal. Attempts to introduce so-called scientific objectives are only fronts for sophisticated continuance of discrimination against the powerless. Decisions concerning guilt and innocence can only reflect the prejudice of the larger society. De facto discrimination, even if individual prejudice could be removed, will occur as long as people suffer from differences in class and money.

The selection of victims by the criminal justice system reflects inequality in the larger society—not only because of prejudice of police or prosecutors, but because the substantive content of the law affects those who are not social equals in quite different ways.

> The brutality of racism and the indignities of second-class citizenship still characterize the administration of criminal justice. The racist ideologies of chattel slavery and of separate but equal have been legally dead but the ugly corpse is not buried. The justice system remains an instrument of white Anglo-Saxon dominance and a barrier to the development of full power within the community of oppressed peoples.

Against this background, the contours of the struggle ahead are clear. That struggle, if correctly waged, must be animated by efforts to bring about a fundamental and decisive reallocation of power and resources. Unless such a reallocation occurs, future reforms and advances within the criminal justice system will and can only mean that the already chronic situation will become worse.

The parole system is as much a tool for controlling the politically dissident as is the more publicized prison system. Both are used "to isolate and control" people who take issue with the established order. To regulate politicized inmates, authorities grant or deny parole in an extra-legal system of "prison justice" that smashes all rights, particularly those of blacks whom staff members brand as militant or revolutionary. D'Army Bailey's explanation of the political utility of parole justifies presentation of his article in this section. He is with Bailey & Bailey in Memphis, Tennessee.

INEQUITIES OF THE PAROLE SYSTEM IN CALIFORNIA

D'Army Bailey

THE PAROLE system cannot be considered as an isolated phenomenon. To give the parole system its proper perspective, the surrounding societal context as well as the internal conditions of the penal institution must here be discussed briefly.

We should not be surprised that crime occurs in a society whose motivating ethic is the dog-eat-dog law of competition. Greed, selfishness, interpersonal fear, distrust, and hate are but extensions of this ethic. Selfishness (or euphemistically put, individualism) serves as an ideology [*sic*] to justify extremely unequal and unjust distributions of wealth and power. This social stratification finds its geographical manifestation in the ghetto—prisons for the victims of racism; the ghetto's barriers and fences are more devious than any physical wall, for its barriers and shackles come to exist in peoples' minds rather than around their ankles. Racism is a crime against the innocent; a society willing to commit this crime should not be surprised to find those whom it victimizes responding criminally.

But this society *is* willing to ignore the injustice of the social order; it is not willing to ignore or understand the crime of the social victim. This victim stands before a system of justice, which by and large, only the rich can afford, and is sentenced. George Jackson was sentenced to ten years in prison for stealing $80 (a glaring example of the inequity of the indeterminate sentence in California). When he refused to be emasculated by the prison system, he was murdered by prison guards.

The horrors of the penal institution need not be mentioned here; however, all efforts must be made to eliminate them. What needs to be mentioned here is the myth that the penal institution is a force for rehabilitation. Prisons are places of punishment, not of rehabilitation. They are meant to serve as a horrifying example to those who would dare to transgress the law of the land. Prisoners become mere pawns in a system of retributive justice which demands an eye for an eye.

Rehabilitation is a big word, but for a small class of prisoners, it has taken on the eerie overtones of Orwell's *1984*. At Atascadero and Vacaville and other "medical facilities" for the criminally insane, Adjustment Centers have been set up. "Criminally insane" can mean and has meant political agitators. Previously and before the advent of modern drugs, beatings, padded cells, strait jackets and the whims of guards were used to insure that the prisoner "adjust" to his setting. In the '50's, these ineffective means were replaced by electric shock, insulin shock, fever treatments, hydrotherapy and spinal injections to increase the possibility of success. Now a drug, Anectine, which produces a sensation of suffocating and dying, as well as a few other averse therapeutic means such as a program for Errorless Extinction of Penile Responses in which the prisoner is shown an erotic picture to give him an erection and is shocked into impotence, are used to insure adjustment. Lobotomies have been discussed to curb the "violent" type. The Adjustment Center, originally a psychiatric dream, has turned into a nightmare. This rehabilitation is directed at some seven hundred men in the California State Prison System. For the rest, a few futile efforts are made to educate. These futile efforts are of course further limited by the lack of adequate funding and sensitive personnel. Eldridge Cleaver, in *Soul on Ice*, relates his utter amusement at the attempts of an instructor to convince him of American justice. When convicted by a criminal society of a crime, it is hard to accept its verdict. It is in this context that we must view the system of parole.

Within the framework of the California penal system, the parole system is an arbitrary tool, designed to destroy political consciousness among inmates. To this end it discriminates against Blacks, and other minority inmates who have become politicized. The mechanism which allows for this in California is the indeterminate sentence, and in the Federal system the practice of discretionary sentencing (i.e. 5-20 years, or the A2 classification which allows for release at the earliest determination of the United States Parole Board). These two sentencing patterns give almost absolute discretionary power to those individuals who make parole determinations. Tangential to the arbitrary release program under both systems is the application or denial of "good time" as a means of control.

In the California state federal system, one is certain not to receive parole if he does not acquiesce in the assumptions of the prison system and the Adult Authority. Thus, an inmate who maintains that he is innocent of the charges brought against him is often considered non-rehabilitated and will almost never receive a date. According to the Adult Authority this is in fact not their practice, but there is strong evidence to the contrary. In addition, many of the programs that an agency like the Adult Authority requires inmates to participate in have no value, or are in fact demeaning to the inmate. The most obvious example is a group psychotherapy. This program is required of all inmates who have received a psychiatric classification by institution staff (all inmates enter the California—prison system through—in Northern California, the Vacaville Medical Facility, and in Southern California, the Chino Institute for Men). Those who refuse to engage in a psychiatric program can expect to not receive a parole date. In addition, it is well known though not documented, that inmates with "psych referrals" (bestowed upon entrance into the system) serve longer time for comparable crimes than those without. The "psych referral" is but another tool for parole denial.

Of the arbitrary practices of the prison system which relate to parole, the most blatant is the arbitrary application of "prison justice." Within the prison systems of this nation, there is an entrenched extra-legal structure, complete with "courts" (disciplinary committees), classification of crimes (i.e. misdemeanor and felony) and sentencing. More than adequate testimony has been brought forward to show how this system of punishment denies inmates all rights afforded defendants under the Constitution. Inmates have no rights with respect to confronting accusers, having legal representation, preparing defense, calling witnesses, etc. On the basis of a guard's whims or prejudices, an inmate may be arbitrarily detained in an "adjustment center" for an institutional violation.

This practice relates directly to the parole system. When one is incarcerated in the "hole" (Adjustment Center-24-hour per day lock-up) he automatically receives a disciplinary write-up which becomes a part of his institutional record. These write-ups become a deterrent to parole since the Board will view the inmate as possessing anti-social traits. Correspondingly, when an individual is placed in the hole, he is denied access to the very programs which the Adult Authority or Parole Board demands that he pursue in order to receive a release date. So, individuals are held in double jeopardy for institutional violations by receiving punishment (lock-up) for the instant offense and by being accountable for these transgressions at their parole hearing; plus they must carry the additional burden of not having been able to participate in programs that would aid in their release.

Within the State prison system it is becoming very much a matter of course that numerous Black inmates are being branded as "Black militants" or "revolutionaries" by the institutional staff. With this accusation, they are placed many times in isolation as a means of "protection for the institution and the other inmates." Quite often this is foisted upon them due to reading material in their possession, their associations, their gestures (clenched fist), or not infrequently, because they are Black. Once in the hole they are subjected to the same problems associated with placement in the hole for specific institutional violations.

Needless to say, this arbitrary power in the hands of the parole authorities and the prison staff militates against any form of political activity or attempts to organize inmates for the betterment of their instant situation, or for preparing them for life on the outside by inter-cultural self-help programs. Those who choose to engage in this type of activity are branded as revolutionaries and troublemakers, and are placed in lock-up facilities.

Taking into account the absolutely abominable conditions of our prison systems, these systems make criminal any action by which an inmate attempts to assert and contribute to a sense of identity and dignity. All of this, once again, relates directly to an inmate's possibilities for parole.

Above and beyond this use of arbitrary power to control the thinking and actions of individuals incarcerated in our penal institutions, prison authorities quite frequently make deals with inmates to affect their parole in exchange for permission to use their minds and bodies for medical experimentation. This occurs most frequently at institutions such as Vacaville Medical Facility. Quite often the medical experimentation is designed to develop nefarious means of controlling dissident inmates (i.e. the Maximum Psychiatric Diagnostic Unit at Vacaville).

The procedures and criteria by which the Adult Authority determines parole readiness are equally as arbitrary and discriminatory as the actions of institutional personnel which affect, in turn, the parole decisions made by the Adult Authority. At parole hearings in California, the subject being considered is not afforded the right to counsel, cannot challenge in any adversary fashion the anonymous write-ups (disciplinary) in his institutional jacket (which is the major piece of evidence working against him) and is quite often not told the reasons for a parole denial if such is forthcoming. I believe that an example at this point would quite clearly articulate the problem that Black people, in particular, face when confronting the parole board.

After serving two years and some months on a 1-6 year sentence for armed robbery (first offense), a young Black inmate at a federal penitentiary placed the following profile before the Board: He had learned three trades during his incarceration, for which he had the unqualified recommendation of the supervisory personnel. He had taken an extension course at a local educational institution, for which he had received the unqualified recommendation of the director. He had three job opportunities awaiting him upon release. He had been a model inmate. He had a sponsor in the local JayCee's. Despite this perfect parole program, he was turned down for two years without receiving a reason as to how he could improve his program—if that was the criterion for his parole.

Although this may be a slightly unique case, it nonetheless significantly represents the type of treatment Blacks are afforded at the hands of parole authorities. To compound the problem, the courts have adopted a hands-off policy, which prevents any form of adequate redress from parole board determinations.

In short, the parole system, in conjunction with the penal institutions of our society have intensified the racism and racist practices of our society. In addition it is becoming used increasingly as a tool for controlling the politically dissident. Statistics are readily available which clearly show that the median time served by Blacks for comparable crimes is significantly higher than for whites. Such information is also available which would show that populations of adjustment centers across the country show significantly higher percentages of Black inmates than the Black prison population, and higher than the population of the general society. The prison and parole system is truly a system designed to isolate and control all those who dissent and digress from the established order of American society.

Let us here take a very brief empirical tour of the standards used to deny parole. A look at the standards used by the California Adult Authority in 1971 . . . in denying parole indicate that a "negative attitude" is the most serious error a prisoner can be guilty of when hoping to gain parole. Given the dehumanizing effects of the prison system and the concurrent futile attempts to rehabilitate, what but a "negative attitude" can be expected?

Lastly, we cannot ignore the question of parole within the context of this technological society. In a recent article, Ralph K. Schwitzgebel of the Harvard School of Law suggests the use of electronic monitoring of parolees. As the system was still a crude prototype, we need not discuss its means of operation. Its purpose, however, would be to map the parolee's behavior by means of determining his location. If he should be detected in a high crime area, an appropriate warning signal would be sent out to him. The parolee becomes locked in a mobile jail. The question of invasion of the parolee's liberty becomes less significant when we consider that techniques designed for specific purposes more often find extended uses in oppressive and destructive rather than positive ways. Abuse of authority is manifest at all levels of society.

Parole, if it is to signify something more than that a man's backbone has been broken or his mind controlled; if it is to signify some real change, can only take place within the context of a supportive environment. The prisons provide no such environment. Prisons should provide intellectual stimulation along with relevant job training, in addition to positive social interactions. . . .

Again, the inequities of the parole system can only be reversed when the over-all prison system has been restructured which, in turn, can only be effected by a society that recognizes that punitive justice is not the cure but the cancer. . . .

Conclusion

Parole is coercive, not educative. Manifests societal attitudes towards the treatment of prisoners. Used as vehicle for political repression.

Recommendation

Although a frequent means of avoiding a problem is the tendency to expand its perimeters, the parole system cannot be effective and equitable without a reorganization of the prison system. The prison system must be made to serve the purpose of rehabilitation rather than punishment. Black leaders and lawmakers must demand representative participation in the reorganization of the prison system in order to protect the largest number of its victims. Societal attitudes towards crime and punishment must, of necessity, also be redirected through education.

Civil law, no less than criminal law, works to the advantage of whites (certainly the well-to-do) and to the disadvantage of blacks (seemingly whatever they do). This is not by chance but by politics: those who have the most get the most of whatever is to be got because or in spite of the law whose enactment and enforcement fall to them and their agents by virtue of their political predominance. The point of all this is made by Judge Mark E. Jones, whose article brings sharply into focus the use of the civil justice machinery by people of means in their highly successful efforts to exploit people of little means. His article exposes elitism at work in the location, rules, hours of court operation, and "all other meaningful things." It serves the additional useful purpose of highlighting the inescapable responsibility that legislators bear for this unfairness. Judge Jones took his AB and JD degrees at Roosevelt University and Loyola University respectively. He is the treasurer of the Judicial Council and at its founding convention in Atlanta, Georgia, on August 5, 1971, read the paper that is reprinted here with permission from him and the *Journal of Public Law* of Emory University. Judge Jones sits on the Circuit Court of Cook County in Chicago.

RACISM IN SPECIAL COURTS

Mark E. Jones

YOU'VE BEEN hearing about racism and classism in the country and in the courts. Many people, for many years, have suggested that while racism surely does exist . . . the principal distinctions between persons in this country are based on reasonable classification and that no one can complain of discrimination which results from such reasonable classification.

But if you're being hurt—if your money or liberty is being taken from you when it ought not to be—then there is little comfort to be gained from the knowledge that the law has decreed that your kind be treated that way, and there are many other people in your class who suffer the same fate, or endure the same injustice. Nevertheless, an understanding of the class structure in our society is necessary if we are to understand the effect of classism and racism in the courts. We might agree that our society is divided into two groups or classes. There is one class from whom comes the rule and lawmakers, those who decide what is legal or illegal. They are legislators, appointive and elective officials and, of course, judges. This class is characterized by being convention-conforming, authority-respecting, family-raising, debt-paying, product-and service-consuming, literate and non-poor. Most of these people—almost all—are white. I shall hereafter refer to these people as Class I or CI.

The second class are people who require different adjectives for description. They are poor; many do not work (although some work very hard with very little to show for it). They are illiterate, convention-upsetting, defiers of the highest authority of church and state. They are welfare-receiving, debt-dodging, draft-dodging and, above all, distracting to some of the rest of us because they aren't like us and don't even want to be. Most of these people are white too, but almost half are non-white. Something like 90 per cent of the non-white population, blacks, browns, and reds belong to this class. Let's call these people CII's.

In addition to producing the legislators, judges, and other elected and appointed officials who decide what is legal or illegal, and when a person has committed an act defined as illegal, the CI's also produce the imagemakers, those who decide proper goals for a country, a city, or state and, of course, proper activities and attitudes, and proper beliefs for its people. Some of the CI's who do this are persons employed in media, officials of trade and manufacturing, religious, fraternal, and veterans organizations.

CI persons, as a rule, will not find it difficult to observe the conventions, strive for the goals, and conform to the restrictions CI's decree. CII persons often find it very difficult.

The CI in power, in most cases, will see the good of the community, the good of mankind, and even God's purpose as being served by those who act like [sic] he does and believe as he does. Conversely, he will see the irreverent and uncooperative CII's as opposed to that which is good and desirable, and may deal with them by decreeing a permanent subordinate status for them.

Thus, the preamble to the Constitution of the United States declares that "in order to . . . establish justice, promote the general welfare, and to secure the blessings of liberty to ourselves and our posterity . . ." that [sic] certain propositions would become the law of the land. Among them was section 9 of article I, which is as follows:

> The migration [or] importation of such persons as any of the states now existing shall think proper to admit, shall not be prohibited by the Congress prior to (1808) but a tax or duty may be imposed on such importation not exceeding Ten Dollars for each person.

Section 2 of article IX further stated:

> No person held to service or labour in one state, under the laws there of escaping into another, shall, in consequence of any law or regulation therein be discharged from such service or labour, but shall be delivered up on claim of the party to whom such service or labour may be due.

Thus we find racism and classism in the basic law of our land. It did not matter to the runaway slave being caught in a free state, and returned to his owner whether it was a "fair and reasonable" class or a "blatantly" racist law that returned him to his chains.

What has all this to do with racism in specialized courts? Nothing, unless it alerts us to the possibility that racism or classism does exist today in our courts as we know it exists in our society.

Almost everything that occurs in our courts, and indeed our courts themselves exist, and are results of acts of the Legislature. Except for the Supreme Court of the United States, the Congress and the various state legislatures establish courts and decree matters cognizable in them. Thus the legislatures of most states and the Congress have decreed that most forms of gambling are illegal and that persons caught gambling shall be prosecuted in courts and on conviction suffer such penalties as the laws prescribe. . . .

For whatever reason, we have laws against gambling but only against some gambling. Anyone may: play the stock market, wager at the race track, or go to Las Vegas or the Caribbean and participate in any game of chance imaginable. It is said that high stake poker, bridge, gin rummy, and other games are played at country clubs and downtown university and health clubs. These activities are participated in principally by CI's, but they are not arrested for them.

The gambling activities participated in by the poor are different. They play the numbers or policy or Bolita. They patronize bookies or shoot dice or play cards in places where they are easier to observe and easier to arrest. It can be argued that our gambling laws are democratic as Anatole France declared laws of France to be, since they "prohibited the rich as well as the poor from begging bread in the streets and from sleeping under bridges at night."

If demonstrative proof is required of racism in this area of the law, then I'd recommend that you take a look at the courts in your jurisdiction where gambling cases are heard. Most or all of the defendants are CII's and any observer would have to conclude that the rich and powerful and white never shoot dice or play cards for money. Similarly, a person observing defendants in "Women's Court" and other courts where prostitutes are prosecuted would conclude that all CI's are moral, since the defendants, day in and day out, are mostly poor and black.

I suggested that my guess would be that more than 90 per cent of the black, Latin, or brown, and Indian people are CII's. When they have any encounter with courts, it's usually to show cause why they shouldn't be punished by fine or jail, or by having a money judgment entered against them. They are almost always there at the instance of some CI, such as a creditor, a landlord, the police, the juvenile authorities, or other government agency.

In the Juvenile Court, he stands before the Judge in most cases because he does not act like [sic] the CI truant officer, case worker, or probationer thinks he ought to act. He ought to like school and to be willing to put up with CI teachers who esteem him lowly, and he should work hard at a non-relevant CI-designed curriculum that assumes a CI cultural background, and CI life expectancies and goals. Yes, he ought to go eagerly into this established thing that everyday shows his shortcomings and deficiencies. Furthermore, he should never ever become influenced by the things he sees on the streets, even though he observes that more often than not crime does pay and that work, when available, does not pay much. He should never steal, rob, push dope, gamble, or commit any of the financially-rewarding activities that he observes some adults commit with impunity and often in connivance with the law.

Even though he has no father to protect him, and even though the law is unable to adequately police the streets and alleys in his neighborhood to keep him from physical harm, he still should never ever join a street gang. It is better to run the risk of being stoned, beaten, or killed than to join a "lawless, crime-committing" street gang.

In Traffic Court the CII does not start out with a presumption of innocence. The official assumption is that the police would not bother anyone who was not guilty of some offense. The harried Judge with 200 cases to hear in one day has heard all the excuses and evasions. If he has to spend too much time with any one defendant's lies, he'll never get through the call. *Besides*, and let no one forget this, those fines, penalties, and costs collected at traffic courts are anticipated by municipal budgets, as are real estate taxes. Unless the anticipated number of CII's are found guilty and fined, cities might not meet their payrolls.

In Small Claims Courts, almost all defendants are CII's.

They are tenants behind in rent, installment purchasers behind in payments to finance companies, or vendors of furniture, food, clothing, autos, or some other necessary item. They are sued because they've been involved in automobile accidents.

Small Claims Courts were, when first set up, created to satisfy the need for a court where small people could have a court designed to offer them a cheap, inexpensive, fast and simple means of settling disputes where money damages should be had by one side over the other.

But these courts are now mainly devices wherein CI creditors have a cheap, inexpensive, and almost sure-fire method of collecting valid, as well as doubtful or spurious, crimes against CII's.

First, the courts are located downtown. Downtown is convenient to most CI's, but most importantly [sic], downtown and the hours are convenient to CI lawyers. It is only CI lawyers (or their secretaries or clerks), who come to court. CI himself seldom has to take the time to come to court.

The story is quite different for CII defendants. They must come to court or suffer judgment in whatever amount CI plaintiff has sued for. Consider the impact of the arrival of a summons and complaint at the home of a CII. He returns home from work or wherever, and finds the "papers." He can read, and so he reads the words on the summons. If you have read all the words on the summons in your jurisdiction you can imagine that implications of its jargon are not fully understood by someone with eighth grade reading ability. Many CII defendants, for reasons known to them, or for no reason, will elect to do nothing and to stay away, perhaps reasoning that no good can come to him from participation in this law suit, and perhaps that if he ignores it, the trouble will go away. Or he may in fact not owe the debt, might never have had a transaction with the plaintiff (but unknown to him has a similar name to someone who did). But unless he takes time off from work and spends carfare or parking lot money to come downtown to file his appearance and pay the appearance fee, "the law" may decree him to be in default, and summarily declare that he owes all the money the plaintiff has asked for. He will discover this unpleasant development when his salary is garnished, or some of his property is repossessed, attached, or sold. But if he goes to the expense of taking a day off, and paying an appearance fee, he only gets information about the date and in what courtroom his case will be heard. The official who has this information has no other information to give him. He returns to court on the date the case is set for trial. If he is an astute observer he will note that as the cases are called, the CI lawyer steps up, and if he observes that no CII defendant is present, will likely answer, "ready," and depending on the proclivity of the Judge he may receive a judgment, or he may only receive the next date. When our CII defendant hears his name, he steps up, and the lawyer will ask that the case be continued, since, after all, it is the first time up and he is entitled to one continuance. The lawyer, law clerk, or whoever appears for the plaintiff, may plead, truthfully, that he does not know enough about the case to discuss it with defendant. Our defendant must then appear for a third time, and it may be that his out-of-pocket money loss may be so great as the claim against him.

What is quite apparent under this system, is that the rules of court, the location of courts, and the times they are open, that all of these things, as are all other meaningful things, are decided by CI's, usually in the interest of and for the convenience of CI's, and that CII's must accommodate to the system or suffer unpleasant consequences.

If CII's had anything at all to say about courts, and if they did not abolish them entirely, they would provide that plaintiffs would have to sue defendants in courts in the neighborhood in which they reside; that there be day courts and night courts; and that defendants could file their appearance either in the day or night court and elect to have his case heard at a time which would not require him to forfeit a day's wage or suffer other hardships. He would, of course, abolish the confession of judgment note, and restore his right to a notice and hearing and a right to make defenses before suffering a judgment and he would abolish the "holder in due course" concept and protect the right to withhold payment from a vendor of shoddy merchandise. . . .

On the bench you are already either adding to the unjust burden society decrees for CII's, or you are giving them as fair a shake as the present laws allow. Again, if you look upon CII's as trouble makers and dead beats, as people who have squandered opportunities because they didn't "make it" and did not turn out like you, you are probably possessed of prejudices from which you might never be disabused. You also have probably developed a protective paranoia which does not admit of its existence. The solution of this problem is difficult to find. It may be that early retirement is the only answer.

Off the bench there are many things you can do. All courts have administrative and rule-making bodies. They decide the time of opening and closing of courts and, depending upon available facilities, where trials will be had. Why not, for example, discuss with your administrative body the advisability of having your city divided into zones and of scheduling Small Claims, Building Code Violations, and Traffic cases for residents of these zones in the courts for those zones. You might consider giving the defendant the option, say at the time of filing his appearance, to elect to have his trial set for the day or evening session.

By far, however, most of the remedies for the relief of CII's must come from the legislature. This is not easy to do because CI's made the laws as they wanted them to be, and generally desire to keep them as they are. It is also a fact that many national prejudices are legislated into law and changes in these areas are slow indeed. . . .

I suggest our purpose here should be to examine the practice of courts in our jurisdictions, to determine whether we commit the offense of racism—classism—and, if so, to end it.

An important stratagem used by whites to deny meaningful political power to blacks is their concerted effort to keep blacks off the bench—and away from the bar, for that matter. On the bench, blacks have varied opportunities to improve the quality of justice for all people by improving it for their own people. Many of them seize those opportunities, not in a prejudicial but in a fair manner. Theirs is no simple task, because whites never fail to set double standards of conduct—one kind for their own, and another more difficult and disrespectful kind for blacks. The idea is to use anything to reduce or eliminate the likelihood that blacks will disrupt the social, economic, and political order by pursuing equal justice. Thus the attorney for Local 542, International Union of Operating Engineers, asked Judge A. Leon Higginbotham, Jr., to disqualify himself in a case in which the union was accused of racial discrimination (see page 62). The request followed Judge Higginbotham's address at the annual meeting of the Association for the Study of Afro-American Life and History on October 25, 1974, in Philadelphia where he sits in the U.S. District Court for the Eastern District of Pennsylvania. The following excerpt is taken from the opinion Judge Higginbotham, a graduate of Antioch and Yale Law School, issued in refusing to withdraw from the case.

DOUBLE STANDARDS FOR BLACK JUDGES

(*Commonwealth of Pennsylvania et al.* v. *Local Union No. 542, International Union of Operating Engineers et al.* 388 F. Supp. 155 [1974]

A. Leon Higginbotham, Jr.

Being Black, and the Appearance of Impartiality

When stripped to its essence, the gravamen of defendants' objection seems primarily based on the following express or implicit allegations:

(1) I am black;

(2) Some of the defendant union's members are white;

(3) The instant case involves a claim of racial discrimination;

(4) "By agreeing to appear before such group (The Association for the Study of Afro-American Life and History) Judge Higginbotham presented himself as a leader in the future course of the black civil rights movement," and

(5) By my appearance at the Association's meeting and/or by the substance of the remarks I actually made or as they were quoted in the newspaper, "the continuation of [Judge Higginbotham] as finder of fact, molder of remedy, and arbiter of all issues constitutes judicial impropriety."

Being Black

I concede that I am black. I do not apologize for that obvious fact. I take rational pride in my heritage, just as most other ethnics take pride in theirs. However, that one is black does not mean, *ipso facto*, that he is anti-white; no more than being Jewish implies being anti-Catholic, or being Catholic implies being anti-Protestant. As do most blacks, I believe that the corridors of history in this country have been lined with countless instances of racial injustice. This is evident by the plain historical fact that for more than two and a half centuries, millions of blacks were slaves under the rule and sanction of law—a fate which confronted no other major minority in this country. Every presidential commission and almost every Supreme Court opinion dealing with racial matters have noted the fact that in this country, there has often been racial injustice for blacks.

Thus a threshold question which might be inferred from defendants' petition is: Since blacks (like most other thoughtful Americans) are aware of the "sordid chapter in American history" of racial injustice, shouldn't black judges be disqualified *per se* from adjudicating cases involving claims of racial discrimination? Defendants do not go so far as to precisely assert that black judges should *per se* be disqualified from hearing cases which involve racial issues, but, as will be demonstrated hereinafter, the absolute consequence and thrust of their rationale would amount to, in practice, a *double standard* within the federal judiciary. By that standard, white judges will be permitted to keep the latitude they have enjoyed for centuries in discussing matters of intellectual substance, even issues of human rights, and because they are white, still be permitted to later decide specific factual situations involving the principles of human rights which they have discussed previously in a generalized fashion. But for black judges, defendants insist on a far more rigid standard, which would preclude black judges from ever discussing race relations even in the generalized fashion that other justices and judges have discussed issues of human rights. Under defendants' standards, if a black judge discusses race relations, he should thereafter be precluded from adjudicating matters involving specific claims of racial discrimination.

To suggest that black judges should be so disqualified would be analogous to suggesting that the slave masters were right when, during tragic hours for this nation, they argued that only they, but not the slaves, could evaluate the harshness or justness of the system. If defendants are not implying this extreme position about blackness *per se* as a basis for disqualification, then one must examine the rationale of their other allegations.

The Perniciousness of Appearing Before the Association for the Study of Afro-American Life and History

The newspaper clipping and the pleadings state that I was speaking to "a group of black historians" at the 59th Annual Meeting of the Association for the Study of Afro-American Life and History. This organization was not a labor group, not an institute of management, not a political party, not the Black Panthers, not any entity which on or off the record has ever had a history antagonistic to those white Americans who believe in equal justice under the law. . . .

. . . Would it have been permissible for a black to have

talked to white historians, or is there something particularly opprobrious about speaking to any group of historians which thereafter taints one's ability to participate in the judicial process? Do petitioners suggest that it is more sinister for a black judge to speak to black historians than for the Chief Justice of the United States Supreme Court to speak to the National Conference of Christians and Jews? Should the distinguished Chief Justice be barred in the future from adjudicating cases where claims of religious or racial bigotry are urged, simply because he spoke to a distinguished group which supports the concepts of the brotherhood of man, the golden rule, and fair play?

Many judges of this court have spoken to bar associations, including those specialized sections of the bar such as the plaintiff's personal injury bar, or the defense bar. Should such judges be forever barred from adjudicating personal injury cases involving plaintiffs or defendants? Is there anything more malevolent in speaking to a group of black historians about equal justice under the law than for a Catholic, Jewish, or Protestant judge to speak in his cathedral, synagogue or church on the Sermon on the Mount, or the Torah? If a Catholic judge spoke to a group of Catholic historians, should he be forever barred from adjudicating cases involving the constitutionality of state appropriations disbursed to parochial schools? Was my speech malevolent because its occasion was a national meeting? Does something inherently more pernicious occur when 100 black historians get together at a national conference than when 20 meet in a local setting?

Is It Permissible for Black Judges to Be Scholars in the Race Relations Field?

. . . Again and again in their petition and memorandum of law, defendants charge that by my appearance before the Association for the Study of Afro-American Life and History "the community at large was, as a consequence, made aware of Judge Higginbotham's significant role as a spokesman, scholar and active supporter of the advancement of the causes of integration." Do defendants think it sinister that some individuals consider me a scholar in the race relations field? Is it that scholarship which is their ultimate grievance? . . .

. . . Complex patent cases in this district were constantly assigned to the late Judge William H. Kirkpatrick. Should he have been disqualified because of his nationally recognized expertise in patent law? Are defendants suggesting that, except for black judges who become scholars on race and the American legal process, all other judges may be scholars in *any* field in which they may later be required to make an adjudication?

Defendants' objection to scholarship again displays their insistence on a different standard for black judges. Presumably defendants should not fear scholarship, but should instead be pleased that they would not have to "educate" a judge on the rudiments of the field.

The Substance of the Speech and Relevant Precedent

If defendants' claim cannot rest on disqualification *per se* because I am black, if it cannot rest on the fact that a black judge spoke to a conference of black historians, if it cannot rest on the fact that some think I have a reputation for scholarship in matters dealing with race and the legal process, then the viability of the motions must depend on the content of the speech, either as actually given or as reported in the newspaper clipping which was attached as an exhibit to their motions.

. . . There is an extraordinary gap between facts as reported in the newspaper article and the inferences, speculation and hunches which defendants assert in their motion for disqualification. Defendants apparently are relying on the newspaper clipping as their basis for disqualification, yet in their brief they make assertions which exemplify more fantasy than logic. As an example, they assert that during his speech Judge Higginbotham spoke in emotional terms of solidarity . . . ; yet not once is the word "solidarity" used or implied in the newspaper clipping, nor was it used in the speech. What is the basis for their inference that I spoke of solidarity in emotional terms? The article notes:

> Judge Higginbotham told the delegates, who interrupted his speech with applause, that his scepticism [of the Supreme Court] had been expressed by Supreme Court Justices. He identified Justice Thurgood Marshall as one of them.

Thus, the core for all of defendants' inferences is the word "applause." But applause does not necessarily mean that a presentation was made in "emotional terms." To imply that it was made in "emotional terms" is predicated on the assumption that several hundred black scholars cannot react with enthusiasm to a rational and non-emotional address. To say that the speaker spoke in terms of "solidarity" must be predicated on a similar assumption, that black scholars cannot react with enthusiasm to a rational presentation until the declarant uses the term "solidarity."

Defendants assert that my use of the term "we" indicates an emotional identification with my audience which requires my disqualification. Perhaps defendants would have wanted me to say "*you* black people must pursue *your* options for equal justice in other forums." Maybe that approach would have been permissible. Perhaps, on the Fourth of July, they would want orators to say "*You* hold these truths to be self evident, that all men are created equal. . . ." but never declare that "*We* hold these truths to be self evident." If defendants' rationale is accepted, whenever an orator says "we" in such a context, he is involved in a conspiracy which precludes his capacity to judge thereafter with impartiality.

Finally, defendants assert that "By agreeing to appear before such a group, Judge Higginbotham presented himself as a leader in the future course of the black civil rights movement." The defendants overstate their case and probably unintentionally denigrate the black civil rights movements. They confuse the civil rights movement with the study of history.

Yet even if the inferences asserted are permissible, the crux of their objection has to be that I dared to speak out on Racism and the American Legal Process to a group of black historians, and that the substance of my comments indicates a bias that will affect this case. . . .

The Precedents of Hastie, Stewart, Alexander and Burger

. . . At the luncheon where I spoke, I was introduced by the late Judge Raymond Pace Alexander, senior judge of the Court of Common Pleas of Philadelphia County, and the first black to be appointed a judge in that court. . . .

One month to the day after he had introduced me before the Association for the Study of Afro-American Life and History, on November 25, 1974, the city and nation suffered the loss of Judge Alexander. The eulogies were endless as the *Philadelphia Inquirer* noted in its lead editorial of November 26, 1974, "His Legacy Is a Better City":

> His death at 76 deprives Philadelphia and the nation of an outstanding fighter against racial discrimination who was equally active in promoting good race relations. Judge Alexander believed in brotherhood, and he made true believers of many, black and white, who were privileged to know him.

Judge Alexander's legacy was partially because of the commitment he kept even after he was a judge. Defendants would probably have been the first to applaud that legacy when it was noted on the obituary page. They might even have sent a card of condolence to the family. But they seem to be oblivious to the fact that this legacy was earned by Judge Alexander's participation in the great events of his lifetime, including his frequent speeches to the Association for the Study of Afro-American Life and History.

One of the many gratifying aspects of Chief Justice Burger's leadership of the federal judicial system has been his intense awareness of the inadequacy of the criminal justice system, particularly as it pertains to corrections, prisons, and jails.

. . . Because Chief Justice Burger has taken such a leadership role in bringing enlightenment to our failures in our correctional institutions, should he be disqualified from adjudicating cases where some wardens or Parole boards feel that the correctional system has not been faulty, at least in a specific case where a prisoner is asking for relief?

The Old and New Order of Things

. . . If, for the reasons previously discussed, defendants' motions are meritless, and since the motions are presumably filed in good faith, what other rationale could explain why defendants so vehemently assert their claim that I be disqualified in the instant case? Perhaps, among some whites, there is an inherent disquietude when they see that occasionally blacks are adjudicating matters pertaining to race relations, and perhaps that anxiety can be eliminated only by having no black judges sit on such matters or, if one cannot escape a black judge, then by having the latter bend over backwards to the detriment of black litigants and black citizens and thus assure that brand of "impartiality" which some whites think they deserve.

Since 1844, when Macon B. Allen became the first black lawyer to be admitted to the bar of any state, and since John S. Rock was admitted to the bar of the United States Supreme Court on February 1, 1865, black lawyers have litigated in the federal courts almost exclusively before white judges, yet they have not urged that white judges should be disqualified on matters of race relations. In fact, in the "good old days" before William H. Hastie was appointed in 1949 to the United States Court of Appeals for the Third Circuit, white litigants throughout America were able to argue before a judiciary from the United States District Courts to the Courts of Appeals to the United States Supreme Court without encountering a single black judge along the entire judicial route; for

until Judge Hastie's appointment there were no black Article
III judges. In fact, until 1961 white litigants in the United
States District Courts never had to ponder the subtle issue
which defendants now raise, because no President had ever
appointed a black as a United States District Judge. If blacks
could accept the fact of their manifest absence from the federal judicial process for almost two centuries, the plain truth is
that white litigants are now going to have to accept the new
day where the judiciary will not be entirely white and where
some black judges will adjudicate cases involving race relations.

Interestingly enough, in my almost eleven years on this
court, Abraham Freedman and his law firm, Freedman,
Borowsky and Lorry, representing claimants and members of
the National Maritime Union and the International Longshoremen's Union, have appeared before me on hundreds of
occasions. Often they were representing black seamen and
black longshoremen. In the process, they have obtained verdicts and settlements before me in behalf of blacks which
cumulatively involve millions of dollars for the litigants and
millions of dollars in fees for their law firm. The rationale on
which they now proceed, if valid, would constitute a basis for
disqualifying me and every other black judge in the nation
who sits on any of the maritime cases which they litigate here
and nationally, because these cases frequently turn on a con-
tested issue of credibility between the allegations of negligence or unseaworthiness by the black seaman or long-
shoreman and the contrary allegations of the stevedore or
maritime officer (who most often are white). Why should
black judges be qualified to sit when defendants' present
counsel are collecting millions of dollars in legal fees from
black seamen and longshoremen, but become instantly disqualified to sit when a predominantly white union represented by the same law firm is charged with racial discrimination?

There is even a more subtle aspect to defendants' argument. It would appear to stem from their possibly subcon-

scious expectations of a black judge's image. They seem highly agitated by the fact that a black judge, with some knowledge of the history of his people, has received sufficient recognition to be invited to speak to a group of black historians. They contend that for him to accept the invitation is to breach his impartiality. Thus, in effect, they are arguing that a black judge cannot convince some whites that he possesses the requisite impartiality unless he shuns associations of black scholars and, *a fortiori*, never speaks to them. Thus by the subtle tone of their objection, they demonstrate either that they want black judges to be robots who are totally isolated from their racial heritage and unconcerned about it, or, more probably, that the impartiality of a black judge can be assured only if he disavows, or does not discuss, the legitimacy of blacks' aspirations to full first class citizenship in their own native land. Again, in the good old days, it was possible to find a retinue of colored leaders who by their speeches, their actions, and their public declarations assured whites, and more specifically the white power structure, that the colored man would not rock the boat on what whites perceived to be their sea of racial tranquility.

. . . Thus, the critical issue is, what conduct by black judges will assure their impartiality? Should they be robots? Should they demean their heritage by asking for less than first class citizenship for other blacks? Should they not tell the truth about past injustices? Of course, there is a dramatic difference between the role which legislators, politicians, and elected officials play in our society, one which is far closer to the cutting edge of policy development, [than] the role which could be tolerated or expected from a federal judge. I willingly accept those limitations; they are inherent in the judicial process. I am aware that Judge Higginbotham should not have to disparage blacks in order to placate whites who otherwise would be fearful of his impartiality.

Obviously, black judges should not decide legal issues on the basis of race. During my ten years on this court, I have not done so. I have, depending on the facts, sentenced numerous black and white criminal defendants to substantial terms of imprisonment. I have placed other criminal defendants, both black and white, on probation. Depending on the relevant facts, some civil cases have been decided in favor of and others against black litigants. In this case, plaintiffs similarly will enjoy no advantage because they are black; defendants will not be disadvantaged because some of them are white. The outcome of this case will be dictated by what the evidence shows, not by the race of the litigants.

I am pleased to see that my distinguished colleagues on the bench who are Jewish serve on committees of the Jewish Community Relations Council, on the boards of Jewish publications, and are active in other affairs of the Jewish community. I respect them, for they recognize that the American experience has often been marred by pervasive anti-Semitism. I would think less of them if they felt that they had to repudiate their heritage in order to be impartial judges.

Many Catholic judges have been active in their church, as have been Episcopalian and other Protestant judges. It would be a tragic day for the nation and the judiciary if a myopic vision of the judge's role should prevail, a vision that required judges to refrain from participating in their churches, in their non-political community affairs, in their universities. So long as Jewish judges preside over matters where Jewish and Gentile litigants disagree; so long as Protestant judges preside over matters where Protestant and Catholic litigants disagree; so long as white judges preside over matters where white and black litigants disagree, I will preside over matters where black and white litigants disagree. Defendants are patently aware of the variety of extra-judicial activities which has been the accepted standard for judges in this District Court, in this circuit, and in the nation. It is inconceivable, then, that rational lawyers would object to the aforementioned speeches made by Chief Justice Burger and Justice Stewart, or even the speech which Justice Douglas made on December 2, 1974, to the Jewish Community Relations Council of Philadelphia.

Conclusion

. . . In many ways this opinion may appear to be too long and prolix. But if defendants' arguments are asserted in good faith and sincerity, they nevertheless represent an almost subconscious expression of their expectation of the deportment of blacks and, more specifically, of black judges. If America is going to have a total rendezvous with justice so that there can be full equality for blacks, other minorities, and women, it is essential that the "instinct" for double standards be completely exposed and hopefully, through analysis, those elements of irrationality can be ultimately eradicated. It is regrettable that in this case I must take substantial time and effort to answer defendants' meritless allegations, but in some respects the motions merely highlight the duality of burdens which blacks have in public life. Blacks must meet not only the normal obligations which confront their colleagues, but often they must spend extraordinary amounts of time in answering irrational positions and assertions before they can fulfill their primary public responsibilities.

My remarks to the Association for the Study of Afro-American Life and History on October 25, 1974, are the factual foundation for defendants' motions. Those remarks reflected a position similar to the one which that distinguished federal jurist from South Carolina, Judge Waring, once took in behalf of equal racial justice. My remarks, like his, showed "at most, zeal for upholding the rights of Negroes under the Constitution and indignation that attempts should be made to deny them their rights. A judge cannot be disqualified merely because he believes in upholding the law, even though he says so with vehemence." . . .

Of course, I do have feelings that this nation must fulfill its theoretical commitment to equal justice under the law. I do not apologize for these feelings, nor do I apologize for my remarks. Given the same opportunity, I would make those remarks again today. If I had not in fact made them, I would wish that I had.

II.

CRIMINAL JUSTICE AND BLACKS

IT IS assumed that we have a system of criminal justice that features three components—law enforcement (police, sheriffs, marshals), the judiciary (judges, prosecutors, defense attorneys), and corrections (prison officials, probation and parole officers).[1] But "system" implies harmonious interaction among components; that we do not have. Rather, we have a "process," a sequence of actions that move accused people from the police to the courts to prison and back to the world outside. Criticism of the process comes from within the so-called system itself; each component castigates and is castigated by the others, providing fodder for the press, which emphasizes friction far more than cooperation.

Perhaps that is because there is little cooperation among criminal justice officials. And perhaps *that*, in turn, is because there are no recognized overall professional bonds among them, because they vie for the same public funds or because crime-control leadership in most cities is lacking. But even if these obstacles were surmounted, two additional ones would still confront the system. One of these is the excessive coverage of human conduct by criminal law,[2] and the other is the separation of the criminal justice process from other efforts intended to attack the root causes of antisocial behavior. Excellent recommendations to correct these and other deficiencies were made by the President's Commission on Law Enforcement and the Administration of Justice in 1967. Their implementation was supposed to have been facilitated by the 1968 Omnibus Crime Control and Safe Streets Act. Not only is that goal yet to be realized, but it is very likely that the flaws in the criminal justice process will be reinforced rather than corrected.[3]

We can foster correction by enlightening the public about the way the criminal justice machinery actually works. Call it our television legacy, but many people believe that the trial is *the* key point in the process. It is not; there is no trial involved in 90 percent of all convictions in many courts.[4] Most defendants plead guilty rather than take their chances in a trial. But this puts us ahead of the starting point, which is the commission of a crime and the arrest of the person suspected of having committed it. This is the first of the instances in which discretion comes into play, for the police have the options of ignoring a situation, making an arrest and releasing the person, or making an arrest and setting the justice machinery into motion. Their exercise of discretion has led to continuous charges of racism against the police.

If prosecution is to follow, the next stage involves bringing the accused before a justice of the peace or lower court judge in state actions and before a federal magistrate in federal actions. At this time the defendant enters a plea of innocence or guilt to the charges brought against him. Most states provide for court appointment of counsel for him if he cannot afford a lawyer. Since it is unlikely that he will plead guilty at this arraignment, the defendant is primarily interested in the amount of bail he will have to post in order to secure his freedom. Theoretically, the amount depends on the likelihood of his appearing for trial; actually, it depends on the seriousness of the crime and often on a desire to punish him even though he has not been found guilty of any crime at all. If he is poor, he will have neither the collateral required for bail nor the means of obtaining it and will be locked up on charges that might be either dismissed later or not proved. Meanwhile, he will be unable to help prepare his own defense. He will run the risk of losing his job; if that happens, he will have less chance of winning probation. Moreover, he is more likely to be found guilty and given a heavier penalty than the accused who posted bail.[5]

After bail has been set at the arraignment or preliminary hearing, the trial will be held—provided it is not avoided as a result of plea bargaining involving the prosecutor, the defense counsel, and, at times, the judge.[6] In these secret negotiations the prosecutor exchanges leniency for a guilty plea. The judge's delicate role is to see to it that the agreement protects both the defendant and the public interest. Plea negotiations, screening (the decision to stop all criminal proceedings prior to plea or trial), and diversion (the decision to encourage individual participation in some particular program or activity under threat, express or implied, of further prosecution) result in administrative rather than judicial dispostion of the overwhelming proportion of cases.[7] But trial remains a crucial step in the administration of justice and in the prosecutor's political strategy, for the press and the public are far more attentive to courtroom victory or defeat than to hallway or office negotiations.

The trial is the scene of battle between the prosecutor and the defense attorney. In accordance with the defendant's wishes, it is held before a judge alone or with a jury. When a jury is to sit, both sides can reject potential jurors because of bias, or, to a limited extent, for no given reason. After each side has presented its case, the judge instructs the jury in the applicable law before it retires to deliberate. Generally, if the jury has been convinced by the prosecutor that the defendant is guilty beyond a reasonable doubt, it returns a verdict of guilty; otherwise, it returns a verdict of not guilty. Then comes sentencing, which concludes matters in most criminal cases.[8]

"For many defendants, everything prior to this decision is prologue," Jacob writes concerning sentencing by the judge. "What counts is what happens to them at this stage." What happens depends on the importance the judge attaches to recommendations by the prosecutor and by probation officers whose presentence reports are supposed to facilitate his deciding the treatment that will be most advantageous to the defendant and to society. The reports are based in part on hearsay evidence about the defendant's background, including family situation, job circumstances, and record of prior involvement with the law. They are not subject to rebuttal by the defense. Since most defendants do not stand trial, the judge is guided by these reports, the prosecutor's suggestions, and the standards set by the legislature.

Some judges themselves are alarmed by the magnitude of their discretionary powers in imposing sentence. For example, to Marvin E. Frankel, a federal judge, these powers are "terrifying and intolerable." Their existence gives lie to the claim that ours is a government of laws, not men; more than that, it leads to "a wild array" of sentences whose inconsistency is contrary to the ideal of equal justice. Legislators are as much at fault as are judges, for they have failed to enact laws that sufficiently guide and govern the judges. Judges require such restriction because by neither training, experience, nor interest are they adequately equipped to perform the awesome task of sentencing. They go their way, imposing sentences (without having to explain the rationale behind them), being tyrannical and lawless.[9]

For a minority of convicted people, the justice machinery grinds on to appellate courts, but for most that final disposition is ruled about by prohibitive costs of time, money, and psychological strain.[10] Rather than appellate court, they enter a correctional system that has a reputation for conversion to and confirmation of criminality, not for correction. The system holds a daily average of almost 1,300,000 offenders, most (95 percent) of whom are young (fifteen to thirty years old) males, almost a third of whom are juveniles, many of whom are from slums, and a disproportionate number of whom are minority group members. Ostensibly, the original purpose of corrections—punishment and retribution—gave way to humanitarianism and reformation. The horrors of prison need not be detailed here; it is enough to note that they reflect the system's failure to be humane and to reform.[11]

One reason for this failure is that parole and probation officers are overburdened with cases and cannot give enough attention to their clients. Often suspected rather than supported by employers, police, school officials, and others whose assistance they need, these officers are too few in number, as are teachers, group workers, vocational instructors, and other specialists. Low salaries, difficult working conditions, and an unfavorable public image dissuade many people from entering those jobs.

Probation is potentially a very effective technique, but usually it is hamstrung by ineffective decision-making in the selection of probationers and by the shortage of sound community programs to serve them. Parole is also marred by faulty decision-making. Parole boards or agencies pretend to base their decisions on an offender's prior history, readiness for release, and need for supervision and assistance. However, in some states they base their decisions on information compiled by caseworkers, whose superficial data gathering seldom goes beyond brief interviews with inmates, skimpy institutional records, and correspondence with officials in the community. In other states, hearings are also held, but these vary widely in quality and in format. Once released, people on parole are both controlled and assisted by parole officers, who, like probation officers, are charged with the incompatible responsibilities of serving as both the court's agent and the convicted person's friend and adviser.

Many of the people caught in the adult criminal justice system started out in its juvenile counterpart. As Eldridge Cleaver writes:

> When you focus on the adult penitentiaries, you're looking at the end of the line, trying to see where a process begins. But if you really want to understand and see what's behind the prisons sytem, you have to look at Juvenile Hall. You have to go down to Juvenile Hall. That's where I started my career, at about the age of twelve, for some charge. . . .
>
> I noticed that every time I went back to jail, the same guys who were in Juvenile Hall with me were also there again.

They arrived there soon after I got there, or a little bit before I left. They always seemed to make the scene. . . .

If you look at the adult prisons, you can't make head or tail out of them. By the time these men get there, they're in for murder, rape, robbery and all the high crimes. But when you look into their pasts, you find Juvenile Hall. You have to ask yourself, why is there not in this country a program for young people that will interest them? . . .[12]

Juvenile proceedings fail to provide several of the safeguards available to adults. For example, publicity and trial by jury may hold discretion in criminal proceedings somewhat in line—but not in juvenile proceedings. Although the latter may result in a child's detention or probation, defense attorneys seldom are present, and a social worker (who is not trained in the law) is the prosecutor, giving the judge information that supports both conviction and mitigation.[13] The court acts against, not for, children. Unlike adults, children need not be accused of specific infractions of the criminal law. They can be hauled into court on vague charges of being wayward, incorrigible, or truant. It is enough to assert that they need care or guidance or that their lives are likely to be immersed in idleness or dissolution. They can be tried for acts that are not cause for court action when committed by adults. They have no right to bail and no protection against hearsay evidence. Criminal court judges cannot overstep the maximum sentence fixed by law, but the juvenile court judge has only the age of twenty-one as the upper limit of the sentence he can impose. Much has yet to be done to grant to children constitutional rights that once belonged to them as well as to adults.[14]

Juvenile courts are sickeningly similar to adult criminal courts in their failure to achieve laudable goals. They are the province of judges whose qualifications are questionable; on a national basis, half have not finished college, a fifth have not even been to college, a fifth are not members of the bar, and three-fourths spend less than a quarter of their time on juvenile and family matters. Most of them have no regular assistance from psychologists and psychiatrists, and their dis-

positional alternatives boil down to outright release, probation, and institutionalization. As likely as not, probation services are either nonexistent or minimal. Institutionalization
means vegetation, for it provides no meaningful education,
vocational training, job counseling or placement, or other
guidance.[15]

Perhaps the most basic problem in juvenile justice is the
refusal of so many of its proponents to acknowledge the
inevitability of compromise between their idealism and their
neighbors' fears. They cling to the ideal of protecting and
rehabilitating children, but their neighbors draw no chro-
nological distinctions among criminals.[16] So juvenile courts,
like adult courts, enforce law that springs from a growing
thirst for "retribution, condemnation, deterrence, incapacita-
tion." These are society's protective weapons, and it uses them
against both children and adults.[17]

"The juvenile court is a court of law, charged like other
agencies of criminal justice with protecting the community
against threatening conduct," the President's Commission on
Law Enforcement and the Administration of Justice reports.[18]
What is the magnitude of the threat? What is its nature? Who
poses it? Among those arrested in 1971 for burglary, larceny,
auto theft, arson, and vandalism, most were under eighteen
years of age. Young people were 22.8 percent of all arrestees
for violent crimes against people and 50.8 percent of all arrestees for crimes against property. They were 25.8 percent of all
those arrested in that year. What's more, they account for the
most rapid increase in crime. From 1964 to 1967, for murder,
forcible rape, robbery, and aggravated assault, arrest rates
increased among urban youths over ten years old (15.4 percent among whites, 23 percent among blacks), and between
ten and seventeen years old (20.6 percent among whites, 48.5
percent among blacks). The percentage of youths under the
age of eighteen among all people arrested for those crimes in
1971 was 22.6 percent and in 1970 22.8 percent.[19]

Who are the delinquents? Who are the adult criminals? Of
all that is to be said about them, it is perhaps most important to

say that (1) many of them are black, but (2) many of them are white—more than official statistics show,[20] and above all (3) their criminal behavior is not a matter of race but of severe socioeconomic plight and of selective design and enforcement of criminal laws. Then in any discussion of blacks and crime, it is instructive to mention their exceedingly high categoric risk. Not only do blacks run a considerably higher risk of being arrested, prosecuted, and convicted than whites who commit the same crimes, but they are locked into the socioeconomic and political slots whose occupants, race notwithstanding, register the highest crime rates.[21]

Crime rates vary among blacks according to economic status, educational level, residential area, and sex. These variations, along with the distinctly legal nature of crime, go far toward countering persistent intimation or outright declaration of some biological cause of black criminality. No comparable aspersion is cast at whites who break the law, often in its name. But no matter. The point is that it is remarkable that given their social situation, blacks do not commit more crime than is attributed to them.[22]

Crime, writes Ramsey Clark, shows more than one face to us. Thus, we have street crime, white-collar crime, crimes of passion, organized crime, violations of regulatory rules, police crime, corruption, and revolutionary crime. We are more likely to see those faces than we are to see the most tragic face of all. And which face is that? "It is the crime of power over impotence—the crime of a society that does not insure equal protection of the laws," Clark answers. "It is crime against people who have no rights—the crime of a society which seeks to maintain order without law."[23]

Clark advises those who want to understand the causes of crime to take a map of their city and mark the areas where health is poorest, education is worst, life expectancy is lowest, unemployment is highest, the average per capita income is 60 percent of the average for the town as a whole, buildings—schools, houses, other structures—are oldest, the population density is twice or more the average for the town, and the occurrence of crime is greatest. This last area is where 10 percent of the people live and the police make two-thirds of their arrests for serious crimes—murder, rape, mugging, robbery, burglary, and assault. It is where dope pushers thrive, prostitutes parade along the streets, and gambling flourishes. It is the same area encircled by all the other marks on the map.[24]

This is not news to us. We have known it all the while. Still, we refuse to wipe out these known causes of crime. What is worse is the prospect that the powerful among us, who suffer least but fear violent crime, will deny to the powerless, who suffer most, the benefits of programs directed against its causes.[25] We know many of the programs required to cut crime rates among blacks and whites, but we prefer to blame the victims of injustice for their misfortune.[26] We tinker with the machinery of justice but never undertake the comprehensive action required to give full truth to our pledge of equal justice under law. In this way we give the lie to the pledge of equality, and justice remains unequal.

Evidence of this hypocrisy and its adverse impact on black people abounds.[27] It does not require full presentation here but merits brief mention. The hypocrisy is hydra-headed and appears in various forms. For example, white judges, prosecutors, and other court personnel often are deliberately discourteous to black lawyers and clients. Their rudeness is a symptom of the hostility that shapes their official action, and this often is important whether the boor is a court clerk or a judge.[28]

The hostility fosters Janus-faced justice, as in the City of Brotherly Love (Philadelphia) where a 1971 study by Barlett and Steele showed that in violent crime cases involving white victims, white defendants were jailed in 45 percent of the cases; black defendants, in 67 percent. Among defendants who pleaded guilty or were convicted in violent crime cases, whites drew jail sentences in 42 percent of the cases; blacks, in 64 percent. The frequency of imposition of a seven-month or longer sentence was lower for whites (49 percent) than for blacks (69 percent). Black defendants accused of a serious crime in a trial before a judge without a jury were more likely to be convicted of the major charge if the victim was white than if the victim was black; the percentages of cases ending in guilty verdicts were 49 and 37 respectively. In nonjury trials concerning violent crimes, black defendants were convicted in 42 percent of the cases before white judges and 32 percent of those before black judges.[29]

Bartlett and Steele's study of the fate of 1,034 persons indicted on charges of murder, rape, aggravated assault, and aggravated robbery led them to conclude that "bail practices in the courts are riddled with discrimination and inequities, and jailing of the innocent." Here, too, charges of the same violent crime resulted in higher bail for blacks than for whites (*e.g.*, 71 percent and 49 percent, respectively, in cases involving bail above $2,000). Moreover, blacks who were charged with having committed a serious crime against whites were put on higher bail than those accused of having committed the same crime against other blacks (*e.g.*, 79 percent and 66 percent, respectively, in cases involving bail of more than $2,000). Additional racial disparities are shown in the chart below.

Bail, by Amount and Race

	Defendants	
	Black	White
Released on Own Recognizance to $2,000	29%	51%
$2,000 to $10,000	21%	20%
More than $10,000 or Held Without Bail	50%	29%

Haywood Burns reports more general disparities in the judicial experiences of blacks and whites. For instance, blacks constituted 53.5 percent of the 3,857 persons who were executed in the United States between 1930 and 1966. The death sentence is actually carried out on more (10 to 20 percent) blacks than whites who receive it. Execution is a form of retribution that seems to give white men peculiar satisfaction when used against black men convicted of raping white women. They view with considerably less outrage the raping of black women by black or white men or of white women by white men.[30] According to Burns, blacks receive less consideration for parole than whites receive, and this helps explain why they constitute about one-tenth of the general population, but about one-third of the prison population.[30]

That wretched population is duplicated in training schools, childen's villages, youth study centers, and other juvenile institutions that generally are warehouses at best and prisons at worst. Often the two populations held in the same cage as juveniles are tossed into prison with adults. A case in point is the Camp Hill Correctional Institution, which is an adult prison near Harrisburg, Pennsylvania. Of the 106 (out of 400) young people at Camp Hill, 99 are black.[31] Blacks are 99 percent of the inmates in the Youth Study Center in Philadelphia, where, reports John Guinther, an award-winning contributing editor on *Philadelphia Magazine*, presumably innocent youngsters are subjected to cruel, unnatural, and even bizarre punishment. For instance, in the Youth Study Center (where it costs $12,775 to keep a child for a year) the temperature regularly is at least 100 degrees in summer. The heating system goes full blast all year long.[32] It has been that way for five years. "If the place were full of white middle-class youths, I can assure you the heatwould've been turned off five years ago," declares Dr. Jerome G. Miller, whose recent appointment as state commissioner of children and youth[33] raises hope that things will get better for young people—even for those in Philadelphia to whom authorities systematically apply a frightful formula: young+black = guilty.[34]

Youths and adults, blacks and nonblacks, males and females, prisoners are an important population. To save that population from certain destruction, some people believe, is to advance toward the goal of providing "safety for society within a frame-work of democratic principles and respect for individual rights." One means of advancement, according to Vernon E. Jordon, executive director of the National Urban

League, is to replace prisons with adequately supported community-based rehabilitation centers. In designing such means —and others mentioned by Jordon, including diversion of people from the criminal justice system and, above all else, forging "a more equal, more just society"—America will be advised to tap the black community as a source of guidance, strength, and assistance. Jordan's apt explanation:

> Black people are doubly victimized: first, by the high incidence of crime against us; and secondly, by the clumsy attempts to exploit the high rates of crimes perpetrated by black people to further isolate us and to further divide this country along racial lines. It is because of our unique position in this society that we can bring to the discussion of crime and its consequences a more rational and realistic viewpoint. As crime's victims, we know how important it is to control it. As victims of a society that has historically been racist and today is still discriminatory, we know how society can warp individuals and close off constructive avenues to them, thus creating criminals. As a people subjected to the capriciousness of the criminal justice system, we know full well the failures of that system and the way it encourages crime.[35]

Judge Bruce McM. Wright is an outspoken critic of the bias against blacks, Puerto Ricans, and poor people that festers in the criminal justice system in New York City. Presented here is the address he gave at the Metropolitan Applied Research Center in New York City on April 3, 1974, which portrays the mixture of racism, classism, and politics that make justice in that city a scarce commodity for people disadvantaged by color or class, or both. Judge Wright was graduated from Lincoln University and New York University Law School. He once sat in the Criminal Court of New York City but was transferred to the Civil Court of New York City.

A VIEW FROM THE BENCH

Bruce McM. Wright

THERE ARE SOME sensitive people who believe that the criminal justice system, so far as the poor are concerned, is more criminal than just.

Many believe that it is not that the blacks and Puerto Ricans in Eastern urban areas are more criminal than others, but that they simply get caught more often because the police spend a great deal more time giving them close attention.

Ask any sensitive leftist, and he will tell you that the terms "law and order," "strict construction," "preventive detention," and "crime in the streets" are all racist code terms, meaning that the niggers and the spics are getting out of hand with an arrogance of knives, guns, cudgels, and lye.

Speak to any Black Panther or surviving veteran of the Black Liberation Army, and you will be told that the police and the FBI pick on anyone who fits the visual profile of a militant, a young lord, or a bad nigger.

The intellectual leftists, brooding in their beards and moods of discontent, will tell you that the Nixon rhetoric on law and order, coupled with his Southern strategy, is nothing but the mirror image of Adolf Hitler, speaking in 1932.

This is not as farfetched as it might seem. Nixon, after all, did many things in the name of national security. Hitler did say, in 1932, that the republic was in danger from within and without. "We need law and order!" he said. "Without law and order, our nation cannot survive."

Early in 1973, the President submitted to Congress his Criminal Law Reform Bill. He said, on that occasion, that there must be "punishment without pity."

There have always been some indications not only that punishment was without pity, but that the entire criminal justice system was without any compassionate understanding of cause and dealt rather impatiently with effect.

The great and tragic emphasis in our courts today is a judicial numbers game. The judges, for the most part, sit in the arraignment parts like Bil Baird puppets, where, for purposes of setting bail, too many judges allow the words of the district attorney to be strings activating their response.

Example: Last August, a sixteen-year-old Puerto Rican youth was arrested and charged with participating in a hold-up. Held in exorbitant bail, he was placed in jail at Rikers Island. There was no time for investigation. The next day he committed suicide. Then the investigation began. It was the after-death discovery that the young lad spoke no English, that he had been in New York but two or three months, and that he had not participated in the holdup at all.

The presumption at his arraignment was that he was guilty.

Do the police really single out the black militant, the man with the afro, exploiting his nonknowledge of Africa and wearing a ferocious afro to prove it? Or are the blacks, longing for the perished glory of crumbled civilizations and mighty chiefs, simply paranoid?

Let's see. P. Jay Sidney, the actor, says that any black man in America who is not paranoid must be sick.

Example: On March 8 of 1974, William B. Saxbe and the FBI revealed that for the last four years, there had been an intensive campaign to harass and disrupt black militant organizations and their leaders. One way in which they did this was the making of repeated arrests of the same people, just to make certain they were off the streets and would finally face bail they could never post.

Most of the poor in our urban situation, are either black or Puerto Rican. In an example of the genetic dirty joke, some Puerto Ricans are not only poor, but black as well.

For many years, every Puerto Rican arrested was automatically described as white on his arrest record, no matter what his pigmentation. For some months in 1970 and 1971 I was assigned to Brooklyn. In case after case, I heard police testify as follows: "I observed the male white Puerto Rican perpetrator," etc. and, without exception, the "male white Puerto Rican perpetrator" sat there before me cleverly masked in a black skin.

After I had carefully dismissed each of the cases by reason of a mistake in identification, I was excommunicated from Brooklyn by District Attorney Eugene Gold, thereby suggesting rather strongly a nasty political taint to the virtue of our lady of justice and the assignment of judges.

The supervising judge in Brooklyn has been heard to certify that edict of banishment and exile by saying that so long as he remains in power, I will never sit in Brooklyn again.

When I faced the czar of all judges in New York City, Mr. Justice David Ross, and foolishly complained about politics making it possible for the district attorneys to shop for judges who would be more responsive to their thinking, as opposed to judges stupid enough to try to think on their own, I was met with a bitter tirade from the justice worthy of a Marine sergeant screaming at a treacherous private.

Thereafter I dealt with his lordship only in writing. In this entirely one-way correspondence, I have yet to have a response.

But back to other examples. The men who run our criminal justice system will know more about this symposium and my naming of names than any of you will remember. They will probably know by tomorrow and have a letter-perfect transcript.

Under our system of jurisprudence, one who is charged with crime is presumed to be innocent until proved guilty beyond a reasonable doubt. What a lovely and crucial fiction! All of us, I am certain, would wish to be presumed innocent, if indicted, as opposed to being presumed guilty, when arrested.

If presumed innocent, then one has the benefit of being paroled, instead of facing bail the size of the national debt. One needs to be free and out of jail in order to line up his witnesses, confer with his attorney, visit the scene of the alleged crime, and prepare a proper defense.

When Burton Roberts was the district attorney for the Bronx, he spoke to me on the question of bail and the presumption of innocence. And this is what he said: "The presumption is no more than a rule of evidence which begins to operate only at the time the trial begins."

Well, the reason for so many riots and dissatisfaction in the Tombs has been that it is so full of blacks and Puerto Ricans who have not been convicted and are simply awaiting trial. They are there because some judge has presumed them guilty and they cannot afford the bail then set.

What happens to presumption?

Apparently, the judges are of the Roberts mind on it. The logic of the Roberts Rule, then, is that when you are arrested, you are presumed guilty and even if it takes two years before your trial is reached, you are still presumed guilty until the trial begins. Then, miracle of judicial miracles, you are presumed innocent as the trial begins, with you still in custody.

This rule has the same quality of logic—ethnic logic, that is—as that expressed by a Housing Authority commissioner some years ago. As I rode up Lenox Avenue one day, I was astonished and unbelieving. I saw a housing project under construction named for Stephen Foster, the all-American composer who celebrated the happiness of the darkies as slaves. I feared that the next project, there in Harlem, would be the Old-Folks-at-Home Project.

An angry letter from me to the Housing Authority resulted

in a reference by the chairman to the man who had named the project. He happened to be the only black member of the authority. I transferred my surprise and wonder to him. He replied as follows:

> Dear Sir: I do not generally answer the letters of cranks. But obviously, you do not know that the songs of Stephen Foster prepared the North for the migration of the Negroes from the South.

I asked what they did for those who remained there, thus managing to get no answers to two questions.

I mention these things only to demonstrate how many people there are in government in positions of power who arbitrarily determine the shape of fate.

The same Burton Roberts who would delay the presumption of innocence is now a State Supreme Court justice and able to enforce his odd theories of justice.

Those of us who know him are not surprised by the prince of the law and the decibels of his ambition.

In 1969, referring to the South Bronx as the "Jungle" and as "Fort Apache," he allowed himself to be quoted in the pages of *New York* magazine, referring to the blacks as *schvartzes,* the Yiddish term for nigger. At the same time, the article described him as rolling his eyes and using a darky accent, a minstrel in white face.

In 1972, just before becoming a Supreme Court justice, Roberts commented on an arrest of two campaign workers for allegedly drawing weapons on the opposition. The New York *Times* report on August 18, 1972, is quoted as follows: "Jesting about the incident, Mr. Roberts remarked: 'That's the way they run elections in the Bronx. What do you think this is, civilization?' "

We may assume that an uncivilized electorate made him first a district attorney and then a Supreme Court justice.

For years people have said that the judges, generally a white and middle-class census of legally created gods, have been hostile to the poor. Is this again the paranoia of the poor, or is it the general rule, showing like a white slip beneath the black robes of the bench?

On December 20, 1970, some federally funded antipoverty law groups revealed that they had filed complaints against several judges, documenting judicial intemperance and prejudice against the poor, coupled with outright hostility. Nothing more has been heard or published on this subject.

It is worth noting, however, that the antipoverty lawyers claimed that the judges favored Establishment individuals—that is, those who most resembled the judges themselves. The judges were, it was said, executing unwritten custom and enforcing rudeness, malice, and prejudice.

And then, late in 1973, a committee of judges themselves issued a printed and bound report in which the justice system was called a failure. The report suggested that the police are more diligent in apprehending blacks than whites. One example of discrimination was underscored, and this should be a warning to all of us who are black parents. It said that the charge most often leveled against a white male in a stolen car case is "unauthorized use of a vehicle." But, "virtually all black males [are] charged with grand larceny, auto."

Unauthorized use is merely a misdemeanor. Grand larceny is a felony.

This is what is called the Dred Scott Syndrome among the judges—not by the judges, of course. Students of the theory of blacks as three-fifths-of-a-man in our constitutional history will remember that Chief Justice Roger Brooke Taney laid down the rule that no Negro had any rights which any white man was bound to respect. Taney was a Roman Catholic zealot, whose devout Christianity nevertheless allowed him to be a slaveowner. It is not known whether the judges today who execute his 1857 theory are slaveowners.

In the summer of 1972 it was revealed that in Villavicencio, Colombia, everybody killed Indians. It was sport. One Colombian, charged with that offense, said, "From childhood, I have been told that everyone kills Indians." Another, amazed that he was charged, said, "All I did was kill the little Indian girl and finish off two who were more dead than alive anyway." Another said, "For me, Indians are animals, like deer. Since way back, Indian hunting has been common practice in these parts."

Translate this into "kill me softly," and you have the Indian scene of South America transferred to the inner cities of America.

An exaggeration? Not really.

Omar Hendrix, in 1972, a member of the city's Correction Department staff, wrote a one-page essay called "Visitations." In horror-stricken nostalgia, he recalled his youth in rural Georgia. Sometimes, he said, on Sundays, the family would visit some of the kinfolk confined to a prison camp. One had been said to have "kilt a nigger." The visit was a picnic affair. After lunch, two white prisoners went off to the Negro section of the jail and brought back two black prisoners. Then the white prisoners encircled the blacks and ordered them to "fight for us." This, Hendrix said, was an old ritual—that is, black men forced to fight for the pleasure of whites.

There is still the mixture as before, with a difference now: We pay the blacks to fight for the whites. . . .

If we live in an atmosphere heavy with built-in discrimination and historical insults, there is little reason to believe that the justice system, which selects most of its judges and district attorneys from the whites who live with the tradition of white supremacy, should be any different on the bench from what they are in private life.

Prisoners, in this respect, are little different from the white judges (and some black ones). A white prisoner who is a bigot seldom emerges from prison transformed into a flaming integrationist. In 1972 there were several stabbings in the New Jersey State Prison at Trenton. An investigation revealed that there was a war between the black and white prisoners. It seems that the whites controlled the drug traffic in the prison and were charging the blacks twice as much for a sale of dope as the white prisoners were charged.

Thus, another mirror image inside the walls of what occurs outside.

I have long urged the abolition of all prisons as they are now constituted. This is not to say that there are nothing but angels out in the streets. Far from it. But the people who really need to be kept in durance vile are not that numerous. And the only reason for prisons and their inhumanity is to avoid and ignore rehabilitation and to encourage recidivism.

Just last month a Congressional subcommittee which has been studying the nation's prison system said that if only the public knew the truth about our prisons, it would demand instant reform.

Shortly after the Attica rebellion I heard a black voice wail over the radio station WBAI, say that he was a survivor, and then, on the question of rehabilitation, asked: "How the hell we gonna be rehabilitated when we ain't never been habilitated in the first place?"

We tend to think of our court system as being pretty much that gloomy and filthy pile of cement known as the Tombs and 100 Centre Street. But the plot against justice infects that lovely granite and marble architecture known as the Federal Courthouse as well.

In a fraud case, involving illegal trading in stock, through numbered Swiss bank accounts, to the tune of $20,000,000, the rich defendant was represented in court by a former federal judge.

The defendant and his firm had received illegal profits of some $225,000, and besides, the defendant had perjured himself during the grand jury investigation. He was fined $30,000, received a suspended jail term, and was placed on probation.

One week later, the same judge had before him an unemployed Negro shipping clerk. The Negro was married, with two children and a prior record of one robbery. He was charged with stealing a television set worth $100 from an interstate shipment. He received one year in jail.

The New York *Times*, in describing this gross disparity in meting out justice by Judge Irving Ben Cooper, noted that the discrimination exhibited was not simply a personal quirk of Judge Cooper, but was a distortion of justice common to his fellow judges.

One needs no help from the lens at Palomar to see the gross distinctions too often made between the wealthy defendant and the poor one.

Wonder still fills the sense and sensibility of many of us who recall the grand manner in which Spiro Agnew arrived at court to say he had no defense to a felony charge. Although the then Attorney General read off a long catalogue of offenses which could have been proved against Agnew, he was allowed to say he had no defense to only one.

He came to court in an expensive suit, in a chauffeured limousine, and with Secret Service bodyguards. He left with what was tantamount to a light rap on his wrist and a fine which was but a tiny fraction of the sum he had embezzled through the years, without paying any taxes on. He left court in the same way he arrived.

But every morning and night black paddy wagons with barred windows arrive at the Criminal Courthouse in Manhattan, to discharge its herd of two-legged beasts, all chained and shackled together as they are hurried into the pens, to await the awful wrath of a harried judge, who will set bail for them and detain them for the crime of being poor, as well as the other crime they must face.

It is a curious experience to see and hear the police in their testimony. The police academy turns out a plastic pattern of the same man with a different name. If all Negroes are said, with false allegiance to a native stereotype, to look alike, it may be said, with more accuracy, that all police sound alike. Invariably, they will say that they "observed the perpetrator," doing whatever the story calls for him having seen.

No cases of streaking have come before me yet, so I can only imagine how they would describe such a "perpetrator." The latter-day annals do, however, report the case of two students from the mainland arrested in San Juan for streaking. Their case was dismissed for insufficient evidence.

The police also generally testify with a masked face—that is, no emotion is tolerated to show through. This serves to camouflage the ancient enmity between the police and the blacks in New York. It began a long time ago and may be roughly dated from the so-called Negro plot of 1741, in New York City. The so-called plot was pretty much the fabrication of an Irish serving girl anxious to win freedom from her indenture and a reward of 100 pounds, then a great fortune.

She invented a story about an interracial plot to burn a local fort and make one plotter king and the Negro New York's governor. Both the police and the militia then began to round up the city's Negroes, whether free, enslaved, or indentured. Most were examined in the most cursory manner, and then justice was speedy. They were ordered lashed to a stake and burned. And they were, by the hundreds.

A report of that fearful era which rivals anything Salem had to offer, says that:

> As every attorney in the city was actively associated with the prosecution, the poor Negroes had no lawyers to defend them. William Smith, in conducting the prosecution, made an impassioned speech on the ingratitude of the Negroes, and expatiated on the kindness and tenderness with which they had always been treated. The Negroes died in agony. The crowd returned home well satisfied.

This early precedent for lynching, as all of you know, later spread to the barbaric South. In any case, it laid a local foundation for treating the lower orders.

The Irish Potato Famine of the 1800's resulted in large numbers of the Irish coming to New York. When they arrived, they were treated as white niggers and barred from many public places and restricted in the kinds of employment available. They competed for the meanest work with the city's

Negroes, and there was great enmity between the niggers, white and black.

The unemployed Irish bully boys, traveling the streets in packs, used to beat up the local police officers. They were appalled to see, walking the city's streets, police dressed as English bobbies. This inflamed the traditional hate between the Irish and the symbol of English authority and persecution.

The bully boys would invariably attack and beat up the police. The head of the police then allowed his officers to serve on duty in ordinary street clothes, wearing a simple star to identify their status. Not fooled by such nonsense, the bully boys continued to beat them up, calling them, derisively, "coppers" from the circumstance of the copper stars they wore. This was later shortened to just "cops," a term which remains to this day.

In desperation, the first metropolitan police commissioner dragooned the bully boys onto the force, thus beginning the continuing tradition and saga of the Irish Mafia on the police force of the city, as well as in Boston. This then gave the Irish armed allies in their combat against the Black Nigger competition for jobs, while leaving some vacancies for the Negroes in night soil chores—the cleaning of backhouses.

It is almost as though the police remember the former competition and their ancestors' designation as white niggers. The getting even process is dramatized daily and nightly in our courts. The police seem to have adopted the antebellum view of Negroes as the "Drones and Pests of Society" and fair prey to the human hunt, or the not-quite-human hunt.

Many blacks, while they may be unaware of any historical basis for police attitudes, are aware of the plain enmity of the police.

No close reading of the draft riots of 1863 is necessary for the blacks to appreciate animosity. It was then that the Irish demonstrated their intention not to go off and fight for the niggers in the Civil War. Then the great poverty sore on the body politic, the Irish themselves, were caught up in poverty and resentment. They had no $300 to purchase freedom from military service, and many set a precedent for the Catonsville raid upon draft records and their destruction. This uprising included the destruction of the colored orphan home here in New York and the killing of some of its helpless infants.

Some among us have attributed our addiction to "black English" to our bitter rejection of social authority—"that is, prestige of public administrators and police." Dr. Clark may recognize the last quotation as an excerpt from his little pamphlet *The Zoot Effect in Personality: A Race Riot Participant.*

It was a reprint from the *Journal of Abnormal and Social Psychology,* issued in 1945, dealing with the 1943 Harlem riot. His coauthor, nearly thirty years ago, was one James Barker, a name not now known to me.

With the proliferation of so-called black studies, to be distinguished from a brown study, blacks are learning more and more about their urban ordeal. I am persuaded that a good deal of their enmity toward the police is reinforced by knowledge of the social isolation of blacks in our society. What Dr. Clark refers to as the zoot personality is perhaps an off-shoot of the chronic humiliation and discrimination against the black skin.

The killing of police officers by some blacks, including some black officers, is evidence that those blacks who cooperate with authority by joining it are lumped with white authority. The police, of course, in avenging their dead must do so with an even hand and include even black officers among their martyrs.

Discussions by the police of black militance is always accompanied by descriptions which give great force to the costumes adopted by so many blacks. Therefore, the ferocious afro, the wearing of beads, teeth, fetish necklaces and the like always define a militant black radical. It is of no matter that these outer camouflages for the black ego and devotion to retrospective glory are no more than a ghetto fashion. These are the stigmata of the enemy to the police.

And even worse, the judges themselves regard such men as dangerous to the commonwealth. If a black man is lucky enough to have made bail or be paroled while his case pends, his luck may end when his case is called and he summons up his compensatory arrogance and bops up to the bench with what the judge interprets as black insolence.

In a study of juries and judges in criminal cases, it was discovered that both jurors and judges bring to the courtroom their personal bias and prejudices. One juror interviewed said: "Niggers have to be taught to behave. I felt that if he hadn't done [what he was accused of], he'd done something else probably even worse and that he should be put out of the way for a good long while."

Another study reveals that there is a subtle interreaction between judgments reached on the basis of poverty and those reached on the basis of racial bias. The trouble is that most of the defendants in criminal proceedings are both poor and black, and without confessions from interviewed jurors and judges, it is difficult to know when there is a basic discrimination against one because of his poverty or because of his race or because of both.

There is little doubt that one is often penalized under our system for being poor. The favorite outcry of the white man who has avoided the relief rolls is that "we were immigrants, too, and we did it, so why can't the colored people be like us." There is little consideration given to the manner of the black immigrant's arrival on these shores or the black codes which regulated him after the fashion of an electronically controlled and obeisant robot.

While there is glorious rhetoric concerning every man's entitlement to counsel of his choice, the government makes very little effort to ensure that the poor have experienced and competent counsel.

While district attorneys are selected with some care to their scholarship, their competence and energy to translate both into successful prosecutions, the legal aid attorney is often employed because he could not get work elsewhere or because, emotionally, his heart is in the right place. So it becomes an uneven battle from the beginning.

Too many judges look with contempt upon the efforts of the attorney assigned to the poor, and that attitude is often communicated to the jurors.

Too often, the public in its snobbery of social distance from the criminal courts, unless they have been ripped off or are jurors, has neglected a secret society which has decimated black reputations and lives. One should not assume that all is well, simply because the pillars of the Temple of Justice, in their imitation of Greek architecture, seem to suggest confidence and a clean ethic.

All of us should pay closer attention to the palaces of justice. If it is true that black men can be expected to be arrested at least once before reaching the age of twenty-five, that ruthless average may reach out for our sons and daughters. I have opened my court to the public and daily have students sitting with me on the bench so they can see the practical side of perjury, lies, cheating, and honest errors.

Some of my learned brothers have deplored this practice and treat me as though I am [sic] a fraternity brother who has advertised the secret society's afterdark practices. They suggest that the presence of strangers on the bench presumes to diminish the judge's power, his discretion, and his prestige.

What they really mean is that it may be publicized what goes on in their Greek revival temples of heedless discretion. One judge said to me that if any community groups came down to spy on him, he would have them thrown out. It is only judicial paranoia which can justify the term "spy" simply because a citizen may wish to discover what happens in the courts which their taxes support.

One of Roberta Flack's managers was in a motor accident last winter and had a fractured arm in a cast for some time. While recuperating, he and a companion went into a Yonkers' liquor store. The owner, seeing two black men enter, one with his arm inside his coat, supported by a sling, immediately pressed an emergency button which told the police that there was a robbery in progress.

The police arrived, roughed up the Flack manager, refractured his arm, and arrested both men, charging them with robbery. Miss Flack, matching action to her sense of outrage, chartered buses and loaded them with black citizens to fill the courtroom for the trial. With such an angry and curious census present for the judge to see, he was transformed into a twentieth-century John Brown. He not only acquitted the defendants, but castigated the police for shabby and discriminatory overzealousness. Yonkers and the police are now being sued for the conduct of the gung-ho police.

Until black citizens fill up courtrooms and look closely at the bench and its conduct, that public institution will remain secret in its work and assume that blacks like to be discriminated against in the courts. There will be the additional assumption, as well, that the black public approves the manner of selecting judges.

That "manner," so far, has neglected thousands of qualities which one might wish to see in a judge. Theoretically, a judge is supposed to be endowed with wisdom, learning, impartiality, and the basics of fairness. He is supposed to be emotionally stable, not troubled by psychological disorders, patient, kind, thoughtful, and courteous.

Even as Diogenes searched in vain for an honest man, his philosophical descendants today might well be hard put to discover such a person on the bench. And now, with urban America's problems being almost synonymous with inner-city problems, the blacks should be even more fascinated by the judicial process.

Why are there not more judges?

Why, among the 100 judges of the Criminal Court in this city, are there only 10 or so who are black, while the defendants who parade before the bench are 85 to 90 percent black?

Why are there only two Puerto Rican judges on that bench?

Why is the court administrator's office all white?

Is this because the whites know all about black rage, black criminal neuroses?

Is it because a white man, Jack Greenberg, is our NAACP Legal Defense Fund leader that we support the theory that a white will have to lift our veil of ignorance and judge us for our black sins?

Is it because so many of us are middle class?

Why is it that black judges become so enthralled by the black robe that they believe that everyone in the courtroom stands because [they enter]?

Why do black judges become distant and superior gods after they ascend the bench?

Why do black judges become autistic on the great debates which derive from the Constitution and stand mute?

Is it because they are happy, satisfied, smug, too upper middle class to identify with those who have not made it?

With preventive detention practiced every day in their courts, by the imposition of bail on the poor which rivals the national debt, why do black judges not cry out and say something?

With professors and researchers writing about racism in the courts and the corruption of justice, why do black judges refuse to rock the boat and demand changes?

Perhaps an excerpt from *Mrs. Wallop*, the Peter DeVries book, may shed some light on this dark judicial diffidence. Examining the American Negro, Mr. DeVries notes that they have progressed from sharecroppers to shareholders. He notes that many of them now have summer homes in Spook (I mean Oak) Bluffs, cottages at Sag Harbour, and sleek yachts in various marinas.

He concludes that the next book written about the suburbanization of the American Negro will have to be entitled *Uncle Tom's Cabin Cruiser*.

One of my fringe benefits from making such remarks is that my learned brothers on the bench do not speak to me.

However, I do have some suggestions for improving the

judges on the bench, which will endear me to them even more.

In certain countries of Europe and in Egypt, judges are selected from among the most brilliant and promising of the law students. During the last year of their law studies these students are allowed to opt for the profession of judging. They then receive special training for that lofty ideal. American law schools should adopt a similar policy.

Then judges in the urban areas could be trained in ethnic sensitivity, basic psychology of the poor, black history in the United States, to permit some knowledge of black heroes and the reason why there are such and institutional racism in the United States. All of this would be in addition to De Tocqueville and Myrdal. They would then have to become familiar with race, crime, and justice, and the Negro in court, all included in the President's Crime Commission Task Force Report in 1967.

There would be courses in the importance of regarding defendants as individuals and human beings, as opposed to faceless ones to be hurried along through the system.

Topping all of this off would be a period of in-depth exposure to a period of psychoanalysis, to determine whether or not the candidate really possessed the emotional stability and strength to sit in judgment of other humans.

Every graduate of a law school who passes his bar examination in New York must first pass a Committee on Character and Fitness before being admitted to practice. Are character and fitness to be of no consequence when a man aspires to that high honor of the law, the bench?

There is too much cronyism in selecting judges these days. It's the old buddy-buddy politics-as-usual thing. Many judges are selected from a clubhouse where they have distinguished themselves by kissing the behind of the district leader or kingmaker. They are safe designees because they have made no waves and have led a career devoid of merit. They have remained neuter, subservient to power and wholly without imagination. They are no threat to anyone.

When I was sent to the committees by Mayor Lindsay for

them to see if I was fit for the bench, the prestige committees looked at my résumé, saw that I had been associated with a Wall Street law firm, and immediately said that I was over-qualified for the Criminal Court bench. No one said a word about the fact that I had never had a criminal case in my life.

When I mentioned my utter lack of experience in criminal law, Mayor Lindsay said that was all to the good because a "fresh" approach was needed at court. Several months later he was heard to say that he never meant quite fresh, and I was accused on television of "judicial insensitivity." This is proof certain that I needed the very instruction I have outlined as necessary for judges.

While I always advocate the abolition of prisons as they [are] now run and operated, I realize that this suggestion, in a time of law and order, may result in my confinement to Bellevue. Therefore, I have an alternative suggestion. While we do have prisons, there should be an upgrading of prison personnel. For the most part, our state prisons are located in rural hinter-lands. They are filled with urban rejects. Both prisoners and their keepers are strangers to each other, neither knowing very much about the other and each suspecting the worst.

Prisons should be closer to the urban areas which feed them, so that the urban experience is not wholly unknown to the keepers. They should be more open and available to the visits of family and friends. The prisons now are dehumaniz-ing institutions in which the prisoners brood about new crimes and getting even with the society which put them there. They are breeding grounds for a cycle of revenge which produces endless recidivism. . . .

The view from the bench, then, is a sad excitement. One sees the walking dead, hapless in their terminal disease of life. I owe it to my selected profession and the honor of judging, to continue to point out my club's imperfections, in the hope that the attention of the public will be aroused enough to bring about the drastic changes so much needed, if the people are to have a calm confidence in both judges and what they do.

If we do not have radical criminology from the black

judges, they can never justify their existence as judges. If we allow our judges, especially our black ones, to be called "your honor," simply because they don the black robe of their high office, then we deserve what we get as the end product. And, if we wish our black judges to be indistinguishable from the white ones, then there is no point in having black ones.

In this season of impeachment rumors in the highest places and fearing that one day soon my head may be upon a platter, I end this reading.

Judge George W. Crockett, Jr., the presiding judge of the Recorder's (Criminal) Court in Detroit, contends that racism and
classism permeate the system of justice at all levels of government
and in all parts of the nation. Crockett believes that black judges
have a special obligation and ability to help change that for the better. He advocates their doing so in order to help return America
to "her true constitutional moorings." Judge Crockett, the
first chairman of the Judicial Council, holds an AB degree from
Morehouse College and an LLB degree from the Detroit College of Law. His article, which is based on remarks made at
the Judicial Council's founding convention in Atlanta, Georgia,
August 5, 1971, is reprinted with permission from him and the
Journal of Public Law of Emory University.

RACISM IN THE COURTS

George W. Crockett, Jr.

RACISM WAS BORN, nurtured, and sustained in the interests of
a few against the many. The economics and the psychology of
slave traders, plantation owners, and large corporate employers is essentially the same and has undergone no basic
change since the first slave ship sailed from Africa to the West
Indies. Thus, what we judges and lawyers observe today in
our courts is more than racism. The poor white derelict, the
indigent, the unemployed, the dispossessed, no matter what
race or color, are given like treatment. While our jails are
filled with mostly blacks, the whites that make up the remaining 5 per cent or 10 per cent of the inmates are seldom persons
of means.

Every impartial study has confirmed the fact that our law
does make distinctions between rich and poor, and these
distinctions are more pronounced where race or color is
encountered. Blacks and non-whites in our society are paid
less, are unemployed and underemployed in greater numbers. They live in worse housing, on dirtier streets, with

poorer medical care and educational opportunities and under far more tension and pressure than any other segment of our population.

Both the President's Crime Commission and the National Advisory Commission on Civil Disorders found that these substandard conditions combine and weld racism and poverty. The former serves to intensify the latter; and the two are directly responsible for our increase in crime and our civil disorders in recent years.

That's not startlingly new information and we didn't have to come to Atlanta to learn the facts we were born with and live with every day. What is revealing, however, is Black America's growing understanding of the inner workings of our social order and the interaction of law and economics. There is apparently an increasing realization by black judges that race discrimination and class discrimination are integral parts of our present-day judicial system; that these twin evils affect profoundly every phase of our work as judges; and—most importantly [sic]—that we ourselves will perpetuate and extend the cancerous effect of these maladies unless we identify and fight them unceasingly.

Racism is evident in our courts whenever and wherever a black litigant is involved. It is indigenous to the law as applied to blacks whether the proceeding be in Michigan or Mississippi, in a Federal or a State tribunal, in a court of civil or criminal jurisdiction, or on the trial or appellate level. Our starting point is not primarily the law itself. The body of law with which we deal is not inherently racist. This does not mean, however, that it is not invidiously class conscious. And this phenomenon deserves our full attention. For America's recognition of itself as a racist institution, and the moral and political offensives now being mounted against racial prejudice and discrimination tend to obscure the underlying root syndrome which is the class struggle.

Racism pervades every area and facet of American life. It is a characteristic of American life; and hence, it is a characteristic of American law.

Those of us who were born and reared in the South know that the courts down here openly acknowledged this fact and have accepted and operated on a racist basis for 350 years. And those of us who hail from other areas of the country know that the courts there have ignored or masked this same salient truth by apologies and by pretending that such racist practices as did exist were accidental and not part of the court system itself.

Since the 1954 decision in *Brown* v. *Board of Education*, there has been a shift in positions in both the North and the South.

In the North today, it is claimed racism no longer exists in our courts; not even accidentally. Notwithstanding it may be a fact in the private sector here and there, the argument goes, it has been eradicated from our courts and from our other public institutions and operations.

The validity of this position (de facto vis-a-vis de jure racism) as it relates to public schools in the North, for example, was posed and was decided adversely to its proponents by our own federal District Judge Damon Keith of Detroit recently in the City of Pontiac School Desegregation case.

The South also has witnessed a change in its position. No longer do you encounter in Southern courts the blatant boasts of Dixie's determination to maintain a racist society buttressed by openly racist laws. Instead, the South has advanced to the astute position formerly maintained in the North; it prefers to pretend now that such racism as does exist is accidental, unintentional and/or unavoidable.

The issue in the Jackson, Mississippi swimming pool case—which split the Fifth Circuit 8 to 7 and the Supreme Court 5 to 4—is typical of this new Southern approach.[4] Court ordered desegregation can be avoided provided the State is willing to penalize the poor whites and blacks equally and thus substitute classism for racism.

While nowhere has America displayed a readiness to confront racism head-on, quite obviously some progress has been made both in the North and in the South. Primary credit is due the members of the Warren Supreme Court and the growing power of the black voter. But adherence to the constitutional guarantees of equal protection of the laws for the poor and the non-white in our society is not yet a reality.

So the struggle continues. During the past five years the battleground has largely shifted from the legislature and repeal or enactment of statute law; and it has shifted from the appellate courts and the invalidation of racially restrictive state action. The battleground today is the trial courts—and especially the lowest trial courts. It is in these tribunals that legally approved racism-classism flourishes in its most virulent form. A few examples will illustrate the point.

In the criminal law area the notorious police practice of stopping citizens for alleged minor traffic offenses and then conducting a humiliating, overly-thorough public search for contraband is generally reserved for black and/or poor people. Also, the prosecution tactic of overcharging as a means of justifying high bail and coercing guilty pleas, is well-known in every ghetto community and accounts in large measure for the grossly disproportionate number of blacks who are kept imprisoned illegally pending trial.

In the civil law area we see courtroom strategy and tactics that are equally onerous and racist. Juries are frequently padded by jury commissioners to distort racial balances. In trials involving a black litigant full use is intentionally made of pre-emptory challenges to eliminate prospective black jurors for reasons other than competency. One consequence of this is that jury verdicts for damages are substantially lower for black litigants than for white.

And in our special courts—such as small claims, domestic relations, traffic, and juvenile—the word of the white process server, the traffic cop or a white social worker seems always to outweigh with most judges the sworn testimony of the black witness.

These are the obvious and more visible racist practices we blacks in the legal profession observe almost every court day. The subtle but no less vicious racism inherent in negotiating a personal injury settlement or bargaining a plea, and in examining a witness or arguing to a jury also is part of the ever-present racist scene in our courts.

If the battleground against racism has shifted to the trial courts, the chief artillery has to be the trial judge himself. He is the one in absolute command; he is the sole repository of that tremendous force for good or evil which we call "judicial discretion."

There are approximately 325 black State and Federal judges out of a total of approximately 12,500 judges of courts of record in the nation. Many of us are convinced that this relative paucity of black judges and the frantic efforts to block the election or appointment of more, stems from the fear in some quarters that this awesome state power which inheres in the trial judge will be used by black judges to correct many of the racist and classist practices of our judicial system.

These fears are not far-fetched. A black New York judge has ruled that a black mother is not an unfit custodian of her child merely because she elects to live in unconfirmed wedlock; a black Detroit judge has held a high-ranking city official in contempt of court for his willful destruction of building code violation records on ghetto housing; this council's Vice-Chairman, Judge [Joseph C.] Howard, gave leadership in defeating a referendum proposal that was calculated to seriously impair the further integration of Maryland's judiciary; and I released 130 black victims of a mass arrest who were detained for six hours in a police garage without benefit of counsel. These and many other non-conformist rulings and actions by blacks confirm that we are the products of our experiences and our environment and that we have not forgotten from whence [sic] we came to our present exalted positions.

One sure remedy for the everyday racist and classist occurrences in our courts is to have more trial court judges who are black and/or non-conformist and who are not afraid to use the authority of their office. A black judge (i.e., one who is "psychologically" as distinguished from "physically" black) will necessarily be more effective in eradicating racism from the judicial process in his court—because he will be able to recognize it when he sees it. Whether he will have the courage in a particular case to use his tremendous judicial power and authority to remedy the situation will depend upon the individual judge, his background, and the support he has in the community he serves. His very presence on the bench and at judges' meetings, however, is likely to make his fellow judges more conscious of their own constitutional responsibilities.

The historical function of the judge is to insure adherence in practice to the guarantees of the constitution and the law. The aim of this Judicial Council is to assist you in doing just that.

This Judicial Council can contribute to the identification of the problems of racism and classism in the court as they affect the administration and dispensation of justice. . . . Justice is supposed to be blind. It treats all individuals alike—rich or poor, black or white, male or female. Well, it's time to remove the blindfold that gives the illusion of fair treatment. We want to expose to the full glare of reality the inequities superimposed on that great but unrealized objective. We want to see its errors, to identify its prejudices and to expose those who would pervert just laws with unjust penalties.

The meaning and the purpose of this conference of the N.B.A. Judicial Council is not to point out, analyze and explore the varied racist practices of our judicial system. Our purpose is to do what no other judicial council or legal gathering has had the courage to do—to engage in a meaningful exchange of experiences that will equip us individually to fashion new judicial approaches and remedies for old racial and class grievances; to consciously plan the re-examination and the eventual overruling of old outmoded legal theories and precedents which no longer serve the legitimate interests of today's new political majority; and, ultimately, to assist judicially in returning America to her true constitutional moorings, to the end that we shall have a Nation and a World at peace.

Milton B. Allen stresses the prosecutor's importance in the justice system. In an interview on January 27, 1974, Mr. Allen provided an insider's views on the politicization of the prosecutor's office, the jury system, plea bargaining, street and white-collar crime, indictment, and black vulnerability to prosecutorial abuse resulting from black political powerlessness. At the time, Mr. Allen, an alumnus of Coppin State College and the University of Maryland Law School, was the state's attorney of Baltimore City.

A BLACK PROSECUTOR'S PERSPECTIVE ON JUSTICE

Milton B. Allen

Q: Why did you run for the office of prosecutor?

A: About 1965, when I had become a fully matured and experienced lawyer, I became very interested in the criminal justice process and the role of the prosecutor because I could see, from my daily contacts with the courts, that the key man in the American system of justice is the prosecutor. It became obvious that whether you had a good justice system or not depended upon whether you had a good prosecutorial system. I could see flaws in our prosecutorial system throughout the country, and in Baltimore I began to work through the Bar Association to try to improve the system. Then, in 1970, by sheer political accident a political situation arose that ended up with me running for office. Running for political office was the thing furthest from my mind. I fully expected to remain outside the system and maintain my status as a critic. But one of those things that makes the prosecutorial system weak happened here in Baltimore.

One of the weaknesses of the prosecutorial system has not matured in the selection and retention of prosecutors. Prosecutors are generally elected. They are elected to the type of political office that is usually the stepping-stone to a higher office. So the people don't stay very long in most of your unenlightened states (and most of your states are unenlightened). A city gets a prosecutor and two, three, or four years when he has begun to get his programs going good, he is plucked out to take a judgeship. That is a pattern that is repeated far too often. So, you never get any sustained periods of time in which you have dedicated prosecutors trying to improve the office.

The same thing applies here in Baltimore. We have never had a prosecutor here more than five or six years. Usually the stay is two or three years. Well, in 1970 the Baltimore prosecutor was appointed to a judgeship, and the bench was required to appoint a successor. The bench appointed a young man who was perfectly capable, but his appointment just hit the community the wrong way. A great cry went up. Cries of political shenanigans filled the media. And the result of all the furor and shouting and conflicting contentions was that five candidates ran for the office. I was one of them. I really didn't intend to run, frankly, but like the public, I was caught up in the waves of protest, and before I knew anything, I was off and running.

Q: Are you glad you ran?

A: Frankly, yes. Running for office, particularly with no political support, is possibly the most challenging experience a mature person can have. Service as prosecutor has been a most rewarding experience. It has also been frustrating in that I think that America's view of the prosecutor has not matured to the point that we can get out of his office all the mileage we can toward improving the system of justice. The prosecutor is at the very center of the whole justice system. He is the person who determines what charges are to be placed and when they are to be placed. He decides what charges are to be tried. He is the one who has to decide whether he will use the powers of his office to persecute people or whether he uses those immense powers to bring about fairness to all the people. If he is a person who is not inclined to be just or looks to his political laurels more than he does to justice, you will not get good prosecution. Unfortunately, it is a lot easier to indict some poor guy and not have the press screaming down your neck than to make a judicial decision and say, "No, in this case it would not be proper to indict."

Q: What is the significance of indictment for the person indicted?

A: Under our system in America, he's dead. Few Americans really believe in the presumption of innocence. Once a person is indicted, so far as most of the public is concerned he is guilty. It is unfortunate, but that's the way it is. Theoretically, indictment is only an accusation, and the person is innocent until proved guilty, but the human mind doesn't work that way. In America, when a person is indicted, he is thought by the populace and by everybody that deals with him to be guilty. An indicted person is restricted in his ability to get and hold a job, for instance. And then, if he is acquitted later on, the fact that he was indicted still hangs over him for the rest of his life. People will say, "He beat it." They will never say, "He was not guilty." The public feels the system let him off some sort of way. So, for all intents and purposes, he is dead once he gets indicted.

A: What happens, if anything, to the prosecutor who brings unsubstantiated indictments?

A: Nothing, absolutely nothing, because of the American way of thinking about justice. It is the same kind of thinking that has produced the gun culture in America. It is the same type of thinking that keeps our police peeping around corners looking for Mafia types when the very guts are being ripped out of our society and economic system by white-collar crime and corruption of or by public officials. It is the type of thinking that goes into producing a bad prosecutor. It is a situation where the public doesn't pay much attention to the real facts but simply deals with the mystique. Yes, prosecutors make plenty of unsubstantiated charges. But it is such a vast job to determine their numbers that nobody except someone running for office could determine how many unsubstantiated charges a prosecutor has brought in any given period of time.

Q: Does the prosecutor alone have the power to determine whether to prosecute?

A: Yes. It is a very important power and a power that can be abused. In some states the prosecutor has very wide discretion. It is his absolute right to nol-pros [choose not to prosecute] a case if he wants to do it, and he can do it simply because he feels that prosecution will not meet the ends of justice, which is a very general all-encompassing definition. You see, he is almost exercising as much power as a judge, maybe more.

Q: I wanted to ask you about the charge that the grand jury is controlled by the prosecutor.

A: Well, it is true. It wasn't designed that way, though. It was designed to be an independent body. But what has happened is this: As the work of the prosecutor's office increased, it became impossible for a grand jury to give every matter the consideration that it needed. So whereas forty or fifty years ago jurors could take all day fooling with one or two cases, now they've got twenty or thirty cases to deal with, and they are all working people, busy people, and you can't have seven or eight grand juries, because the cost would be prohibitive. So the grand jury's function has deteriorated over the years to a point where instead of having all of the key witnesses in the case presented what you get is a summary from the policeman or from the state's attorney. The grand jury doesn't need to have the type of evidence a judge needs to convict. To indict they can use hearsay, even third- or fourth-hand hearsay. The grand jury ends up relying on the prosecutor because they just don't have enough time to give everything due consideration. They sit only three or four months in most states. They are usually all laymen, and in many states they are selected by computer. Usually by the time they learn the system their tenure is over.

The average grand jury in a busy city does not have the

time, the money, or the facilities to perform the functions it is supposed to perform. So, what happens is that an assistant goes before the grand jury and runs through twenty or thirty cases and spends a couple of hours, and lets the grand jurors go home, or go back to work, wherever they may wish to go. The pressure to move cases swiftly is the watchword. Jurors have very little knowledge of the law, the grand jury system, or the justice system. They are forced to rely almost entirely on the state's attorney for guidance on the very issues they are sworn to resolve.

Q: Given the importance of indictment itself, would you say that this is a serious flaw in the justice system?

A: It is an extremely serious flaw, because you get overzealous prosecutors. Most prosecutors will confess to you off the record that they can get out of the grand jury any indictment that they want. So, if you have a prosecutor that is politically ambitious, or he is just a bad fellow or a bad prosecutor, he can misuse the grand jury terribly to his own advantage. Now, you can't get a city or state to put enough money, time, and attention into its grand jury system to revive it and to restore it to its proper use.

I don't think the indictment process should be left to the prosecutor. I would rather leave it to twenty-three laymen. But in order to do that, you've got to have the proper amount of time, space, and manpower to let the grand jurors make these weighty decisions. It is a huge bill to make the grand jury system work as it is supposed to. But that's what we need. See, one of our problems about the justice system is we have always played pinchpenny with it. We have never spent enough money on it. Sometimes grand juries are rubber stamps, because they just don't have time to be anything else. You simply can't give adequate consideration to a murder case in four or five minutes. If you have a reliable prosecutor, then you get fairly good indictments. If you don't, then you get bad indictments. And you see by the percentage of convictions whether he is doing a good job or not. Because, if he is running around 50 or 60 percent it means that he is doing a bad job.

What they keep talking about in these various states is that rather than make the grand jury concept viable, we should abandon it and let the prosecutor do it all, since he is doing it anyway. However, the prosecutor is often such a weak figure that I wouldn't be willing to trust indictment to the prosecutor in most states. In many states you have fine prosecutors, but the system is self-defeating. A good prosecutor seldom stays around long enough to be trusted with the awesome responsibility of indicting people for crime. Unfortunately, the system breeds a lot of young prosecutors who are on their way somewhere and are trying to make a record for themselves. Because of the powerful incentive for self-aggrandizement and the abundant opportunity for the same, trusting the entire indictment process to a prosecutor could be a dangerous practice.

Q: What's the significance of all this for blacks in Baltimore and other cities?

A: Well, the victims of an archaic system are usually the people at the bottom of the scale: blacks, poor whites, whoever they might be. A weak or bad prosecutorial system victimizes the people with the short end of the stick, and they are usually blacks in our cities where you've got a lot of blacks. So, if there is overindictment, there are blacks being overindicted, whoever is at the lower end, because those people don't fight back. They don't have any political clout, and so if a prosecutor wants to make a little hay, he usually makes it on the people he can make it on easily. Blacks are accessible, they all live in the inner city, they don't have anything, and that may account for the peculiar weight of your prison population.

A racist prosecution and police system and judiciary, for many, many, years, may account for that. I refuse to believe that blacks are just bad people. But more blacks are arrested, more blacks are prosecuted, more blacks go to jail. Because the inefficient system preys on the weak, and, of course, the poor do commit more crimes. They commit a lot of crimes because they are mad at society and they commit a lot of crimes because they feel it's all right to take from a society that has shortchanged you. If you kick people in the backside for three or four hundred years, you know, you get a pretty vicious individual at the end of that time. He is really anti-society, and he is going to react like that. If society can rip him off, he is going to rip society off. So you get a lot of anti-society people, and they are easy targets for law enforcement.

None of the people at the lower end of the strata and none of the disenchanted go in for sophisticated crime. Either they don't have the ability or training or patience or they can't get access to the opportunities, so they don't go in for white-collar crime. They go in for selling narcotics. They steal; they sell hot goods; and you'll find that 95 percent of your criminal court dockets are made up of routine crimes: murder, rape, robbery, narcotics, larceny. But anyone with two eyes would know that the trouble with America today is not routine crime, but white-collar crime and official corruption.

But if the powers that run this country can keep the people's attention on street crimes, Americans can be stolen blind. That's what is happening. We are worrying about the guy mugging somebody (and nobody ever hears statistics about your chances of being mugged). Meanwhile, the white-collar criminal is sucking us dry, and no one even wants to talk about that. We are beginning to see some of it now as a result of what is happening around the country in various jurisdictions, at various levels of government, particularly in Washington. I think that people will begin to realize that we lose more in white-collar crime in a couple of days than we do in a couple of years by routine crime.

Now, what blacks should be thinking about around the country is that being at the lower end of the economic scale, they would most likely be victimized by an inefficient system of justice. And it is important for young blacks to think about going into prosecution because that's where the control is. Young blacks often say to me in argument that they don't want to take any part in prosecuting black folk, and I point out to them that as a prosecutor they are bound to deal fairly with all folk—much more so than as a private lawyer. Simply by fulfilling the duties of your office and acting fairly, you can bring more justice in five minutes than you can in five years as a private lawyer. Now, [we need somebody] in that office to pull the coattails of the powers, saying, "Wait a minute, fellows, you don't have any evidence in that case. Why are you prose cuting that man?" Because, you see, it's so easy to prosecute and so hard not to prosecute. If for valid reasons you refuse to prosecute a notorious case, the police get on you, the press gets on you, and some of your political enemies get on you. If you, as a chief prosecutor, feel that a case should not be prosecuted because it would not serve the ends of justice or you can't prove the case, but it happens to be a notorious case, you are in for big trouble. Now, it's a question of whether you have the guts to stand it. Now, if you've got the guts to handle the trouble, fine, but if you don't, if you are a little weak, the easiest thing to do is say "Let's indict the guy anyway and let the judge worry about it." And that happens over and over again.

So, eventually, this poor guy stays in jail two years perhaps. He comes up for trial after all the hue and cry dies down and some judge says to your successor in the prosecutor's office, "Who the devil indicted this man in this case?" The prosecutor answers, "This is what Judge Ware did when he was state's attorney." Well, now it's too late. The man's been harmed. He's dead. He has been in prison for two years. He is bitter. And he will never forgive society. I don't know how many blacks or how many poor people have passed through the system like that. Kept in jail a month, two months, three years, because somebody said, "It's easier to indict the guy and keep the press off our backs." I don't know how many people have been victimized over these United States like that. Perhaps millions.

Each one of those people is a walking time bomb against the system. They will never believe in the system again—never. About the best example is the series of cases brought by the federal government in the last ten years or so, like the Chicago Seven case, like the case up in Connecticut against the Panthers, the case here against the Panthers, the case on the coast against the Panthers, the Berrigan case, the Ellsberg case. Those cases where a federal prosecutor indicted these people because it was something that had to be done, politically—not because he could prove a case. The cases show how abusive prosecution can be and how the grand jury process can be abused. Now all of those cases around the country—and there were dozens of them—were just the ones you know about. Those are all federal. Now, on the state level how many times, how many such cases do you have?

Q: How about William Yates, the prosecutor in Cambridge [Maryland], and Rap Brown?

A: Same thing, the exact same thing. Rap Brown should be classified among those cases like the Berrigan brothers. Now look at the reverberations of that case. Yates indicts Rap Brown and charges him with a felony that's impossible to prove. Yates talked with the state's attorney of Harford County, who claims that Yates said he only brought the felony charge to bring it under federal jurisdiction so he could extradite Rap Brown. Yates said he didn't say that. They went to trial about that thing, and Yates was found in contempt of court for discussing the case contrary to court order.

Q: I remember talking to State Attorney General Francis Burch from Cambridge a number of times, telling him that there was widespread feeling in Cambridge that Yates was using arrest and exorbitant bail to intimidate blacks. Burch told me there was nothing he could do about it because of Yates' autonomy. It was interesting to me to see Burch become involved in the effort to discipline Kinlein by Yates' former deputy] once Kinlein had made those assertions about Yates.

A: Legally there was nothing Burch could do about it. He can't tell Yates what to do. But it is not unusual for the attorney general to suggest to a prosecutor what should be done in a case or how some things can be done. He is not technically the prosecutor's boss, but he is regarded as being some sort of superior legal officer. So, if he calls the prosecutor up and says, "Prosecutor, if I were you I would proceed to indict in such-and-such a case," the prosecutor might take his suggestion. It depends upon the political situation. Now, in Maryland, it's not likely that would happen because some prosecutors don't particularly like Burch and would not be likely to follow his suggestions.

Q: What are some of the principle results achieved since you have been in office?

A: It's kind of hard to measure impact. You can see, for instance, that we are trying cases faster. We are keeping the people in jail less time awaiting trial. You can see that the indictment processes have probably improved a lot because we get a high conviction rate, which means that we are not improperly indicting a lot of people. Things like the level of professionalism have risen a lot because people are staying longer in office. We are getting a better quality of prosecution. But in three years' time it's kind of hard to put your hand on definitive things and say this is a proved thing.

Q: Has the number of indictments dropped?

A: The number of pending indictments. But that, too, can be an illusion. The popular figure around here they used to use was 6,000 indictments pending. Well, 6,000 indictments are more than a year's work for our courts. We usually run from eight to twelve courts. That's a year's work. Now, obviously if we have 6,000 indictments and we are turning out another 500 every month, we are a year behind. That's the way it looks. If we really have 6,000 indictments, see. But I've contended from the very beginning that we have never had a backlog here. What we've had is a poorly managed caseload. Now, they did have 6,000 indictments, but this is what we did the first year I was in office. We went through these indictments and found out exactly what they were. It took a year to do that. And what we found was that a lot of cases were where people had been indicted who had never been arrested. To indict a guy and never take him into custody is accomplishing nothing. You aren't doing anything. But that's the way to get the press off your tail, see. A man kills someone and he escapes and somebody says, "Tom Brown did it." So you go ahead and indict Tom Brown based on that statement. So it appears in the paper, "Tom Brown indicted for the murder of Bill Smith." So that Tom Brown case is solved as far as the public is concerned. Now this man may be in China for the rest of his life. He may be dead. But that goes into your file as part of your backlog because, first of all, the theory about searching for fugitives is all television drama. Once a man gets out of this state, brother, he's gone unless he gets arrested in another state. He's gone. Nobody runs people down the way Cannon does on TV. Now, if he gets locked up in another state, then they got him. But that's the only way they'll get him.

In this backlog we found a lot of cases where defendants had never been arrested or had been arrested but had jumped bail and the bondsman was made to pay. We found a lot of cases where persons went into the hospital, had been in the hospital, or had escaped. Well, what it amounted to was a lot of cases that could never be tried anyhow. So they should have been gotten out of the system years ago. We found one case back in 1948. What are we going to do with a 1948 case in the 1970's? It was a rape case, the man was indicted and went to a mental hospital, and he is still there and will be for the rest of his life, and it is still an open case on the books. By the time we cleaned this debris out of the dockets, what was left were the real, triable cases, and I attacked them by assigning them to teams of prosecutors and checking and rechecking until they were tried. I forced them to court and got them tried. So what have I got now? I've got about 2,000 cases, which is a normal caseload. But those are real cases and most of them will be tried.

Q: Did you get much support from the black community in your campaign?

A: Not from black organizations. But in the black community there was a lot of enthusiasm about my running for election. It was sort of like magic. Everybody was caught up in it. A lot of people who were never involved in campaigns before got involved in it. I didn't have any money except for a few dollars of my own—I had no source of raising funds. I had no organized political support. It was a spontaneous outpouring of the black community that got me elected. They didn't have any money, but they all came out and they put up signs. They put on bumper stickers; they did everything. I got a lot of support from clients of my law office, which had to number thousands of people.

The primary was just about entirely run by black folk and some white firebrands. I've been here all my life, you know. I was fifty-two years old at the time, and they became caught up in the idea that here was a black guy who could tackle the system seriously. I just did squeeze by the primary election, but I won pretty big in the general election.

Q: Do black political figures, the pros, seem to appreciate judicial politics?

A; No. They don't. Apparently, our civilization has gotten too complicated for anybody to understand, except for a very few people. I really believe that the system is so big and so complicated that we can only understand a part of it at a time, and that a lot of the black politicians would like me to be state's attorney because I'm a black guy, not because they realize that a black guy can be very effective in helping them in the administration of justice. It's because they like me and they say, "Well, I want to see him win."

Q: So, it's a personal thing—

A: It's personal, sure. Just like I like to see a black judge on the bench. I like to see black judges there because I know how effective it's going to be in straightening out a lot of problems we've got. Not because he's a good guy and I like to see him with a $35,000 job and you feel proud of him when he walks down the street. That's not why I want to see him on the bench. I know that if we get enough black judges on the bench, it would change this damn system around. And I know if you get black prosecutors around the country in enough of these good-size cities, and they stay there for some time, you are going to gradually see a change in the proper administration of justice. And I am glad to see it because blacks, unless they are the blacks who were reared entirely in a white society, have a feeling about justice that whites just don't have. What is just to people who grew up in a white society and what is just to a black man are two different things. I frankly believe that we've got a perception that other people don't have, particularly about fairness and unfairness.

Q: But you find that young black lawyers veer away from prosecutorial work?

A: Yes. They are fascinated by private practice. They are their own boss. They can make a lot of money, because there are so few black lawyers, and with the new black pride more people are going to black lawyers. They are particularly fascinated with criminal practice. A few of them are veering into business practice, getting in on the ground floor of corporate work. They are doing all right, individually, but for blacks they aren't doing much. I mean, you can make a lot of money, but that just means one man is successful. I contend that what a young black just out of law school should be thinking about hard is prosecution. Prosecution has such a widespread effect on the whole system, on everything. And if we could get four or five blacks in the chief prosecutor's office, like we have mayors, they would be a hell of a lot more effective than mayors could ever be.

Q: What is there to be said for and against plea bargaining?

A: It is both a good thing and a bad thing; it is mixed. It's good or bad, depending upon what jurisdiction is doing it and how they are doing it. If you are plea bargaining because your caseload is so heavy that you must plea bargain to keep it down, then it's bad. But there is nothing wrong with a plea bargain or, as they call it, a "plea negotiation," if you're doing it based on the facts of the case rather than the exigencies of the docket. There are many things that happen in cases that make bargaining the most sensible approach. For instance, it is very seldom that the state has a perfect case. There are so many mistakes that can be made from the time you learn that the man is arrested until the time you bring him to trial—there are so many things that can affect the case—that you really need a prosecutor from the very beginning. So what happens is, if you end up with a case with any defects in it, the prosecutor knows that he might very easily lose the case, or he knows that his chances are maybe seventy to thirty or fifty-fifty. It depends upon what the defects are, and there are always some defects. On the other hand, the defense also knows that he might lose the case. Plea bargaining is bad or good depending upon who is doing it. And, of course, plea bargaining is different from pleading; let's not forget that.

Q: How about the judge who might want to clear his docket or speed up his list?

A: Well, some judges push people to plea bargaining. It depends upon the judge. Now sometimes it's justified if you have a bunch of inefficient lawyers on both sides, and it's likely that the prosecutors will be inefficient because they are often so young. Right now, you have a dearth of good trial lawyers all over the country so you can end up with two lawyers not really knowing their case too well. Very often inexperienced lawyers simply do not see the issues in a case. An experienced judge will often advise counsel for both sides of the true parameters of the evidence and the probable verdict. Very often a reasonable plea is suggested and often accepted. So, instead of having a trial take a week, the trial takes fifteen minutes. So plea bargaining comes about by the judge expressing his opinion based on his experience, by the experience or lack of it of the parties, and by the necessities of the case.

Q: What are blacks in the law doing collectively to improve the system of justice?

A: You would expect black lawyers to be a very cohesive, self-help oriented group, but the attitude of mutual protection does not exist as much as you would expect. Lawyers have not surged to the front as community leaders, at least not here in Baltimore. The black judges are probably more oriented toward the community, but they operate under such a strict code of ethics that they cannot exert nearly as much influence as I am sure they would like to.

The lawyers are a different lot, however. They seem to be strongly oriented toward developing lucrative private practices as rapidly as possible. I suppose this arises from the scarcity of black lawyers and the economic background of blacks as a whole. There are few black lawyers I know who did not feel the pinches of poverty coming through law school. Consequently, once they are admitted to practice, they seem to want to get into a lucrative practice just about immediately. This may be a mistake on the part of many because one thing you do not learn in law school is how to practice law. I simply do not think a young lawyer is equipped to take a full-time practice the minute he's admitted.

Today an aggressive black lawyer can be off and running with a sizable practice in a very short time because of the scarcity of black lawyers and tendency of black people to turn more toward black lawyers than they did in former years. The consequences of this is that few black lawyers are content to work in programs that will give them a good basic training in the practice of law. You find very few of them in prosecutors' offices, city solicitors' offices, or legal aid offices. They often prefer to pass up this initial two- or three-year paid additional preparation and go directly into law practice. The consequence is insufficient participation in community affairs, little participation in the legislative process, and almost no input at the policy-making level of our city and state governments.

The place where a black lawyer can perform the most good for black people is first in the legislature; secondly, in the prosecutor's or city solicitor's office; and thirdly, in legal aid work. In each of these endeavors he can materially affect the progress of black people by influencing massive changes in practices generally harmful to poor people and particularly harmful to black people. In my limited contact on the national level I seem to detect the same type of thinking: a fanatic attraction to private practice and little interest or understanding of self-commitment to programs designed to get involved at policy-making levels of government.

Q: Does the local chapter of the NBA have any meaningful input into that process?

A: We think so, yes. The judges seek our support and help, and the governor pays attention to what the Bar Association says sometimes. For instance, I don't think they would appoint a man that the NBA would be dead set against because he is a racist.

Q: Is this a fairly recent sensitivity, though?

A: Yes. But there weren't that many lawyers around here ten or twelve years ago.

Q: Would an increase in the number of black lawyers foster cohesion among them?

A: I don't really know. I am hopeful. But the clannishness of black lawyers and the fact that they are so tied up in their own personal careers and they are not oriented toward the new black awareness as much as I think they should be, except individually, of course, probably would prevent us from having the type of force that we should have. And I don't know if these youngbloods want to join us. You know, they feel they are different.

Q: Do you know of anybody in the black legal community who is monitoring the revision of the Maryland Criminal Code?

A: No. No one is monitoring the revision of the Maryland Criminal Code. No blacks are on the committee. I, in my capacity as state's attorney, am monitoring it as much as physically possible without being on the committee. It would be a good thing if the black community could muster the manpower to monitor several areas of concern, but we simply do not have the horses. Our law firms are usually very small and could not spare a man to deal with a certain area, such as the legislature, for instance. We are still a greatly economically disadvantaged class of people. The business of survival occupies all of our time, attention, and energy.

Q: And the NBA, does it have anybody doing it?

A: I know of no such effort by the NBA or any other group in the black community. The same thing that afflicts the black bar afflicts every other black institution, body or group. We're in a perpetual economic crunch. We have no money for special projects. First, we must survive; then we must wipe the last traces of racism from the face of the earth. Then, and only then, can we start thinking about special projects.

Q: How about legal services here in Baltimore?

A: We have a very good legal services program for the poor here, except that it is going to be cut down, momentarily. Now that's an area where we don't have many blacks and that's where black lawyers could be a lot of help, if they're really sincere in helping black folk. But I find that my black brothers have a constant struggle within themselves as to whether they want to help black folk or whether they want to help themselves. Now they'll defend some black folk if they are charged with a crime, but that's not helping black folk in general. The people that really need the help are the poor people, in the worst way. And that's purely a labor of love. You don't get paid much money, and you do an awful lot of work and an awful lot of good.

If the young black lawyers were sincere in helping black folk at all, they would get in those poverty programs and those legal aid to the poor programs because those are the people who really get the dirty end of the stick from those white-collar criminals. Exploitation of the poor is big business. If something happened to all the poor people overnight, there would be a lot of people out of business because their entire business is exploitation of the poor, and they do well on it. Short weight, shoddy merchandise, rent fraud, slum rentals, repair fraud are crimes of exploitation of the poor, and no city has sufficient law enforcement manpower to deal with the individual crimes or with the criminal practice. This is an area that needs imaginative law enforcement, perhaps a suit to force law enforcement authorities to enforce the law or some other bold plan showing verve, creativeness, and imagination.

Q: Have you been able to do many of the things in your role as prosecutor that you would have liked to have seen done during those years you were working on the other side?

A: It's amazing even to myself. After three years I had really done everything I set out to do except for one thing: I have not completely professionalized the office. See, the big battle in America is between a professional prosecutor and the catch-as-catch-can prosecutor, the part-time prosecutor. That's the big battle. Prosecutors know that you must have professionals to do a good job—you must have a guy who has been around for some time, gets a good salary, and is a professional prosecutor to compete with the defense lawyer who is a professional. But the system in most states is that the prosecutor is a young fellow, fresh out of law school who is just there to get some intermediate training (to get his feet wet as they call it), and that often your chief prosecutor is a politician on his way up, who will be a judge as soon as possible.

Now, under that present system, you simply do not get that quality in a prosecutor I think in my office I should have. Out of ninety-six prosecutors I think I have maybe thirty professional prosecutors who are there to make a career. The rest of them are these young people that simply churn through the system. When I am obligated to try a serious case, I think the state's entitled to a professional. That is the one thing I haven't been able to achieve. I have moved in that direction, I have noted some improvement, but it will take a lot of doing to convince the city and state fathers that the prosecutor's office is not the proper place to serve as a postgraduate training ground for young lawyers.

Q: Isn't another bit of thinking that the prosecutor is in the business of just winning cases, not weeding out cases?

A: Well, that's the concept of too many people. The concept is incorrect, of course, as the prosecutor is charged with the responsibility of protecting the innocent as well as prosecuting the guilty. He is also charged with investigating criminal activity and rooting out corruption. If you prosecute by police arrests, you have an unjust system because the police arrest a lot of people against whom there is no case. They arrest on probable cause, which is not enough to convict usually. A lot of unpopular people and a lot of queer people get arrested. A lot of oddball folk who are simply unpopular get arrested; a lot of modern-thinking kids get arrested; people who drive sports cars get arrested. A lot of people get arrested who are neither factually nor legally guilty and the police often charge them improperly. Often arrests are made in explosive situations or emergency situations. It would be a great injustice to simply assume the correctness of an arrest and put the defendant to trial.

The proper prosecutor will weigh a case before putting the defendant to trial. It is unfair to do otherwise. But this is another area where the prosecutor has to make a hard choice. He has to run for election and some people don't like public servants who don't conform to their preconceived ideas. It is a temptation to some prosecutors to take the easiest way. The safest way is to charge the defendant and let the judge worry about it. Simply don't exercise your discretion; try everything the police bring up; and then if it fails, blame the police. This is playing politics. It's prostituting the office of the prosecutor. I will not do it, whatever the cost.

Q: Finally, what about the kids, juveniles?

A: Well, the same things that affect the adult system affect the juvenile system, except it is worse there. The juvenile systems are allegedly civil systems to provide care for children in trouble, but the practice is so far from the theory. I think those responsible for the system are so completely frustrated by its weaknesses and utter failures that they don't know what to do. The incarceration of juveniles is notoriously poor all around the country.

Now most people agree that if there is anything you can do with a person headed for a criminal career, it has to happen in the juvenile stage. But we don't do it. It is written in our code, but we have never had enough institutions, we have never had enough probation officers, parole facilities, or court facilities.

We have never had enough of anything. We have devoted very little money to the juvenile system in this country.

If we could devote the proper amount of money to the juvenile system, the effect on the adult system would be dramatic. But we don't have enough of anything. So what happens? You just churn the kids through there, and they go on probation. They are not supervised properly, and some of them may survive, and some of them may not. More than likely they come back as adult criminals. There isn't a vast amount of difference except that I don't guess it gets as much attention as the adult system because the kids grow up in three or four years and they no longer are in the juvenile system. You are a juvenile problem last year, you are an adult problem next year. We are dealing with thirty or forty years of a man's life, and they are only dealing with three or four years in the juvenile system.

What I expect to happen in the juvenile system is a Supreme Court decision to require complete reworking of the juvenile system. It will cost billions of dollars. It will be like the *Miranda* decision in impact, but the states have had years of warning. I also expect a taxpayer-type suit or Common Cause-type suit against the juvenile system in some state for the same purpose of getting some action on an insoluble problem because we are so far from its original aims that it's not even funny. . . .

Judge Joseph C. Howard is critical of the administration of justice in Baltimore and in Maryland. His article centers on sentencing in rape cases. It documents the prevalence of racial disparities, disclosing, for example, that the rapist receive a harsher sentence when he is black and the victim is white than in any other instance. Judge Howard also reveals that the imposition of the death penalty on blacks convicted of raping whites has been disproportionate and inequitable. Conceivably, the disparities could be explained in terms of variables, including the ages of the assailant and the victim, the commission of concomitant capital offenses, and previous sexual offense convictions, to mention several. But Judge Howard demonstrates that race is the key variable. A former chairman of the Judicial Council, Judge Howard is on the Supreme Bench of Baltimore City. He is an alumnus of the University of Iowa (BS), University of Washington (JD), and Drake University (MS).

ADMINISTRATION OF RAPE CASES IN THE CITY OF BALTIMORE AND THE STATE OF MARYLAND

Joseph C. Howard

THE PURPOSE of this report is to document the existence of pervasive and persistent inequities in the administration of justice in rape cases in the City of Baltimore and the State of Maryland. . . . The value of this report will lie in its usefulness as a stimulus for effecting changes in the administration of justice which result in the virtual elimination of the duality of standards predicated upon race or, for that matter, any other nebulous rationalization. . . .

Inequities discussed in the body of the text comprise a set of problems in which the judiciary participates. First, it participates passively by refusing to recognize that dual standards of justice exist in the administration of rape and other criminal cases in Maryland. Secondly, the judiciary quiescently contributes to these problems by failing to recognize that dual standards of justice give birth to dual standards of morality. Thirdly, because the judiciary is so estranged from the black community, it complicates the problem by not visualizing the extent to which it contributes to disrespect for the law and to civil disobedience. Finally, the judiciary participates in the problem by remaining oblivious to the fact that the system of justice has not won the respect and cooperation of all citizens because of its unwillingness to eliminate injustice. If a criminal system of justice is to succeed, people of all kinds and on all levels must be involved in its planning and execution. . . .

Every effort has been directed toward making the survey as exhaustive and complete as possible within the limits of known and accessible materials. The findings and discussions thereof are presented in two sections: (1) the General Administration of Rape Cases in the City of Baltimore, 1962-1966, and (2) Capital Sentencing in Rape Cases in Maryland Since 1923.

The General Administration of Rape Cases in the City of Baltimore, 1962-1966

This section of the report presents a panoramic picture of the handling of rape cases in the City of Baltimore since January 1, 1962, inherent in and associated with the administration of interracial and intraracial rape cases. Consequently, the analysis involves numbers rather than names. In the administration of the rape statutes in Baltimore City over the last five years, it may be assumed that there has been no significant racial discrimination. In other words, it suggests that there is no differential treatment accorded Negro defendants. It is the central purpose of this inquiry to examine the available evidence and determine the validity of such an assumption. This section of the report will examine the following categories of information pertinent to this aspect of the study: (a) indictment-trial and trial-conviction relationships and ratios; (b) probation before verdict; and (c) suspension of sentence and granting of probation. Certain rape cases have been excluded from this report either because they are incomplete or because their inclusion would have introduced considerable distortion. These exclusions are: (1) indictments returned by the grand jury in 1966 which were either not tried or completely disposed of at the time of this survey; (2) other cases between 1962 and 1965 which were begun but not completed for one reason or another; (3) all cases involving murder indictments growing out of the killing of the rape victim or a third party; (4) the twelve indictments which make up the Paoli Series involving numerous attacks by one individual;[1] and (5) cases abated by death of the defendants prior to trial.

The data presented here were obtained from schedules made of each case in which an indictment was returned by the grand jury and prosecution was instituted by the state's attorney's office. In this survey, each attack of a male upon a female is considered as one rape. Cases in which a male is charged with attacking two females are counted as two separate rapes. Similarly, cases in which two men are charged with raping one woman are recorded as two rapes. When not otherwise specified, the term "rape" shall include: rape, assault with intent to rape, statutory rape, and assault with intent to commit statutory rape, all of which carry the possible penalty of death. . . .

Suspension of Sentence and Granting of Probation

During the survey period, there were 263 convictions for sexual attacks on Negro victims and 107 for such attacks on white victims. If the rape of a Negro woman is considered as seriously as the rape of a white woman, then no difference can be expected in the rate at which sentences are suspended and probation invoked. Yet the available data indicate that as a general proposition, considering all of these racially categorized rapes with respect to the suspension of sentences and the institution of probation, it can be concluded that in no racially combined rape case is a defendant accorded so little consideration and the act deemed so serious as the one involving a Negro defendant in an interracial rape.

Of the 26 Negroes convicted of sexual offenses against whites, only one (less than 4.0 percent) had his sentence suspended and probation invoked. This suspended sentence involved a girl who also charged two white boys with the same type of attack. On the other hand, of the 258 Negroes convicted of similar offenses against Negroes, 120, constituting 46.5 percent, were immediately returned to the community. A comparable analysis concerning the white rapist since January, 1962, shows that of the 141 white-white rapes or rape-related offenses tried, 38 (27 percent) had their sentences suspended and were placed on probation. Of the six similarly indicted white-Negro cases tried during the same period, one (16.7 percent) was released on probation. As a matter of fact, these statistics show that of the 9 cases charging white males with sexual attacks on Negro females, only 5 reached the sentencing stage of trial.

Sentencing Patterns

For all practical purposes, a Negro's sexual attack on a white woman in Baltimore City results in a sentence carrying the possible death penalty. This close relationship of capital convictions in interracial rape cases should be borne in mind throughout the following discussion. In this report, our analysis considers the average sentence imposed and the classification of sentences imposed, ranging from less than five years up to and including the death penalty. All cases in which the sentence imposed was as much as eighteen months were recorded as two years. All sentences less than one year were figured at one year. All fines and suspended sentences were recorded as 0.

The average sentence imposed on a Negro who rapes a white is approximately five times as great as when a Negro rapes a Negro or a white rapes a white. Excluding life, death, and suspended sentence, the Negro-white average sentence is approximately three times as great as all other racially combined rapes. Excluding life and death sentences, the Negro-white rape sentence is approximately four times greater than the Negro-Negro rape sentence and at least three times greater than all others. A classification of dispositions made in rape cases reveals a persistent, inequitable pattern of penalty.

Only one Negro convicted of rape or a rape-related offense involving a white defendant received less than five years or a suspended sentence. That one involved a prosecuting witness who charged two white boys with the same type of an offense. The overwhelming majority of all other racially composed cases fall in this category of minimal punishment. At the lethal end of the pole, excluding cases in which a person was killed, the number of death penalties imposed in all the combined Negro-Negro, white-white, and white-Negro rapes does not exceed those imposed in the Negro-white situation. One death penalty was imposed upon a seventeen-year-old Negro for raping a white; the other Negro was sentenced for raping a Negro, but was also convicted earlier for an attack upon a white.

As one moves from the death penalty to life imprisonment, the pattern persists. The number of Negroes receiving life sentences for raping whites equals the total number of defendants who received life for all other racially combined rapes. Moving again to the twenty-years-to-life classification, the same situation continues. Thirteen of these sentences were meted out to Negroes who attacked whites, while fifteen were imposed upon all others who committed similar offenses.

An inspection of the penalties imposed upon Negroes who raped whites as opposed to whites who rape Negroes reveals that none of the twenty-five Negroes who served time for their offenses was sentenced to less than five years. But three of the four whites who raped Negroes fell into this bracket. Furthermore, where only one of the five whites who raped Negroes received fifteen years for such capital offenses, four Negroes received life or death, seventeen received twenty.

years or more, and nineteen, or almost four-fifths, received fifteen years or more.

In all racial categories, except the rape of a white by a Negro, the penalties are relatively minor. Over three-fourths of the Negroes who raped Negroes, 70.3 percent of the whites who raped whites, and 80.0 percent of the whites who raped Negroes received less than five years, while only 3.8 percent of the Negroes who raped whites fell in this category. Of those defendants receiving less than ten years, the records show that while 86.0 percent of the Negroes who raped Negroes, 81.4 percent of the whites who raped whites, and 80.0 percent of the whites who raped Negroes received less than 10 years, only 15.3 percent of the Negroes who raped whites fell in this sentence bracket.

An analysis of the more severe sentences imposed indicates that such sentences have been imposed almost exclusively in cases involving attacks on white females. Of all such attacks, 17.7 percent have resulted in life or death sentences, whereas only 0.6 percent of all attacks on Negro women have resulted in similar sentences, and no whites who raped Negroes were so sentenced. The same differential exists in the area of those sentenced from twenty years to death. Of the Negroes who raped whites, 65.3 percent have fallen into this extended sentence category while only 4.8 percent of the whites who raped whites, 5.6 percent of the Negroes who raped Negroes, and none of the whites who raped Negroes were so penalized. Of the 263 males who raped Negroes, 121, representing 46.0 percent, were given no prison term whatsoever, and 198, constituting 75.2 percent, received less than five years. Of the 107 males convicted of raping white victims, 39, amounting to 36.4 percent, had their sentences suspended, and 58, constituting 54.2 percent, were sentenced to less than five years.

It becomes apparent, then, that the nature and extent of penalty in these rape cases are dependent primarily upon one and only one factor—race. Finally, it might be noted that in not one single case where a Negro raped a white was the sentence reduced. This rigidity has not been maintained in intraracial rape situations.

In summary, this analysis justifies several conclusions: The rape of a white by a Negro is treated as a far more serious crime than any other racially categorized rape. Negroes charged with sexual attacks on white victims are disproportionately denied probation before verdict. . . . Negroes convicted of sexual attacks on white victims are disproportionately denied probation by way of suspension of sentence. . . . Negroes convicted of rape or rape-related offenses against whites are disproportionately sentenced to death, life, and extended prison terms. . . . Negroes convicted of rape or rape-related offenses against whites are disproportionately denied nominal prison terms. White defendants convicted of rape or rape-related offenses against Negroes are given less extended sentences than Negroes convicted of similar attacks on whites.

Capital Sentencing in Rape Cases in Maryland, 1923-1966

This section changes the focus of the preceding section in three important ways. It enlarges the scope to extend to the whole State of Maryland and expands the period covered to include the years since 1923. . . . This survey analyzes the treatment accorded Negro and white sex offenders whose crimes resulted in the imposition of the death penalty. As previously indicated, any rape that is accompanied by the killing of the victim or any third person present carries the additional indictment of murder. In such cases, the death penalty becomes understandable, if not justifiable. For this reason, all such cases are completely excluded from this analysis. . . .

Numerical Examination

Of the fifty-five males who, between 1923 and 1966, were sentenced to death in Maryland for rape or assault with the intent, forty-six were Negroes, two were other nonwhites, seven were white, one was Mexican, and another was Puerto Rican. Of the thirty who were executed, twenty-three were Negro, five were white, and two were other non-whites. All thirty offenders who were executed were convicted and sentenced for rape or assault with intent to rape a white female. This latter category accounts for seven of the twenty-three Negroes executed. No white was executed for assault with intent to rape. Of the seven males on death row or awaiting further disposition of their cases as of August, 1967, all were Negro and all but one was sentenced for the rape of a white female. The one Negro facing death at that time for the rape of a Negro was also convicted, weeks earlier, by a jury of assault with intent to rape a white woman. However, the jury recommended mercy in the earlier case, thereby restricting the sentence to a maximum of twenty years.

Eighteen sex offenders had their sentences commuted from death to life imprisonment. Sixteen of the commutations were granted to Negroes and two to whites. Of the sixteen Negroes, twelve were convicted of sexual attacks on white victims, one for raping both a white and a Negro, one for raping two Negroes and held for the rape of a white victim and the sexual molestation of a white child, and two for the rape of Negro victims. The two whites whose sentences were commuted were convicted of raping white females.

Of the fifty-five recipients of the death penalty between 1923 and 1966, all but two either directly or indirectly involved white females. In Maryland no man, white or black, was executed for the rape of a Negro female. Against nonwhite offenders, the death penalty has been imposed almost seven times as often and carried out nearly five times as often as against white offenders.

Death Penalties, 1940-1966

A look at these figures from another perspective brings to light a somewhat different view of the death penalty. It might be contended by some that although a dual standard of justice with respect to rape and race did, in fact, exist in the 1920's and 1930's, such inequities are no longer extant. Going back to 1960, the death penalty for rape was imposed eleven times in the State of Maryland. Each time it was imposed on a Negro. Going back to 1955, the death penalty has been imposed seventeen times in rape cases. On only one of those occasions was it used against a white defendant and sixteen times against Negroes. Between 1950 and 1966 the death sentence was decreed twenty-two times, with only two of the defendants being white. Capital punishment for rape, then, has been imposed forty-seven times between 1940 and 1966, involving thirty-eight Negroes, two other nonwhites, and seven whites. The imposition of the death penalty against Negroes reached its lowest ebb during the 1950's. There was also a diminution during this period for whites. Such impositions against Negroes during the first six years of the 1960's reached the epic proportions of the 1940's, but for the whites they continued the diminishing trend to the point of no such convictions. The decrease in death penalty impositions during the fifties coincides with the aforementioned term of the governor who disapproved of capital punishment.

Some might be tempted to conclude from the data that rape by whites is on the decline or that they have not committed the more serious sexual offenses which permit the death penalty. However, neither of these conclusions is accurate. Records show that the incidence of rape among both Negroes and whites continues to grow, and that during 1960-1966 in Baltimore City alone, forty-nine white defendants were convicted of capital sex offenses. One of these was convicted of twelve separate such offenses. Yet in none of these forty-nine capital convictions was death decreed. If capital convictions secured in the counties over this same period and those for both the counties and the city during the preceding two decades were added, the discrepancy would be even more pronounced. Thus, there appears to be neither a logical nor a justifiable reason for the disproportionate use of the death penalty in a manner that systematically includes Negroes and excludes whites.

Racial Composition of Death Penalty Cases, 1940-1966

Of the forty-seven death penalties decreed, thirty-five were interracial; twelve, intraracial. This amounts to almost three times as many impositions of the penalty in interracial rape cases as in intraracial ones. It could be contended that the apparent disproportionate imposition of the death penalty against Negroes who rape whites does not in itself demonstrate discrimination because such rapes are more heinous and as a result more detestable than any other racial combination. But to substantiate this contention, and thereby justify the disproportionate use of the death penalty against Negroes, it must be shown that the Negro rapist is more closely associated with the following extremes or aggravations:

1. Attacks on the young or very old
2. Commission of concomitant capital offenses
3. Age of defendant
4. Previous sexual offense convictions
5. Participating in multiple sexual attacks upon one victim
6. Forced perverted act in addition to rape
7. Display of a deadly weapon
8. Brutalization of the victim
9. Multiple victims attacked by a single defendant

An examination of the nature and extent of the sexual attacks committed by Negro and white defendants in light of these nine variables is instructive.

1. AGE OF VICTIM

Among Negro defendants, less than 25.0 percent of their victims were young or very old, while 85.7 percent of the white defendants/victims were in this age category. From these statistics, it is apparent that Negroes are not significantly associated with sexual attacks on the young or the very old. Therefore, the ages of the victims in terms of the extremes of the age range do not coincide with the disproportionate imposition of the death penalty against Negroes. This inverse relationship is not true of the situation for white defendants. On the contrary, as indicated above, there is a high correlation between the imposition of the death penalty against them and the extremes of the age range for their victims.

2. CONCOMITANT CAPITAL OFFENSES

An inspection of the fifty-five rape cases with respect to the concomitant commission of other capital offenses reveals that not one involved another capital offense. It should be remembered, however, that murder-rape cases have been completely excluded from this report. The commission of concurrent capital offenses, then, is not a justifiable basis for the disproportionate utilization of the death penalty against Negroes.

3. AGE OF DEFENDANT

The age of the defendant, especially if he is extremely young, often serves as the basis for affording him consideration. Of the total of forty-six Negro offenders sentenced to death, nine (19.6 percent), were in their teens; twenty-four (52.2 percent), were under twenty-four years of age; and the ages of four of the defendants (8.6 percent) were unknown. No teenage white was sentenced to death, much less executed, for rape. As noted, Negroes fifteen, sixteen, and seventeen years of age have been sentenced to death for rape, and an eighteen-year-old Negro youth was executed for the rape of a white female. Both the youngest white offender executed and the youngest sentenced to death were twenty-three years old. Justification, then, of the disproportionate number of death sentences meted out to Negroes cannot be founded on the theory that these defendants are older and thus more responsible for their acts. When the victim is white and the offender is Negro, the age of the latter is an important factor neither in mitigation of the offense nor in the disposition of the case.

4. PREVIOUS SEXUAL OFFENSE CONVICTION

Examination of existing records shows that of the twenty-three Negroes executed, none had previous convictions for sexual offenses. One of the seven under imposition of the death penalty, on death row, and one of the sixteen whose sentences were commuted to life had such prior convictions. One of the five whites executed and one of the two currently serving commuted sentences had previous records of sex offenses. Again, there is no evidence that previous convictions played an important part in the disproportionate number of death penalties imposed upon Negroes.

5. MULTIPLE SEXUAL ATTACKS

An examination of the frequency with which two or more rapists attack a single victim indicates that this is the case for only four, representing 8.7 percent, of the forty-six Negro defendants receiving the death penalty. On the other hand, among the seven cases with white defendants, one (14.2 percent) involved more than one rapist. Thus, there is no significant association between this phenomenon and either racial group. Consequently, the evidence does not lend any credence to the assumption that the Negro is more of an offender in this respect.

6. PERVERTED ACT

In none of the fifty-five death penalty rape cases involving both Negro and white offenders was a defendant charged with committing a perverted act. This type of aggravation appears to have no impact upon the issue under consideration.

7. DEADLY WEAPON

The term "deadly weapon" refers to guns, knives, bricks, sticks, or any other instrument that could become lethal if used in a sufficiently violent manner. Although display is not synonymous with use, any indication on the part of the prosecuting witness that a weapon was displayed in the course of the attack is sufficient to bring the case within the scope of this investigation. Four of the twenty-three Negroes executed (17.3 percent) displayed deadly weapons. Three (42.8 percent) of the seven Negroes currently on death row displayed such weapons. Of the sixteen Negroes serving commuted sentences, four (25.0 percent) displayed them. In total, then, eleven of the forty-six Negroes sentenced to death, representing 23.9 percent, displayed such lethal instruments. Of the seven whites sentenced to death, none displayed a deadly weapon. . . .

The display of a deadly weapon during commission of rape appears to be somewhat more associated with Negro offenders than with whites. It does not appear, however, that the display of a deadly weapon with respect to the Negro defendant is significantly associated with the sentence of death. In fact, 35 (over three-fourths) of the Negroes who received the death penalty displayed no weapon of any kind. Thus, what might at first be regarded as an important variable leading to an understandable basis for the disproportionate sentencing of Negroes to death for rape is negated

8. BRUTALIZATION

The variable involving brutality is impossible to analyze without definition. The penetration of a child or aged female, in and of itself, may be regarded by some as brutality. Others regard brutality as encompassing such acts as striking or throwing to the ground a member of the weaker sex. However, for the purpose of this analysis, the term "brutality" will be restricted to those cases in which the victim required medical treatment or sustained some sort of permanent injury or disfiguration as a result of the attack.

Brutality was associated with attacks by 71.4 percent of the white and 13 percent of the black defendants. The comparative infrequency among Negro defendants makes it impossible to justify the high rate of harsh penalties or to support an assumption that such cases are more detestable than those involving whites.

9. MULTIPLE VICTIMS

The following frequencies were found with respect to single defendants attacking more than one victim. Of the forty-three interracial rape convictions, one charged the defendant with attacking two or more females. Of the total of twelve intraracial rapes, one was so charged. Among the white-white classification there were no such charges.

We have considered nine variables which might logically justify imposition of the death penalty for rape. An inspection of these nine variables indicates that all of the white defendants were associated with one or more of them. However, among those Negroes sentenced to death, nine of the twenty-three executed, one of the seven currently on death row, and six of the sixteen whose sentences were commuted, a total of sixteen of the forty-six cases (34.7 percent) were associated with none of these extreme or aggravated conditions.

The white intraracial cases tend to be polarized in areas characterized as extreme. Interracial rape cases involving Negro defendants do not appear, generally, to be attended by extreme or aggravated circumstances. For this reason, the assumption that the interracial rape committed by Negroes is more serious and therefore more deserving of different treatment must be rejected. Moreover, inasmuch as the Negro-white rape is not strongly associated with any of the considered extremes or aggravations, there is no equitable standard or understandable rationale for the sentences imposed. It can be concluded, therefore, that Negroes receive little consideration based upon the nine variables discussed above when the victim is white.

Several additional conclusions are unavoidable. Negroes who have been convicted of raping white victims have been disproportionately and inequitably sentenced to death during the years 1923-66 in Maryland. The death penalty has been used exclusively against Negroes and those few whites who perpetrated the most extreme and aggravated sexual attacks. There is no evidence that the administration of the death penalty, where Negro defendants are concerned, has tended to become more equitable over the last forty years. On the contrary, it appears that the degree of equity has tended to lessen over that period, especially more recently.

Not the least among the issues involved in penal reform are those regarding the rights of prisoners and the proper role of courts and judges in the matter. Traditionally, penal officials have gone about their work with little interference from the judges, who entrust other lives to their care. But recent surges of judicial activism have put judges squarely in the thick of the controversy over the treatment of prisoners. No jurist is more prominent in this enlightened insistence on protection of prisoners than Judge Constance Baker Motley, who has displayed the courage for which she was noted as a civil rights lawyer before she became a judge. The following article is excerpted from her opinion in a case that has particular implications for blacks as well as importance for non-blacks. Judge Motley is an alumna of New York University and Columbia University Law School. She sits on the U.S. District Court for the Southern District of New York.

PRISONERS' RIGHTS

(*Sostre v. Rockefeller,* 312 F. Supp. 863 [1970])

Constance Baker Motley

. . . THERE is also no real dispute as to the conditions which obtained in punitive segregation during plaintiff's year long stay. There was only one other person incarcerated in the same group of cells as plaintiff (about four out of thirteen months) from August 14, 1968, to December 20, 1968. . . . One prisoner brought to solitary and placed in another group of cells committed suicide the next day. . . . Plaintiff was deprived of second portions of food (T.887-888) and all desserts as a punishment for the entire time. . . . He remained in his cell for 24 hours per day. He was allowed one hour per day of recreation in a small, completely enclosed yard. Sostre refused this privilege because it was conditioned upon submission each day to a mandatory "strip frisk" (completely naked) which included a rectal examination. . . . He was permitted to shower and shave with *hot* water only once a week. . . . He was not permitted to use the prison library, read newspapers, see movies, or attend school or training programs. . . . He was not allowed to work. . . . Prisoners in the general population who work are able to earn money with which they may purchase items from the prison commissary, or purchase books, or subscribe to newspapers. . . . Prisoners in punitive segregation have access to only a few novels and "shoot-'em-ups" selected for them. . . . But, as plaintiff and defendant's counsel put it, the crux of the matter is human isolation—the loss of "group privileges.". . . Release from segregation is wholly within the discretion of the Warden. However, a recommendation from a non-professional, so-called, group therapy counselor might help. . . .

This court finds that punitive segregation under the conditions to which plaintiff was subjected at Green Haven is physically harsh, destructive of morale, dehumanizing in the sense that it is needlessly degrading and dangerous to the maintenance of sanity when continued for more than a short period of time which should certainly not exceed 15 days. . . .

. . . On or about August 3, 1969, plaintiff was again disciplined for having "inflammatory racist literature" in his cell. The punishment was deprivation of yard and movie privileges for 60 days. . . . The so-called "inflammatory racist literature" consisted of handwritten political articles by Sostre, some of which contained excerpts from articles printed in newspapers and magazines in general circulation in the prison (T.72-77; Pl. Exh. 23) and lists of officers of the Black Panther Party and the Republic of New Africa [RNA] copied from similar articles in *Esquire* and other magazines. . . .

This court finds from all of the facts and circumstances of this case, as set forth above, that Sostre was sent to punitive segregation and kept there until released by court order not because of any serious infraction of the rules of prison discipline, or even for any minor infraction, but because Sostre was being punished specially by the Warden because of his legal and Black Muslim activities during his 1952-64 incarceration, because of his threat to file a law suit against the Warden to secure his right to unrestricted correspondence with his attorney and to aid his codefendant . . . and because he is, unquestionably, a black militant who persists in writing and expressing his militant and radical ideas in prison. . . .

. . . The court also holds that the totality of the circumstances to which Sostre was subjected for more than a year was cruel and unusual punishment when tested against "the evolving standards of decency that mark the progress of a maturing society. . . ."

. . . Subjecting a prisoner to the demonstrated risk of the loss of his sanity as punishment for any offense in prison is plainly cruel and unusual punishment as judged by present standards of decency. . . . In order to be constitutional, punitive segregation as practiced in Green Haven must be limited to no more than fifteen days and may be imposed only for serious infractions of the rules.

. . . This court holds that plaintiff was, in effect, "sentenced" to more than a year in punitive segregation without the minimal procedural safeguards required for the imposition of such drastic punishment upon a prisoner. This punishment not only caused plaintiff physical deprivation, needless degradation, loss of work, training and self improvement opportunities, and mental suffering, but materially affected the length of time he must serve under his court-imposed sentence.

. . . There is no question that defendants cannot unreasonably restrict the right of plaintiff to apply to the state court for relief. . . .

. . . Exactly how the exercise of this right will undermine prison discipline and authority is not made clear. The Attorney General alleges that "prisoners would be able to carry on unauthorized activities through communications from prisoners to their attorneys and hence to third parties." Uncensored communications, however, presently occur on personal visits to the prison by the prisoner's attorney and members of his family, without any apparent undermining of prison discipline. In any event, the right of a prisoner to unexpurgated communications with his attorney is so significant that it outweighs the danger of frustration of prison rules regarding outside activities in the rare case where an attorney—an officer of the court—would assist a prisoner in avoiding legitimate prison regulations.

. . . About a month after this court ordered plaintiff's release from solitary confinement on July 2, 1969, plaintiff was charged with the possession of contraband found in his cell. This consisted of political literature, such as a list of officers of the Black Panther Party and Republic of New Africa, and "Revolutionary Thoughts" put on paper by plaintiff. Some of this matter was copied from newspapers and magazines which had been legally and regularly circulated in the prison. . . . This information was characterized by the Deputy Warden as racist and, consequently, contraband. . . . The Deputy Warden found plaintiff guilty of possession of such contraband and punished him by the denial of 60 days of yard time and movies. . . . This action on the part of defendants must be considered in conjunction with the Warden's sending Sostre to solitary confinement initially because of the statement made in the letter to his sister and because of Sostre's refusal to answer questions about RNA. Thus considered, there is no room for doubt that Sostre's troubles with defendants stem not from his acts or threats to prison security, but from his political thoughts and beliefs, as expressed in the literature he reads and the letters he writes. . . . Sostre was not charged with organizing a chapter of RNA in prison, making inflammatory racist speeches to other prisoners, or urging revolt by inmates against prison officials prior or subsequent to being sent to punitive segregation. Sostre had been previously sent to segregation because of something he had written to his sister and because of his refusal to answer questions about a political organization. And even the August 3, 1969, charge was that of mere possession of "racist" literature.

. . . The First Amendment to the Constitution is a guarantee that freedom of the mind shall have the same protection as freedom of religion and that "[g]reat secular causes, with small ones, are guarded" against unreasonable governmental infringement. Other case . . . make clear that a prisoner retains his right to access to the courts, freedom from cruel and unusual punishment, and certain procedural due process rights. The right to freedom of political thought and expression is also among those rights which a prisoner takes with him to prison (subject to reasonable rules and regulations necessary to maintain prison discipline) since, as the court reminded us in *La Vallee, supra,* 293 F. 2d at 235, when we talk about First Amendment rights we are talking about "preferred" constitutional rights.

. . . The undisputed evidence established that shortly before trial defendants voluntarily transferred plaintiff to another state prison, Wallkill, where he would be nearer his attorney for the purposes of preparing for trial. At Wallkill, Sostre has been permitted to help organize a Black Studies program, an Afro-American Cultural Society and an Afro-Asian Book Shop. He is able to read, share his books, obtain books and possess political literature of the very kind for which he was punished at Green Haven. . . . As a matter of fact, the undisputed testimony was that the Warden at Wallkill had approved Sostre's Afro-American Society program and was seeking professional help as a model for other prisons. . . .

. . . Under the rationale of Johnson v. Avery, *supra,* a man may not be punished for reasonably exercising his First Amendment rights, as here, or any other federally protected right. It is not a function of our prison system to make prisoners conform in their political thought and belief to ideas acceptable to their jailers. On the other hand, one function is to try to rehabilitate the lawbreaker by convincing him of the validity of our legal system. There is little chance that such an objective will be achieved if prisoners are entrusted to those who likewise break the law by denying prisoners their basic constitutional rights. This court holds that Sostre's confinement to punitive segregation for the letters he wrote and for refusal to answer questions about a political organization, and his subsequent punishment for mere possession of political literature, were unreasonable punishments and violated his First Amendment right to freedom of political expression.

. . . Sostre was, in fact, subjected to cruel and unusual punishment because he insisted upon exercising his constitutional rights. The multiplicity of charges against him was a pretext for his long punishment. And as set forth above, even if some of the charges found to be false were true, the long punishment for such offenses and the failure to take into account the Supreme Court's decision in Johnson v. Avery, *supra*, demolish any claim of good faith.

Judges are the primary audience for Judge Sherman W. Smith's article about racism and classism in corrections, but all of us will benefit from his observations about bail, community rehabilitation programs, recommendations from probation departments, and public information activities. Judge Smith deals with disparities in sentencing in cases involving auto theft, larceny, and assault and robbery, attributing these disparities to both racial and cultural gaps between white law enforcement officials and black defendants. He bases his observations largely on his experience as a judge on the Superior Court of Los Angeles. Judge Smith is a graduate of West Virginia State College and Howard University Law School.

JUDICIAL AND ADMINISTRATIVE ACTION TO AVOID RACISM IN POST-TRIAL CRIMINAL PRACTICES AND PROCEDURES

Sherman W. Smith

IN a discussion of judicial and administrative action to avoid racism implicit therein is the conclusion that such racism exists. One of the first things that a judge must do is to recognize this fact. It is also to be recognized by the agencies dealing with "less chance" (minority-group) people that there is racism in post-trial criminal practices and procedures. There are few objective studies of these problems. None is a nationwide study. Not all of them recognize the economic status of the defendant or the lawyer he obtains, the effect of a prior criminal record, regional factors, and others, which add considerably to the complexity of testing the hypothesis on the relationship between race and sentencing. However, there is enough evidence accumulated throughout the years that there is a problem in connection with disparity of sentences between "less chance" people and "greater chance" (non-minority-group) people.

Instances have come to light in which defendants differing only by race have received remarkably disparate sentences for essentially the same crime. In one jurisdiction a Negro defendant accused of raping a white woman received the death sentence in the same courtroom in which three months before a white man had received five years for raping an eleven-year-old Negro girl. One Negro teenager drew a seven-year-sentence for forging a $10 check.

On the front page of the Los Angeles *Times* which carried the story about the Supreme Court's decision in connection with the death penalty, a prominent picture of a black teenager was displayed as one whose life was saved after he had been given the death sentence for raping a sixty-seven-year-old white woman in Texas. In Maryland during the period between 1940 and 1961, when Negroes constituted less than one-third of the total population, forty-seven persons received the death penalty, and forty of these were Negroes.

There are other instances of abuse in sentencing which have led to a widespread belief that less-chance groups, particularly blacks, are likely to receive harsher sentences when the pertinent crime is committed against a white person and lesser sentences when the crime is committed by one Negro against another and that the white person is not likely to be severely punished for a crime against a Negro.

From a study made in St. Louis in recent years for the crimes of homicide and rape, everyone convicted was sent to prison. For burglary equal proportions of blacks and whites received penitentiary sentences. In other areas the proportions are somewhat startling. For auto theft, for example, 56 percent of the whites were granted probation, but 82 percent of the blacks were sent to prison. For larceny, 82 percent of the blacks were sent to prison, compared to only 54 percent of the whites. A substantially higher proportion of Negroes to whites were sentenced to prison for assault and robbery. Overall, 75 percent of the convicted blacks went to prison, compared to 61 percent of the whites. Even more

remarkable is the fact that the ratio of those granted probation was almost twice as high for whites as for Negroes (37
percent to 19 percent).

Aside from overt racial discrimination, there is another
kind of bias which occurs because white lawyers, judges, and
juries can't deal with, and the judicial system makes no provision for, the cultural gulf between black and white America.
Black people living in ghettos, isolated from white society,
have developed styles of grooming and dress, a vocabulary,
and a set of traditions that are strange and incomprehensible
to most whites. A white jury called upon to evaluate the
evidence surrounding an incident involving black people in
their own community faces a very difficult task because of
cultural barriers. Our judicial system, which is based upon a
system of cultural homogeneity, does nothing to alleviate the
problem. The reaction of white judges to the proud, aloof
black youths with tight pants and "naturals," which they
associate with black power and rebellious violence, is that . . .
such assertion of cultural difference [is] . . . a threat to the
established order.

Justice James Cobey, of the California Court of Appeal, in a
recent dissent in *Adams* v. *Superior Court,* 2 Civil No. 40086, in
a case which discusses the propriety of jurors from county-
wide draw sitting on central district juries, stated:

> The central district is apparently, for the most part, a
> ghetto of low income working-class families. The people
> within it have little mobility and live, work and exist almost
> completely within the district. Their way of life is largely
> unique when it is compared to the ways of life obtaining in
> the other districts. This uniqueness extends to life style,
> environment, problems, perception of life and even, to
> some extent, to language.

Also, there has to be an understanding of the causes of
criminality. A long-term effect of segregation upon lower-
class Negroes has been a blocking off of their self-assertion,

economically, socially, and psychologically. Open expression of their resentment against second-class status has been blocked off in both the South and the North. This damning up of resentment is one reason for the high incidence of crime among lower-class Negroes. It is further supported by the fact that the vast majority of violent acts by Negroes is directed toward other Negroes. To put it another way, one might say that for the lower-class Negroes avenues have been closed off by the social structures so that violent crime against members of their own race is one of the channels of least resistance open to him for the expression of aggression. . . .

It would not follow that men who take the oath as judges will automatically shed all of their conscious and subconscious bias, predispositions, and predilections simply because they ascend the bench, although they may assume that they are acting in good faith at all times and will attempt to dispense justice with fairness and impartiality. Judges have been and usually are near the upper middle to older group of lawyers when appointed to the bench. In too many instances, they have been and are men who at the time of their appointment to the bench had been in the forefront of holding the line and creating "intellectual barriers" for the growth of civil liberties. . . .

In any discussion of post-trial proceedings, it is assumed that the conscientious judge has taken the proper steps to see that the defendant has been released on bail or on his own recognizance in a proper case and that he has received a fair trial, including the selection of a representative jury. In discussing what a judge may do to avoid racism, classism, or any other type of "ism," which prevents justice and equal treatment under the law, I wish to suggest several categories:

1. What the judge may do within the law as provided for by applicable city, state, and federal code.

2. What the judge may do without sanction of any specific applicable law but within discretion inherent within his office.

3. What the judge may, can, and should do in directing,

influencing, persuading, and working with other agencies given the responsibility in post-conviction programs.

4. What the judge may, can, and should do in the way that he handles himself, and his general demeanor and philosophy as a judge in the total aspects of his personality on and off the bench. . . .

All judges and persons in corrections must come to know that there are certain fundamental disciplines and opportunities which must be afforded every human being in order for him to lead a healthy and normal life. These include love and a proper comprehension of its opposite, hate; independence and the right kind of independence; constructive use of imagination and truth; achievement and learning how to meet failure; identity and a decent humility which recognizes the dignity of individuals; intimacy and its opposite, discrimination; creativity and constructive criticism; integration and concentration.

The judge must be continually aware of all of the programs of rehabilitation within the community, the specific areas in which the program can be most helpful and the type of individual most suited for the program. . . . It would follow that any enlightened program for rehabilitation helps to alleviate racism as an overwhelming disproportionate number of less-chance people are within the correction system, as subjects and inmates, and thus would be substantial beneficiaries.

After conviction, should a defendant who has been on bail be remanded and the bail revoked? Unless the offense is of a very serious nature and some reliable intelligence has come to the attention of the court that the defendant may leave the jurisdiction, then he should be able to remain at liberty. In California, in felony cases, unless there is a waiver from the defendant, it is mandatory that the case be referred to the probation department for its recommendation as to what in their opinion is the best program, best suited for the defendant, considering the interest of society and the rehabilitation prospects for the defendant. This takes three weeks. Within this period of time, if he is remanded, he may lose his job when in the final determination the court may decide to place the defendant on probation without any time in custody. To less-chance people, to remain at liberty as long as possible is very important because the job market having a shrunken scope so far as they are concerned. One of the greatest safeguards [against] recidivism is to promote and encourage every program to help maintain and secure work. Further, that period of time keeps the family intact, which of course has its great social value, and, particularly, will perhaps keep the family off the welfare rolls. . . .

In consideration of any motion for a new trial the judge should consider the question of whether or not there has been any element of racism or poverty, spoken of or suggested in a disparaging or prejudicial way, either by the defense, prosecution, jury, or witness, as to raise some doubt as to the propriety of the guilty verdict of the jury. If so, the judge should not hesitate to grant the motion for a new trial. Of course, if there is a court trial, the judge should never hesitate to do justice by acquitting where there is a showing of fundamental unfairness which amounts to denial of the due process of law in the prosecution of a case because of racism, classism, or poverty.

Sometimes, in lieu of a motion for new trial, the offense can be reduced to a lesser offense; in meritorious cases, from a felony to a misdemeanor or from a greater felony to a lesser felony. This can help with the problem of getting a job or entering into college, which again is very important to members of the less-chance group.

Further, we must also consider the type of individual whom we are now to help. Is this individual a menace or threat to society? Does he need to be sent to state prison to protect society? . . . [What is] the probability or possibility of his rehabilitation in the community? Is he the type of individual who should be retained in the community and offered the services of the probation department and other agencies to aid him in his rehabilitation? Does he deserve a combination of local jail time plus probation services? Further, whether he should be placed on summary probation—that is, without the responsibility of having to report to the probation department—or whether he is an individual who has enough strength not to need any probation at all and perhaps his sentence can be suspended with or without a fine?

All people, particularly less-chance people, need to be heard and have the feeling that they are being considered as individuals and that the judge is not taking action because of racism or classism.

Justice Louis H. Burke, of the California Supreme Court, in speaking to the 1970 sentencing institute for superior court judges, said:

> It seems to me that the attitude of the judge at the time of sentencing is extremely important. I was helped in my concept of it by one who explained that it is not the function of the judge to determine what he is to *do to* the man for the crime that he has committed, but what he can *do for* him.
> . . . This change in attitude from what the judge can *do to* the man, as compared to what he can *do for* him, does not result in diminishing the number of persons sent to prisons, but it does have a direct bearing upon the impressions which remain with a man of his day of sentence. Usually he has many days of enforced idleness ahead within which he probably reflect on what was said and done. . . . It is not sufficient that justice be done on the day of sentence but that to every extent possible what is done will have the appearance of justice. . . .

Judges should avoid having a guilt complex or any other state of mind toward less-chance people which allows them to walk out of the courtroom upon conviction and not establish some type of control, the lack of which was the cause for his being there. There is and has been a serious problem of lack of discipline in the less-chance homes, and much criminality within this group is because of this. Therefore, the conscientious judge, in order to avoid a type of inverse racism, will in a proper case use the powers inherent in his office to see that the defendant is placed on probation and should order that he do one or all of the following things, which may be applicable, to make the defendant more secure, thus enhancing the probability of discontinuing his course toward criminality. Some of the things would be to order him to get a job, to complete his education, to support his dependents, stay away from drugs, narcotics, etc. and report to the probation officer regularly, and the court can require periodical reports in reference to this program. If the defendant fails to comply, the judge should modify the terms of his probation and place him in the county jail as a condition of probation for such period of time as is deemed necessary for the defendant to get the message.

Before any judgment is rendered, in order to aid the defendant in his rehabilitation, the court may wish to make a finding that, in consideration of sentence and of the defendant as an individual, all of the record which appeared before the court, which included the arrests of the defendant not amounting to convictions, should be ignored and that he is to be considered as any other citizen who did not have these arrests. In *Gregory* v. *Litton Systems, Inc.*, 316 Fed. Supp. 401 (1970), a California district court examined the practice of excluding from employment persons who had suffered a number of arrests without having been convicted. The plaintiff, a Negro, was successful in having the court grant monetary relief and enjoining Litton from seeking, obtaining, and considering in connection with employment any information concerning arrests of applicants which did not result in conviction. An applicant, despite his general qualifications for the job, is effectively barred from employment opportunities when an employer's policy automatically eliminates applicants with prior arrest records from further consideration. Moreover, even if the applicant is not barred from employment opportunities because of a prior arrest record, he is likely to be viewed by an employer as less suitable for employment than an applicant with similar qualifications but no record of prior arrests. The court in Gregory was able to establish an adverse racial impact by finding that the arrest record criteria utilized by Litton discriminated against less-chance people and was particularly significant in the case of blacks.

Numerically, more whites are arrested than blacks, but proportionately blacks have a significantly higher rate of arrests than do whites in almost all offense categories. Arrest statistics support the court's assertion that:

> Negroes are arrested substantially more frequently than whites in proportion to their numbers. While blacks represented only 11% of the nation's population in 1969, they constituted 27% of all persons arrested. The arrest problem is exceptionally critical for blacks living in the inner cities where as high as 90% of the male ghetto residents may have an arrest record. Litton's practice of denying employment to applicants whose records showed a number of arrests will apparently bar many of these ghetto residents from any employment consideration.

The prison is a public institution, and the preclusion against segregation applies in full force to it. . . .

After years of attempting to deal with the critical issue of institutional racism via departmental memos and general training sessions, the California Department of Corrections, through its affirmative action program, decided to meet the problem head on. The director of corrections issued orders calling for an affirmative action program to (1) increase the number of minority employees at all levels; (2) establish a method to assure an equitable ethnic distribution of jobs among institution inmates; and (3) set up a viable and meaningful channel of communication for minority inmates and employees to express their concerns. The mandate also called for all departing less-chance employees to be given exit interviews to obtain their impressions of work conditions. Lastly, the mandate encouraged creation of ethnic groups among institution inmates.

The department concluded that a written examination for personnel eliminated candidates who might make good officers, including persons from less-chance races. Many otherwise qualified candidates were screened out because of an apparent inability to succeed in written exercise. A request was made to the State Personnel Board to modify the examination. Steps were taken to afford a greater opportunity to persons applying for jobs to reach the oral interview. Steps were also taken to help interviewers work through whatever unconscious racial bias they may tend to exhibit during the interviewing process. Special orientation sessions were set up to acquaint interviewers with basic different characteristics which might be exhibited by the interviewees. Items such as speech patterns, dress, and grooming styles received attention. Candidates who are successful are given special instruction as to some of the basic sociocultural traits of minority groups to aid both the probationers and supervisors. For instance, one session dealt with the tendency of Mexican-Americans to relate only a "feeling level" as opposed to an intellectual level.

Within the last two years, there has been a great influx of young Vietnam veterans who bring with them a brand of independence that often is interpreted by supervisors as insubordination. This appears particularly true of blacks. Orders were issued to hire more blacks than browns in specific categories and also in general. A policy calling for equitable distribution of inmates' assignment was instituted. The ethnic breakdown in the California prison population for many years has been about 50 percent white, 30 percent black, and 19 percent Mexican-American, or Chicano. The remaining 1 percent covers other ethnic minority group members, such as Asians and native Americans. Thus the new policy required that of every ten men assigned to a job five should be white, three black, and two Mexican-American, or Chicano.

Realizing [sic] that ethnic minority inmates face special kinds of problems, the formation of ethnic inmate self-help groups was encouraged. In each correctional institution there is a variety of self-help groups including such standbys as Alcoholics Anonymous and Gamblers Anonymous. However, these groups apparently fail to adjust to the special kind of problems facing the community by minority inmates. Names like Self Advancement Through Education, a black group at San Quentin, and EMPLEO, a job-placement-oriented group at the California Medical Facility, began to spring up in several institutions. The department learned rather quickly how ill prepared it was to manage and lead groups of this nature. Learned also was the fact that inmates were not well prepared to handle constructively the new role of probation. The reasons appeared to rest in the component racism itself. The system long had ignored the collective personality of ethnic minority inmates, and consequently they had failed to learn from the system. . . .

It was mandated that each institution and parole region would develop a recruitment action plan and that efforts would be directed toward actively seeking out minority recruits and encouraging job retention by creating a realistic climate for equal opportunity in the department. When personnel begin to treat others as equals, there will be little need for exit interviews or special handling of complaint letters. In order to keep the director informed, beginning July 10, 1969, and monthly thereafter, a report was required to be submitted which reflected the personnel actions for the preceding month. Such report was required to show: (a) first of month total staff Caucasians, Negroes, Orientals, Mexican-Americans, and others; (b) employee movement during the month showing the name and position of all employees who were hired, transferred, promoted, resigned, or otherwise separated; and (c) a brief narrative on every complaint which had racial employment implications.

The Los Angeles County probation department requires all work locations to be integrated even though certain offices will have a larger number of staff of one ethnic group or another following the pattern of ethnic composition of the particular area. No office is to be staffed with only one ethnic group. The department is currently drafting an affirmative action policy which will speak to the subject of integration and how it is intended to be implemented. Written examinations have been eliminated for the probation series based on a study that written examinations were culturally and ethnically biased. No written exams will be given until the Department of Personnel comes up with an unbiased examination. Also of interest was the entry level exam for Spanish-speaking personnel. . . .

The probation departm3nt sees the major problems currently existing as: (a) a lack of awareness in ethnic self-cultures, (the training office is currently involved in an inter-cultural awareness program which will eventually cover the entire department), and (b) a lack of minority brown staff to work with Mexican-American families (the current thrust is in the area to recruit brown staff as to create a readily available pool. . . .)

The work furlough program in California has been highly successful, particularly in Los Angeles County. It was inaugurated in California in 1957 and in Los Angeles County in 1964. It is estimated that 20 percent to 35 percent of the furloughees' families would have been receiving welfare had the inmates' sentences been served in full custody instead of the work furlough program. Some benefits of work furlough are: (1) Upon release, furloughees are able to continue their regular jobs, thus saving vocational and professional careers; (2) the urgency of finding a job following normal release from jail and accounting to a new employer for the interruption of his work history is relieved; (3) in addition to supporting his family, the furloughee is able to offset his custodial costs by reimbursing the county $4 for each workday; (4) there is the added psychological advantage to the inmate of providing financial security for his family while in custody; and (5) undoubtedly many marriages have been saved and many family units preserved by virtue of this program. . . .

Judges must assume greater leadership because apparently the other two coordinate branches of government may not. Some other specific suggestions in reference to what the judge may do to avoid racism or classism would be:

1. To refuse to follow the recommendation of the probation department or anyone else wherein it is recommended that the defendant be sent to an institution or placed in any program which maintains an atmosphere of dehumanizing less-chance people.

2. To require correctional agencies to make periodic reports to the court in referring to its human relations policy, personnel hiring, and general administration policies, as it particularly affects less-chance people. . . .

3. To play the role of a "change agent" in all of the areas of rehabilitation and correction.

4. To attend with probation and corrections officers sentencing institutes which provide panel discussions in reference to corrections, latent prejudices, psychological tests to be administered to judges in an effort to discover any latent prejudices against less-chance people, and promulgation of human relations policies.

5. To write articles for legal publications read by judges in reference to the problem of racism and classism in connection with sentencing.

6. To participate more in making the public aware of the need for more humane programs for giving people the best chance to reform. Perhaps the legislative and executive branches of government would be more responsive in this area if judges took more of a position.

Judges, lawyers, correctional officers, and all others connected with the criminal justice system can and should speak out on issues which affect the law and which will point up some suggestions for change to stabilize our communities in this day of serious crisis. In a day when the resolution of the crisis in criminal justice may very well determine the course of, and indeed the very survival of, this country, the talent which we have on the bench should not be reserved exclusively to the deciding of cases.

Judges have a special responsibility. Men become judges because they are respected in their communities, have been successful practitioners, and are considered men of great courage and honesty. We owe it to our profession, to the dignity of our office, to those who look to us for leadership, and particularly those frustrated, frightened less-chance people who stand before us looking for help, and as we quietly say to ourselves: "There but for the grace of God stand I!"

The defendants with whom Joyce I. London is concerned are disadvantaged by reason of age as well as race and class. To curb adult criminality, she writes, we must reduce juvenile delinquency, and our ability to do that is conditioned by our willingness to rid the juvenile justice system of racism, classism, and insensitivity. She addresses to black jurists a special plea "to save the children" and suggests several courses of action for their consideration. Ms. London completed her education at Howard University and the New England Law School. She holds a Reginald Heber Smith Community Lawyer Fellowship and is assigned to the Boston Legal Assistance Project.

BLACK JURISTS/BLACK JUVENILES

Joyce I. London

IT is axiomatic that young offenders grow older. If we would reduce the ranks of adult criminals, we must look to the youthful contacts of an offender with the juvenile justice system. Society can do more to prevent the tragic commonplace of a delinquent maturing into a bitter and expert felon. Social injustice is ill served unless practical alternatives to incarceration and punishment are provided to individuals at every phase of their youth.

The broader premise here to be explored is that society can do more for its children in the juvenile courts. Racism, classism, and insensitivity are ugly traps that oftentimes catch young offenders, keeping them in life patterns that are destructive to themselves and to others. To reduce crime and to uplift young lives, it is essential that we remove these traps from our juvenile justice system.

In a recent study on the New York State system entitled "Juvenile Injustice," seven past and present New York juvenile judges have charged that yet another generation of children is in danger of destruction unless changes are made. Citing blatant examples of discriminatory education, racist administration of justice system, and grossly inadequate youth guidance services, the report warned: "We must cease sowing the seeds of Attica." In furtherance of the premise, a recent report in the Boston *Globe* stated that one-third of the inmates at Walpole State prison are alumni of the juvenile system. The report, reflecting different viewpoints, also noted that recidivism and failure rates of juvenile crimes and rehabilitation ranged from 48 percent to 90 percent in the years 1971 and 1972. Likewise, Judge Lois G. Forer has stated that "our court system, our institutions for children have neither deterred crimes nor rehabilitated these children."

To demonstrate further the fact that juvenile justice is a problem receiving nationwide attention, former Commissioner of the Bureau of Children and Youth in Pennsylvania Larry D. Barker in a newspaper article stated "the institutions are inconsistent with modern correctional philosophy. They perpetuate a system, which has shown little, if any, results in curbing delinquency patterns." The aforementioned statements must shock all people of good conscience and all people interested in reducing crime. To those who truly feel the call to "save the children," the appalling statistics of recidivism spell out clearly the need for immense and immediate reform.

What, then, is a way out of this bleak picture? It seems clear from past results and present plight that punishment of juveniles is ineffective. Rather, our hope appears to lie in downplaying the authoritarian role of the juvenile court and enhancing its role as surrogate parent figure. This approach decries that type of bogus proceeding where, under the guise of *parens patriae*, the system attempts to sidestep constitutional safeguards in juvenile hearings. Indeed, when used as a cover instead of a cure for various ills, *parens patriae*, as Judge Forer says, is "an old Latin term misapplied to a juvenile court judge, who may or may not be learned in the law, which gives him the power to send any child in his jurisdiction to a correctional institution (jail). The phrase transforms a judge into a wise kindly father to thousands of boys and girls whom he sees for as little as three, four or five minutes."

Such hard-won juvenile rights as the right to counsel (in Re Gault) are never contrary to the optimum workings of justice. Rights are swords that cut through injustice; they are shields, insurance against possible failures of integrity within the system. The enforcement of rights of children, then, is necessary and proper; regarding rights does not contravene judicial benevolence. Children with rights remain children who are properly to be treated as such. That judge who is most truly the parent surrogate will respect rights; he wants, as does the good parent, to foster proud individuality. He does not need to manifest judicial might in a monarchial atmosphere of cloying dependency because to do so opens a superiority-inferiority door through which racism and classism creep in.

There is no room in a heterogeneous society for a system wherein the traditional white middle-class judge may attempt, although unwittingly, to homogenize and rob of individuality diverse racial and social elements. It is obviously most difficult for a defendant to identify "the man" as someone out to help and not to punish. A solution lies in having a juvenile court system that in its personnel and in its goals is broadly representative of the real parenthood of the community.

Treating juveniles as children to be protected rather than as adults to be punished results in daring innovation. An example of this occurs in Massachusetts, where former Commissioner Jerome G. Miller of the State Department of Youth Services attempted to abandon the custodial and authoritarian model. Miller inaugurated a community-based juvenile correctional network that is characterized by group homes and rehabilitation services. Juvenile correctional institutions —the "reform" schools that did not reform—have been closed down. Now, under the new system, there are more than twice as many juveniles in foster homes and residential and nonresidential programs. The programs are generally operated under private guidance and funded by the department of youth services. In Roxbury, for example, a black community in Boston, the YMCA heads the Roxbury Tracking Program which provides counseling, recreation, tutoring and work experience for eighty-seven boys and girls. Hastings House in Cambridge is a group home for eleven boys where, according to the statement of one youthful resident, "you don't have to be locked up. They don't throw you out if you screw up. They give chances."

The rehabilitative model featuring community-based treatment is an idea whose time is now. In the Massachusetts experiment it is still too early to have any definitive results. Although the tendency is for less recidivism, the system still has to work itself out. The important thing, which forecasts a bright future for Massachusetts youth and youth everywhere, is that a good start has been made. Yet one unfortunate result of the Massachusetts innovation has been increased bind-over of teenagers from the juvenile court system for Superior Court trials. Bind-over, if advised, can be a device for side-stepping the parent-surrogate function of the court. There is little doubt that extreme circumstances may warrant extreme measures. However, the use of bind-over other than as a rarity points out the insensitivity to youth of too many juvenile court judges. Pontius Pilate did not alleviate the problem by washing his hands of it; neither do our judges do well by passing the more seriously criminalized youth into an adult system.

The revised rule in Massachusetts under which bind-over is undertaken points out the manifold problems created by vaguely worded, liberal-seeming legislation. This rule gives the juvenile court almost unfettered discretion to wash its hands of situations that may seem sticky. In 1969 and 1970, Dorchester, Boston, Springfield, and Worcester juvenile courts bound over 66 juveniles. In 1971 and 1972, after the Massachusetts reform of the department of youth services, courts bound over 246 youthful offenders. Although these statistics do not reflect the number of juvenile offenders actually incarcerated in adult institutions, they do indicate an unfortunate judicial tendency to treat juveniles as adults.

There is no doubt that some kind of institutionalization may be needed for a small percentage of incorrigibles. Statistics indicate that in Massachusetts, the word "incorrigible" can be applied to only about 5 percent to 8 percent of youth appearing in court. Institutionalization need not be punishment. It is unreasonable to treat people like animals and expect them to improve. Good, humane, small treatment centers would protect society from the incorrigible while giving the latter a healthy look at what it means to be a respected, well-treated member of society. With such proper juvenile-oriented restraining facilities, there can be no excuse for widespread use of bind-over.

The bind-over backlash in Massachusetts, while showing the need for contemporary institutions proper to community reform, also accentuates the need for better legislation. If we have statutes that provide little actual guidance that are in effect vague, rhetorical flourishes, then court-won rights are correspondingly vitiated. Judges, although often well intentioned and sometimes even profound, may often be seen as possessing certain entrenched mentalities. They need guidance to keep their thoughts and actions current. They must be kept responsive to the will of the electorate. Judicial power is like a gun and the person holding it, the judge, must be acutely aware of his every pertinent action. We have grave statistics that show how many people have died from misuse of guns. How much more staggering would be the number of lives lost from misuse of judicial power. The key idea here is that a judge is only and also a man or woman, that we must help our judges become better judges.

Racism and classism can and must be eradicated from our legal system. It is not necessary that different groups receive unequal treatment, although admittedly the cure can seem utopian. Racism and classism are false solutions to very real social differences.

A broadly representative juvenile justice system and heightened sensitivity of its personnel are the only truly practical and long-term solvents that will preserve the good element of racial and class individuality, while eliminating the bad. Justice is a result of good laws administered by good men and women.

Our juvenile justice personnel must be men and women who are sensitive to the needs of youth. Judges, probation officers, prosecutors, police, and all others in contact with the youth must be made aware of their own possible bias and educated out of it. Qualifications of juvenile court personnel assume a paramount importance. The day of the political appointee as a *civil* servant is, we hope, nearing its end. Just as we would not entrust delicate medical surgery to an unqualified, albeit well-connected individual, so neither can we trust our children to such persons. Our national resources in sensitivity and brotherly love are vast, and we must call on them in this vital area.

Sensitivity is a two-way street: Defendants are sensitive too. Thus, it is necessary that the outward manifestation of the "quasi" criminal justice system be proportionate to society. For instance, a young black brother is going to feel that the black judge and probation officer understands him more than do the whites. In fact, since outward signs are suggestive, although not dispositive, of inward states, the brother may be right more often than wrong in his choice.

The racially and socially diverse justice system can offer more resources and role models for a child; it can give us a real possibility for social change by drawing on the practical experience of each involved individual. . . .

We need not fear what is to come if we enhance our juvenile system. A rethinking and reworking of our juvenile justice system can result in the reshaping of our children's very future. Contact with the juvenile justice system can be the first positive gleam in a hitherto-negative young life. This is done as society turns away from punishment to view the courts as wise-parent surrogates. Legislation must promote benevolence and guard against prejudice, vagueness, and judicial arbitrariness. The court personnel must be outwardly and inwardly representative of the diverse elements of society.

There are some good practical things for the black bench

and bar to do at once to make these ideas a reality. The National Bar Association, National Conference of Black Lawyers, and the local black bar associations must not merely study the problems of judicial selection in the juvenile system but should start formulating concrete criteria for choosing these judges, especially where such choice is made by appointment of the governors in various jurisdictions. Ways must be sought creatively to program our ends through the system. We must call on the electorate and legislatures to take considerably more care in drafting legislation. The bench and bar, especially, should make themselves available as role models to our youth through contact with educational and social institutions. This contact must be substantive; in other words, we must educate our youth of their rights and responsibilities.

The black bench and bar should, ideally, get more press than black criminals. That has not happened in the past. This can be reversed by a mass publicity called to redress lack of minority representation throughout the juvenile justice system. As the community base of the system comes to be broader, it will be more truly a parent-surrogate.

Black attorneys and judges must not rest on professional laurels. We must become involved in institutional safeguards, in good judicial appointments, and in good government in general. Judge Forer's book title aptly captures the essence of the juvenile justice system—*No One Will Lissen*; it will be an even sadder commentary on the plight of our youth if, regarding the black bench and bar, "no one will act."

For almost half a century, Judge William H. Hastie has been a tower among jurists. His excellence as a student, teacher, law school dean, government official, lawyer, and judge has ensured his place in history. His life and work remind us that it is entirely possible to put long years into the quest for equal justice, contributing immeasurably to advancement toward that ideal, all the while being noted for both style and substance too rarely displayed. In an interview with the editor on July 19, 1971, Judge Hastie drew on his rich experience to comment on such timely topics as the possibility of a fair trial for blacks today, plea bargaining, political prisoners, "law and order," counsel for the poor, and black judicial activism. An alumnus of Amherst College, Harvard University Law School, he is senior judge, U.S. Court of Appeals, Third District, in Philadelphia.

OBSERVATIONS ON THE JUDICIAL PROCESS

William H. Hastie

Q: Can a black man get a fair trial in this country?

A: Maybe it would be useful to start with the situation that got so much publicity when Kingman Brewster, the president of Yale, made his observation that there was doubt in his mind whether or not the black person in the situation of the Black Panther leaders could get a fair trial. Of course, one interesting thing is there seems to be no question now that Bobby Seale did get a fair trial. But more important than that, we can be talking about so many different things when we speak about "fair trial." Particularly, we may be talking about what a jury will do, or we may be talking about what a judge will do, and I think we should distinguish those sharply. The jury is very often faced with the task of whom to believe—the testimony of the prosecution is to one effect, and the testimony of the defense denies it. In the Bobby Seale case there was one witness who testified positively that Seale had given certain orders, and Seale and others denied that he had given those orders.

Now, to what extent does race or radical policy, poor person versus rich person, influence a jury, even subconsciously, in reaching a decision as whom they will believe? I don't know any way that we can establish or measure that. Certainly, traditionally in the South, if a white person told one story and a black person told another story, the white person's story was credited and the black's was discredited. There are certainly some jurors who, if a policeman tells one story and a poor citizen—be he black or white and even more so if he's black— tells a contrary story, their disposition is to credit the police. So in that aspect one would certainly have to say the experience is that there are at least many situations which turn upon whose story is credited and in which the jury tends to accept the white person against the black person or the policeman as the representative of authority against the disadvantaged individual, often the prepossessing and unimpressive individual who tells the opposite story. I don't know how the social scientist can get at that in any statistical way, but I think anyone who has been around courtrooms, any lawyer or any judge, would say that in many cases you can observe that tendency. So that's one aspect of the courtroom situation.

Now as far as the judge is concerned, the judge, of course, gives the jury formal instructions as to the law and the rules that they are to follow. We all know it is possible for the judge—by tone of voice, by a shrug of the shoulder, or by innuendo—to indicate his own belief and the view he thinks the jury should take without his making any kind of biased statement. And undoubtedly there are cases in which the judge will exert that kind of influence upon the jury. But as far as the basic thing of the judge making an incorrect, prejudiced, or unfair statement of what the law is, your appellate courts come in and correct this and I would say that by and large, when there is an obviously biased or incorrect statement of ruling of law by the judge, it gets corrected. However, we still have the situations you refer to—that the great majority of cases, both civil and criminal, in the minor courts never get appealed for any correction. The decision of the lower court is the final decision.

Q: Are there ways in which a judge can abuse his power?

A: Yes, he could abuse his role by either excluding certain evidence which properly would come in or admitting certain evidence which does not come into the case. Take an extreme situation, evidence of prior criminal conduct, which is normally not admitted in a criminal trial. The only time it is admitted ordinarily is when the defendant himself takes the stand and the evidence of prior criminal conduct is to discredit his statement. But with very limited exceptions of that sort, evidence that the accused person has been convicted of crime before is not, under the law, admissible, and again the appellate court would correct that. But you might well get in a situation in a lower court where something of that sort is permitted and the matter is never appealed. And there are many other rulings of law that might be made that are technically incorrect and prejudicial to the accused which don't get corrected.

Q: One defendant in the Black Panther trial in New York City has spoken bitterly of the use of bail as ransom. Would you characterize it that way?

A: Well, the objectionable thing is not so much use of bail as ransom but use of extremely high bail to keep the accused in prison and thus inflict as punishment before the person is even convicted. That is the basic evil and the basic effect of denying bail while the person is still awaiting trial. That, of course, has been the basis of the still-continuing very bitter fight on the whole notion of preventive detention; a person is being punished by the deprival of his liberties before his guilt or innocence has been determined. There again, by and large, when the matter is appealed, I think the appellate courts have been more liberal than the trial courts in ordering the accused admitted to bail. Theoretically, the basis of denying bail is the fear that despite heavy bail, the accused might flee and not be available, but there are other things. There may be a case where the accused has threatened a witness and there is reason to suspect that he might carry out that threat if he is allowed to be free. The really controversial situations occur when there is speculation that if the accused is admitted on bail, he will go out and commit some other crime. I think the most difficult situation arises where the person is a pusher or in some way engaged in the business of selling narcotics, and a sensible argument is made that if the accused is released on bail, he will resume the narcotics traffic to the great harm of other people. And I would say that in recent years, probably, disposition to deny bail or do the same thing—set it so high that the person cannot make the bail—has increased more in narcotics cases than in any other situation. I think it is a difficult decision for the fair-minded judge to make, whether a person who is substantially engaged in narcotics traffic should be released on an amount of bail that he can make pending his trial. A number of the courts have set bail in a prohibitive figure, but required that the person be brought to trial within thirty days or some other short period of time.

Q: Reduction of court backlogs is a growing priority in some areas. Can such preoccupation jeopardize basic rights?

A: Oh, there is no question that such danger is very real [in] the whole matter of speeding up trials. Certainly, we can make real improvement in bringing people to trial faster. On the other hand, the speedup can, in some circumstances, operate unfairly in not giving the accused an adequate opportunity to prepare his defense. An interesting thing that is a sidelight and isn't part of your thesis is that often the prosecutor wants to delay the trial because he does not feel he has built up a strong enough case yet. So it is not always the accused who is delaying the trial.

Q: Some observers attach similar risk to plea bargaining.

A: Well, many responsible observers think that plea bargaining is not inherently an evil. The American Bar Association has approved it under proper regulation. Indeed . . . without it the administration of criminal justice would break down from the sheer weight of the number of cases to be tried. The question of whether one approves or disapproves of plea bargaining also is tied up with the notion of what the purpose of conviction is anyhow. In many cases it may well be just as much in the interest of society to accept a plea for a lesser offense or even probation than just lock the person up for ten years. And that raises the related fact, the very terrible fact, that experience shows us tragically large numbers of prisoners who come out of jail worse than they were when they went in. Thus, the conviction and incarceration of many persons, instead of doing social good, have done social harm.

Q: Do you agree with the argument that courts concern themselves more with property rights than with human rights?

A: That's a historic argument. There is no question if we go back fifty years we can trace the dominance of property concerns in many cases. And yet the so-called great cases of the past twenty years have basically been cases of the vindication of the personal rights of the individual.

Q: Much is now said about blacks being, in effect, political prisoners. How does one separate the rhetoric of that statement from the reality of the situation, or is it impossible to separate the two?

A: It is possible to separate them. I would agree that at times there is a great deal of rhetoric involved in the argument. I think one way to get at it is to ask: "Assume a person who is not a radical or does not have unpopular political views had done the same thing. How different would he be treated?" Now, again taking the Panther case in New Haven, the Bobby Seale case, if a group of persons not black and not political should get in trouble, some fraternal order or secret order, and there was evidence that somebody had disclosed the secrets of the order and the person was tortured and killed by members of the order and allegedly one of the leaders of the order had directed it, I have no doubt that that person would be prose-cuted and prosecuted vigorously for murder.

So, though I think that it is hard to answer the question, the question I would in turn ask is whether there is reason to believe that if a person who did not have radical political views, or was not black, had done the same thing, would he be charged with the crime and vigorously prosecuted? Take the Angela Davis case, which is still going on; there was no doubt that there was a shoot-out in the courtroom, and tragically some people were killed, and had it happened in an entirely nonpolitical context that there would have been a vigorous prosecution. My point is that there are certain types of of-fenses against society against which the public authorities are going to move vigorously regardless of whether the culprit is black or politically unpopular. Now there will be others where there will be a real question whether a person would be prose-cuted if he were not of some unpopular or disadvantaged group. I think that's about all I can say on the separation of rhetoric from the realities.

Q: The phrase "law and order" has been either used or taken as code words for racial repression. Does its usage by politicians advance or impede the cause of justice?

A: Certainly, there have been many occasions when from the lips of various people, including your former boss [Spiro T. Agnew], the law and order phraseology has had veiled but well-understood appeal to whites—that we've got to take a tough line and keep these blacks in their place. Unquestion-ably, it is so read and understood by many people, white and black. At the same time there are very real problems in our culture, our society, of protecting the citizen who walks the street, or the householder who is in his home, from crimes, from robbery, from muggings. Those are real problems. But again, so often the rhetoric which develops out of those real problems is a cloak or inviting whites, particularly, to keep blacks quiet and in line.

Q: It seems that many people who urge blacks to vote

for—and to become—candidates for public office emphasize executive and legislative position far more than judicial positions. Is there a serious imbalance in this kind of politics that underrates judicial power?

A: I am not sure—are you speaking of the relative importance of blacks in other types of public office, on the one hand, and blacks on the bench, on the other hand? I don't know. I must confess I never particularly thought in those relative terms. I suspect larger opportunity of influencing the way government behaves toward the disadvantaged exists in the case of people who are appointed to executive or legislative positions than judicial positions. I suppose a black prosecutor has a larger opportunity to influence the fairness of the prosecution than the judge does, and the people who are responsible for the development of housing, slum clearance, and urban renewal programs and policies have more directly and largely affected the disadvantaged and the black than the judge on the bench.

Q: The Chief Justice of the Supreme Court, Warren Burger, has said that, in his view, the courts are not properly considered agents for social change. But should we consider courts agents of social change, of racial justice?

A: Well, they are; they are in fact, and I think they inevitably are. Of course, the court only comes in when a particular case comes before it and then makes the ruling that applies not only to that case but also controls similar cases. I can give you examples from many years ago. Back in the twenties and thirties many people thought, and I think rightfully so, that particularly in the South blacks would make no really major progress or major breakthrough as masters of their own fate in the South until in law and in fact blacks had a free franchise. Now the courts were deeply involved in that process. The first thing that had to be done was outlaw the various formerly approved devices for keeping blacks from voting, most conspicuous among them the white primary, which by state legislation or later by rule of the local Democratic Party, prevented blacks from voting in the Democratic elections. As long as that was the law, blacks were just stymied, and could not be a political force. So the major breakthrough had to be one by the courts ruling that those restrictions were invalid. Now there were many other things that had to follow after that, but the other things could not come until those prohibitions were struck down.

I think the same is true of this matter of malapportionment. Until the courts struck down certain types of malapportionment it was inevitable that the franchise would not mean as much as it should to many people. I am sure we could go through the catalogue and find any number of similar cases. So all I can say is that there are particular problems and particular stages in trying to solve those problems where the intervention of the courts is essential before headway can be made. But then after the courts have made the breakthrough, other persons and forces have to solve the problem. Courts merely put others in position where they can work effectively.

Q: In a recent CBS-TV series, Judge J. Skelly Wright said that if, in criminal proceedings, he had to pick one thing to underline in the interest of going furthest toward protecting the rights of the disadvantaged, he would want to guarantee the provision of counsel that is adequate in every respect. Would you concur in that view, or is there a different feature you would speak to?

A: Well, for the minute, I cannot think of any one thing I would consider more important. During the recent American Bar Association convention a speaker deplored the rule of the *Miranda* case guaranteeing the right of counsel as a serious interference with the police doing their job. Of course, it interferes with their doing it in a particular way. It may be harder to overcome the unwillingness of a person to talk after he has had the guidance of counsel. But the whole theory of our law of confessions is distorted unless the suspect makes a free and intelligent choice of whether or not he will speak. If the guidance of counsel in making that choice is an interference with the police, it is an interference that seems to be mandated by our concept of fair criminal procedure.

Q: Plans are being made to organize black judges in a collective effort to influence legal processes. What impact would such a group have?

A: Well, I am going to Atlanta in a couple of weeks where there is going to be a meeting of the National Bar Association and black judges are scheduled to assemble in substantial numbers. I think I prefer not to prognosticate until I see a little more of what such a group hopes to accomplish and how this develops. There may be a difference between the periodic informal getting together of blacks who have a common experience of judges and discussing the problems they have faced and are likely to face on the one hand, and, on the other, a formal organized group. I rather suppose that many of us would be pretty disturbed if there was an organization of Catholic judges or Jewish judges, though we recognize that there are very real religious problems or problems of religious groups just as there are of racial groups. I suppose that we would be worried that this might become a move toward making racial considerations dominant in the administration of justice. And while no one can control his subconscious, it is certainly to be hoped that the judge, regardless of his race or religion, tries fairly to adjudicate between the parties who are litigating the matter, rather than making [sic] race a dominant factor in his decision. Any suggestion that black judges do or are planning to make race a dominant factor in their decisions would certainly be unfortunate.

Q: When I learned of that development, I began thinking more about blacks on the bench, and a nagging question came to mind: Does it make any difference to the black defendant to come before a black judge than a white judge?

A: I would say that in many cases the defendant will feel that it does. He will feel that the black judge understands his motivations, understands the plight which led him into whatever social conduct he is charged with, and so on. But on the other hand, I am sure that if I were a defendant, there would be certain white judges that I would certainly rather come before than some black judges, and vice versa.

Q: To your way of thinking, do black judges have any special kind of obligations toward fellow blacks, maybe within the judicial arena and maybe without?

A: I can express in general terms that his obligation to the black is essentially the same as his obligation to the white: to see that they are fairly treated in the courts—in and by the courts. Now it may be that the judge has certain understanding as a result of his experience as a black person in the community that is helpful to him in determining what is a just solution, but I think that is as far as I am going. But sometimes a black judge dealing with a black person who claims unfair play will be in a better situation to understand the unfairness the person is talking about. To that extent, sometimes a person would appropriately hope that there might be a black judge passing on his case.

Q: What are we to make of accusations that judges are soft on crime?

A: Well, sometimes people mean by that the judge doesn't let the prosecutor have his own way. The judge does not play the role of the person who is helping the prosecutor to get a conviction, and of course, it is not his role to help the prosecutor in getting a conviction any more than it is his role to try to see that the accused is freed. There we come back to what we were talking about—the judge's own concept of what is just in accordance with the law.

Q: Are there any particular areas in the matter of justice or court administration which seem to you to warrant particular attention by researchers?

A: Let me think a minute. I do think of one thing that is pretty obvious—that charges and countercharges as to what happens are much better evaluated if one has some responsible statistical study of what happens to criminal cases. Let me give you an example: I suppose that I'm safe in saying that nationwide more than half of our reported crimes are never solved. I mean by that that there never is enough evidence to bring anybody to trial. Moreover, of those people who actually are charged, the overwhelming majority plead

guilty. I think the figures usually given are somewhere between 65 and 80 percent plead guilty. So the court never has
to intervene in the determination of guilt at all. Then, if you
take that 20 or 30 percent who are convicted obviously there
are at least a few who deserve to be acquitted. So when you get
down to the ultimate of how many crimes result in the acquittal of a guilty person, percentage-wise it has to be very small.

Q: A general question: You are not a Johnny-come-lately to
the battle of trying to use the law to advance social causes—

A: No. I have been at it about forty years now.

Q: Looking back over your long experience, are there any
real high or low points along the way that you'd like to
mention?

A: Well, I can remember, I guess nearly twenty-five or
thirty years ago, when the Supreme Court knocked out voting
restrictions in the South, I felt then that that was quite the
most important breakthrough we had been able to make.
Offhand, I don't think of another single episode which im-
pressed me quite the way that that one did. I may think of
some others that are more comparable in my view of their
significance. The 1954 education cases, of course, were the
culmination of something over a long period of time. Many of
us thought these decisions were rather clearly foreshadowed
by some of the earlier cases, most notably the *Sweatt* case from
Texas and the *McLaurin* case from Oklahoma. But I'm not
sure that that is what you are aiming at in your question.

Q: How about developments outside the courts?

A: Well, I think in historic perspective, one of the worst
things that happened was what occurred during the ten years
immediately after the Second World War when we had the
first really massive growth and rehousing of what had been
our urban population featured by tremendous development
of suburban housing on the outskirts of our cities. That was
attended by the deliberate and effective exclusion of blacks
from that entire normal population movement and dispersal,
with concomitant concentration of blacks in the least desirable
housing that is left in the center cities. That, I think, has been,

during my lifetime the most far-reaching and critical adverse development that has hurt the black community and its rights and its progress. It is difficult to believe, for example, right here in Philadelphia, we would have the starving of the school system that is going on, if the public schools weren't becoming all the time more and more a service for black children.

The vice-chairman of the Democratic National Committee, Basil A. Paterson, urges blacks to obtain "heavy political muscle," for it is politics that determines the quality of justice—or injustice. Judges, prosecutors, police commissioners, and wardens gain their positions by way of politics. "That is the direction we must proceed in," said Paterson in these remarks at the National Bar Association's convention in San Francisco, California, on August 1, 1973. Mr. Paterson holds degrees from St. John's College and St. John's Law School.

BLACKS AND THE JUSTICE SYSTEM

Basil A. Paterson

IT IS for me a moment of signal honor to be able to speak to you on a subject that is of fundamental concern to us all—justice.

For when we talk of blacks and the justice system, I am reminded of the admonition of one young black scholar who when asked, "How can blacks avoid the inequities of the criminal justice system?" answered, "Don't get in it."

Somehow that answer seems almost natural, particularly when it applies to blacks . . . For we have long come to understand that blacks do not expect to receive justice in our criminal justice system, although they may hope for the best.

I daresay few of you here believe that blacks are not discriminated against, both as perpetrators and as victims. And the statistics support your perception of the imbalance of the criminal justice system as it applies to blacks. First, blacks are "overrepresented" as clients. The chance that a black person will be arrested is four times that of a white person. Moreover, blacks are more likely to be prosecuted than whites. They are more likely to be found guilty than whites. They are more likely to receive stiffer sentences than whites. They are more likely to be imprisoned than whites. Indeed, blacks are pronounced guilty 42 percent of the time. Whites, on the other hand, are judged to be guilty 28 percent of the time. And if this were not enough, blacks accused of felonies are less likely to receive probation than their white counterparts.

But the real horror and oppressiveness of our justice system can only truly be measured by what it does to our children. In the book *Delinquency in a Birth Cohort*, it was pointed out that of the nonwhites born in Philadelphia in 1945, of those who resided in the city from their tenth birthday until their eighteenth, 56 percent of them had been arrested at least once. As staggering—and sobering—and saddening as these figures are, there is little appreciation of the true horror of what the justice system represents until you examine the statistics compiled by sociologist [Marvin C.] Wolfgang, author of the book [*Crime and Race*]. Mr. Wolfgang informs us graphically that not only is the juvenile justice system ineffective, but the more frequently the system is used, the more likelihood the juvenile will be indicted. So you see a juvenile's introduction to the juvenile justice system may in all likelihood result in his being penalized by that system.

Empirically, blacks have always had a different view of the nation's criminal justice system which traditionally meted out "justice" quite differently for those Americans who were blacks and those who were white. To be sure, a 1972 study informs us that the average sentence of a white person in a federal penitentiary is 43.3 months, while for blacks it is 58.7 months. At the same time, a 1970 study revealed that of the 479 men on death row, 40 percent of them were black. Nor has discrimination in sentencing been limited to those crimes where a victim was involved—the so-called violent crime. In the area of victimless crime, black offenders received penalties that were twice as severe as those meted out to whites. For instance, in 1970, whites convicted of income tax evasion received 12.8 months, while blacks convicted of the same offense received an average of 28.6 months.

If the criminal justice system seeks to operate against blacks, it is also persistently antipoor. A study by the administrative office of the United States courts had this to say: People who could not afford private counsel could depend on receiving twice as severe a sentence. Blacks by their very economic level were assured of this very "special" distinction.

But the inequities of our system of justice are not just limited to offenders and victims. While we are overrepresented as clients of the system, we are grossly underrepresented as attorneys and officers of the court and on decision-making levels. Today there are only about 3,000 black lawyers in the country out of a total of approximately 300,000. One percent. One percent who are black and possibly understanding and knowledgeable about what it means to be black and poor—and often uneducated and caught in our criminal justice system. Clearly, 3,000 lawyers are not enough to service the needs of the poor and black. And so we have the court-appointed legal aid. By all estimates, it is only half as effective as private counsel, but it is 1,000 percent better than no counsel at all. Yet today we have the spectacle in Washington, D.C., the nation's capital, where the chief judge of the D.C. superior court system is begging the United States Congress to allocate funds for the indigent who are in need of legal assistance in the District.

Not only are blacks underrepresented in the courts, they are seriously lacking in visibility on the nation's police forces, the traditional first encounter with the criminal justice system. Ramsey Clark, the former Attorney General, is the author of a book, *Crime in America,* in which he talks of the fast-emerging black urban majorities in cities like Washington, D.C., Atlanta, Richmond, New York City, Newark, Detroit, and Cleveland. But even as these cities bulge with new black faces, the complexion of the police departments have not changed. They remain predominantly white, guardians of the status quo, sentinels of conformity.

It is surprising, though really it shouldn't be, that only 3.5 percent of the nation's police force is black. In New York an estimated 35 percent of the population is listed as nonwhite.

Yet the police force is only 7 percent black and only 9 percent nonwhite. In the nation's capital, which is believed to have a black population of almost 84 percent, only 36 percent of the police force is black. The rest of the force is made up of persons who reside in Virginia and Maryland, but not in the District.

The question is, of course: How should our police force be constituted? Should it be a community-based law enforcement unit? Should it reflect the makeup of that community, or should it be composed of outsiders who merely patrol the community during the day or night and return to the sanctuary of their communities at night? The question is: Can we have an absentee police force that is paid simply to maintain the status quo, but is not involved in the dynamics of everyday living? Put bluntly, the essential question is: Can the total community be adequately served by a police force that is not representative of the total community?

Given our knowledge of the history of the administration of justice in our communities, the uneven treatment from time of apprehension, to the police station, to the courtrooms, to the penitentiaries, we have little reason for placing any real faith in the system as it presently operates. Shouldn't we ask ourselves: Who should patrol the black community? Who should be the apprehenders? Who can best serve the interest of our communities as prosecutor, judge, jury, counselor, probation officer? Isn't it reasonable to assume that black correctional officers would better understand the problems of a community where the majority of the perpetrators and the victims are black? But only 8 percent of the nation's correction personnel are black. Why with a prison population that has a sizable number of blacks do we have the spectacle of Attica, New York, where only one staff member was black, and he was not even a guard?

I submit that we will never have justice in the criminal justice system until blacks are more equitably represented. Why, for instance, is it that we have only a handful of black judges and *no* prosecutors? The absence of such persons reflects more than anything I can say here, the politics and power of our justice system, a system that excludes and victimizes the powerless while rewarding the powerful. . . . The response to an inequitable judicial system is not only better trained and better motivated lawyers. Basically, it is the election or appointment of better trained and better motivated judges.

But how do we get to that point? How do we effectuate the election and selection of judges, prosecutors, police chiefs and precinct commanders, wardens, chief probation officers, and parole board members? The answer comes out easy, but the doing is difficult. We as a community have got to find the technique for achieving heavy political muscle. For it is politics, damnable word that it has become, which is the vehicle for influencing the destinies of our communities. Judges and prosecutors are not born; they are made . . . by political leaders! Mayors and governors appoint police chiefs and wardens and parole boards.

That is the direction we must proceed in. What we need today is an agenda that serves the needs of the so-called minorities, those who have been shut out from any meaningful participation in this society, those of us who have been asked to act responsibly while those who hold the real power act irresponsibly. In every black community across the nation, we are beset by problems: poor housing, drug addiction, crime, unemployment and underemployment, poor or non-existent health care and sanitation services, poor educational facilities, and a government—on all levels—that is indifferent to our problems. We have been told at various stages that there were one or two rather simple solutions to our problems. Jobs, we were told at one point, were the answer. Then we were advised that education really held the key. Later integration was touted as the panacea for our ills.

But what we found was what some of us had known all along. We didn't do the separating and didn't have the power to do any integrating. Now there is much talk about separatism. It's supposed to be a dirty word. But black people have been forced to accept a separate society and separate accommodations all our lives. Two societies—separate but unequal—are facts of life we have understood and fought against. Only today the rhetoric has changed. What I am saying is that ever since we were brought to these shores, we have in one way or another been forced to react to the forces outside our community. . . .

There is no need to further recount the litany of abuse and deprivation we as a people have experienced at the hands of a system allegedly designed to serve "all the people." There is no need to further recite the failures of that system. That is a story indelibly imprinted in the minds of us all. There is a need, in fact, a compelling urgency, for those of us who occupy roles of leadership, large or small, *to lead.* What we must seek to do is to use the political system, as it has been used, is being used, and will continue to be used, for the benefit of certain people—but the certain people we are concerned about are all the underprivileged, underrepresented, and unresponded-to of the nation.

The people who were brought to this country in chains now have a chance to set it free. And the opportune time is now! I am, of course, referring to the fallout of Watergate. Barbara Mikulski is chairman of the Delegate Selection Commission of the Democratic National Committee. When asked if Watergate represented an advantage for the Democratic Party, she said "No! After all—people didn't flock to the airlines when the *Titanic* sank, did they?" We all, of course, know that there were no airplanes when that tragic event took place. But the point is well taken. People will not automatically flock to the Democratic Party because of the misgivings of a cynical few.

We should recognize, though, that Watergate does represent an opportunity to the black and other minority communities of this country. Blacks were damn near ignored when we screamed about police brutality and police graft. Maybe no one was listening when we complained about Martin Luther King's phone being tapped. When blacks in politics bemoaned the lopsided effect of big money on elections, we were told "reforms take time." So-called black problems become urban crises only when the maladies of the ghetto are found to be contagious. We then discover that human misery cannot be contained or cordoned off. As the plague of narcotics vaulted ghetto walls, so again has that truism been demonstrated by the revelations of the Knapp Commission in New York, the police scandals in Boston and Detroit, and now finally . . . the Watergates of the nation.

The fertility created by this new national awareness of the frailties of the system offers hope. Maybe, just maybe, others are listening. Now, when we gather together to break bread and to discourse on the tragedies inherent in the judicial system, we may not be alone.

We have not been the prophets of doom, but the seers and reporters of reality.

III.

CIVIL JUSTICE AND BLACKS

THE LAW is harsh on poor people in general and on black people in particular. In courts and administrative agencies, its bias against them is revealed by the advantages that it gives to others in their dealings with them and by its provision for treating on an individual basis problems that must be solved on a collective basis if meaningful relief is to be had by them.[1] It enables others to run roughshod over them. For example, it is legal for a seller to have customers sign a confession of judgment when they sign a contract and, once a payment is missed, to sue them—without notice—for the unpaid balance. Armed with that judgment, he can obtain a lien against their property, garnishee their wages, and retain collection agencies that threaten them and harass their employers, thus jeopardizing their jobs.[2]

It is also legal for landlords to charge exorbitant rent for apartments and houses that are unfit for habitation. Tenants sign a thirty-day lease, disclaim any guarantee of habitability, agree to make necessary repairs, and free the landlord of any accountability for negligence. The landlord can evict them—without notice—should they default on the rent. They soon learn that the law "gives little succor" to them whether it is applied by courts or administrative agencies.[3]

Some administrative agencies purport to assist the indigent, but it is questionable whether they do. For instance, public housing typically is not more than a notch above slum quarters. Only the most desirable applicants get past overzealous administrators, and then they face long waiting periods because public housing is always in short supply. Public educa-

191

tion has a well-deserved reputation as the handmaid of poverty. Its run-down facilities, underachieving teachers, insensitive administrators, and antiquated equipment are notorious for their part in mutilating the lives of countless students.[4]

The welfare system is the special oppressor of the poor. With its ironclad control over all facets of their lives and its invitation to politicians and the public to heap abuse upon them, it provides firm support for Downie's proposition that "Almost as though it were a law of nature, every program devised for the benefit of the poor seems destined to be captured by another interest and twisted, with no interference from the courts, until it works against the poor."[5]

Welfare recipients have no monopoly on the receipt of government assistance. Even greater aid is given to radio and television station owners, shippers, and airline owners, farmers, transportation firms, small businessmen, builders, home buyers, and wealthy citizens at tax-paying time. These welfare recipients, unlike the poor ones, are not confronted with eligibility criteria that are arbitrarily devised and enforced in behalf of interests that are inimical to their own. Unlike their poor counterparts, they are not hounded by investigators who pry into the depths of their lives. Nor are they stigmatized, degraded, and terrorized as are the poor recipients. The courts enforce for them legal rights that are refused to the poor.[6]

Welfare departments and some other agencies that are supposed to help destitute people harm them instead; such is their prejudice against their clientele. Public housing authorities and some other agencies that are supposed to protect destitute people fail to do so; such is their passivity. Ostensibly buttressing housing code authorities are consumer fraud bureaus and human relations and antidiscrimination commissions. These agencies are deficient in money, manpower, and mandate. Because they wait for complaints to be filed before taking action, enforcement is episodic, fragmented, and even discriminatory. The poor often are too afraid, skeptical, or busy trying to earn a living to file complaints, and the agencies are too timid, weak, and politically vulnerable to go beyond negotiation and mediation. Thus, housing code authorities give landlords periods of grace and extension that may result in the tenant's living in cold and damp (or wet) quarters for as long as eighteen months before repairs are made. Seldom are recalcitrant landlords jailed or fined heavily, because judges prefer not to apply the criminal penalties that are the only remedies provided in most housing codes.[7]

In the courtroom, which is the ultimate arena for the resolution of conflict, the poor are at further disadvantage. "Justice is not free," a lawyer in New Hampshire reminds us. "It's a luxury you have to pay for."[8] The costs add up quickly to much more than the poor can afford. For example, appointed counsel may cost the defendant in an uncontested court case $100, and a blood test in a paternity suit may cost $50. Each appearance of an expert witness may cost up to $300. Each hour of an investigator's time may cost $10, and a retainer must be paid. Other general and special costs are almost too numerous to mention. Perhaps the point can be made simply by observing that all too often the poor cannot even pay the fee to initiate suit. *Forma pauperis* laws that exempt some fees for poor people typically apply to filing, court officials, and clerks, but not to independent entrepreneurs (*e.g.*, medical experts, court reporters, and surety companies) whose involvement is prerequisite to litigation. Their application is usually a matter of judicial discretion that often is exercised unfavorably toward the poor.[9]

The poor are also handicapped by their failure to obtain counsel in time to prepare for battle in our adversary justice system. Without such counsel provided by competent and responsible lawyers, the poor have no chance of winning in court or before administrative agencies. But they don't know many able and reliable lawyers, and in the main, their dependence on legal aid societies is unsatisfactory because those agencies are not equal to the tremendous task of assisting them.[10]

The magnitude of this challenge is not the only reason that legal aid agencies are unable to meet it. Overextended and understaffed, these agencies are beset by the organized bar and business interests. The bar tries to use eligibility criteria so as to prevent a cut into the supply of clients available for private attorneys, and businesses try to protect merchants and landlords against litigation and to see to it that bankruptcy cases are handled by private attorneys. The results are caution, passivity, and accommodation by legal aid attorneys, who frequently consider their services to be a matter of charity and not a right for people whom they consider to be irresponsible and immature. "For the poor client," Carlin and his colleagues believe, "Legal Aid often becomes another line to wait in another humiliating experience and a further reminder that the law is unresponsive to, if not opposed to, his interests."[11]

The long wait for help in legal aid offices is itself indicative of difficulties confronting their staffs. The attorneys have to sort out the cases that they are authorized to accept. That takes a lot of time. So does the unavoidable Mickey Mouse work: explaining nonacceptance of cases, staying abreast of dockets, waiting around courts, and doing paperwork. All the while they must fend off criticisms from the left and the right.[12] And they must carry on without appreciable relief from private attorneys. Relatively few private attorneys serve the poor, and those who do are known for their ineffectiveness, exploitation of clients, and propensity to accept only cases that contain certainty of payment.[13]

What accounts for the reluctance of the private bar to serve poor people? The answer, in part, lies in their lack of money, status, and value as a source of referral of satisfactory clients.[14] But it goes beyond that to the training that conditions lawyers to endorse the status quo without serious qualm. "Law schools rarely teach their students to become advocates of presently unrepresented interests or to become social engineers in behalf of interests other than the predominant ones," Jacob alleges.[15] Undoubtedly, this conditioning explains partially the organized bar's failure to rally around the most obvious victims of injustice, or, for that matter, to give serious thought to its obligation to the general public. To some degree, this is changing, with the bar recognizing such an obligation—but more regarding criminal than civil cases and still in such marginal fashion that a study made by the American Bar Foundation holds that the legal services program dramatizes the profession's "failure to democratize the means of access to the legal system."[16]

What does it matter that lawyers are used more by the rich than by the poor, by whites than by blacks, by landlords than by tenants, and by creditors than by debtors? Of what importance are differentials in the quality of representation? These variations are significant because they determine both the nature and presentation of civil cases in court and affect their settlement out of court.[17]

The poor seldom take someone else to court. Usually, someone takes them to court to accomplish one or more of the purposes of civil suits. These purposes are to have the court either (1) simply declare that certain rights are his, (2) prevent threatened harm to him, (3) undo harm already done, (4) in lieu thereof, order monetary compensation to him for it, or (5) provide special remedies that fall outside the preceding classifications.[18]

Civil proceedings start when a plaintiff files with the clerk of a court a request for favorable action concerning the grievances specified. The complaint must show that he has been or will be injured by the defendant and that statutory or common law empowers the court to take preventive or corrective action. Usually, the defendant has a month after the complaint has been served on him to respond. He may deny the allegations, defend his action, argue that the court has no jurisdiction in the matter, or file counterallegations. If he enters a countercomplaint, the plaintiff is allowed to reply.

Attorneys for each side follow up the completion of the filing of complaints, replies, countercomplaints, and answers by gathering pertinent information from documents and witnesses. Federal and some state courts provide for extensive discovery procedures that enable each side to ascertain much of the other side's case.[19] Very often the next development is the pretrial conference that the judge orders (and sometimes attends) to enable opposing counsel to agree on undisputed facts, narrow the issues of fact and law to be taken up at the trial, and try to work out a settlement. If no settlement is achieved or if no pretrial conference is held, the case is heard by a judge or by a judge and jury. In jury trials, proceedings are considerably more subject to the judge's direction than in criminal cases. But jury trials are rare. Indeed, civil trials are far from common. Most disputes are settled outside the courtroom.

Civil disputes may center on personal life or public policy, and the litigants may be private people or public officials. Jacobs' typology of civil cases shows one category involving private persons in controversies generally viewed as private matters, such as those concerning personal injury, divorce, collection, business contracts, wills, and land settlement. The second group involves public officials in court either to settle such private matters or to obtain orders against private people (for example, public housing officials trying to evict tenants). The third group consists of suits brought by private people to affect the course of governmental action. And in the fourth category are suits initiated by public officials against other officials, governmental agencies, or private parties over public policy issues.

As Jacob notes, civil litigation is not as closely linked to politics as is criminal prosecution, which is the work of public officials in the furtherance of public policy. This is not to say, however, that the linkage does not exist; it does, for civil justice also concerns the distribution of material and nonmaterial values, with the might of the government backing it up.

An equally important connection to acknowledge is that between civil justice and criminal justice. The denial of the first, as with governmental toleration of the exploitation of consumers by merchants, often is a contributing factor to consumer or tenant behavior that violates the criminal law, as with the burning and looting of stores during urban disorders. As the Kerner Commission put it:

> Much of the violence in recent civil disorders has been directed at stores and other commercial establishments in disadvantaged Negro areas. In some cases, rioters focused on stores operated by white merchants who, they apparrently believed, had been charging exorbitant prices or selling inferior goods. Not all the violence against these stores can be attributed to "revenge" for such practices. Yet it is clear that many residents of disadvantaged Negro neighborhoods believe they suffer constant abuses by local merchants.[20]

Urban disorders are born of the life conditions that foster the hopelessness that—legally—choke the poor. Downie tells us the summer rioters of the 1960's had as their primary targets "the ghetto merchants, who had always stood impregnably behind the law in their dishonest business dealings, and the police, who serve as the most visible symbol of the law in the inner city." [21] The late Dr. Ralph Bunche, a Nobel Peace Prize recipient and Under Secretary of the United Nations, stated that the conditions of despair must be improved to prevent race riots. "Thus as the Kerner Commission indicated, pursuing the same courses of white racism and what [Daniel P.] Moynihan calls benign neglect could have only the easily predictable results—riots—and police oppression as a justifiable response," Samuel F. Yette reasons. Troops and policemen, by their presence and conduct, had an incendiary effect on troubled communities in cities across the nation. "This the green-shirted youth in Newark would call 'Whitey tactics,' resulting, at best, in nondeliberate genocide."[22]

There is cruelty in tacit or open governmental sanction of

unjust practices that provoke predictable and preventable
violation of the law.[23] And there is a certain irony in it, for most
of those who suffer under poverty are white—just like most of
those who have the wherewithal but not the will to reduce or
eliminate the suffering. Perhaps it is because the rebellion
against classism, like that against racism, is a black enterprise
that so many people seem to think that blacks would be the
major beneficiaries of a victorious war on poverty. Actually,
far more whites would profit, for they are two-thirds of the
poor. In 1968 about half of all the nation's poor lived in
metropolitan areas. Of those who lived in the suburbs, more
than 90 percent were white. That percentage dropped to 57 in
the central cities, where 43 percent of the poor were black.
Nonwhites, blacks included, were disproportionately represented among the nation's poor in that they were 32.2 percent
of that group but only 15.3 percent of the total population.[24]
Still, most of the poor were and are white. And if their fellow
whites in power will not spare them the wretchedness of
poverty and injustice, what hope is there for blacks? Not much
if we are to go by past experience in helping blacks overcome
discrimination in employment and in the enforcement of law.
Alan Batchelder holds that a drop in black unemployment
rates is prerequisite to the attainment of economic and civil
parity.[25] But Herbert Hill paints a grim picture of job opportunities for blacks, saying, for instance, that a huge portion of
"an entire generation of young blacks" will go through the
1970's without ever being employed—unless "drastic and
rapid" alteration occurs in the labor market.[26]

Comparable change is also required (and unexpected) in
law enforcement to prevent its working to the further detriment of people of color. Poverty and prejudice in combination account for that injustice so much so that attribution of it
to class rather than race is commonplace. But that is a mis-
leading and dangerous assertion, as Burns' comment suggests:

On its face, the structural inequality [in the law] relates
largely to differences in the economic status of individuals,

but it has a peculiarly racial dimension since such a widely disproportionate number of the poor in this country is nonwhite. Even without bad motives on the part of those who administer the system of justice, the continued application of the legal system in this way is racist because of the way in which it perpetuates past racial wrongs. It battens upon blacks' depressed condition, for which racial injustices were largely responsible in the first place.[27]

If change, timely and sufficient, is to be made in the present dismal justice picture, it will have to be largely the work of the legal profession. Public programs should be enlarged to provide improved legal aid to the indigent, but we should also establish complaint centers and consumer fraud bureaus to make government correct its own faults and reform sales practice. We should place ombudsmen in government at all levels to monitor its accountability to citizens, and we should experiment with lay mediators, legal paraprofessionals, community courts, and arbitration in landlord-tenant controversy. Tenant councils, welfare rights organizations, and institutes funded by private foundations to carry out research and litigation on urban issues are additional instruments for coping with injustice. But the private bar's response to this crisis is essential to its resolution.[28] That response has been, at best, mixed and, typically, far from encouraging. Perhaps the best assessment of it is made in an American Bar Foundation study:

> The organized bar has not played a central role in defining, initiating, leading, or coordinating new responses to public demand or public need. This is not to say that the organized bar has not recognized the need for new responses. In some instances it has even exercised leadership. But it has not played a central part in either the overall response or in the overall address of the profession to questions of professional responsibility to the public.[29]

Some black jurists are eager to shake the organized bar, black and white, out of its lethargy and irresponsibility. Many

of them know what it is to be poor and powerless. That Judge
Solomon Baylor knows this is made clear in the following
extract from the paper he prepared for this book:

> We were always keenly aware of the "boundaries" where
> the black community ended and the white community
> began. Theirs was where the better houses existed; where
> the people with good jobs, better education, better dress
> and greater influence lived; where it was not wise or safe
> for black persons—other than domestic servants or de-
> livery men—to linger; where the streets were quieter,
> cleaner, and less congested; and where commercial estab-
> lishments were considerably fewer in number. Ours was
> where the streets and alleys were poorly kept; where huck-
> sters bellowed loud and long in efforts to dispose of their
> various wares; where door-to-door salesmen, usually
> white, flooded the area with bad deals and thereby helped
> to drain it of the meager earnings which trickled in and
> which were seldom adequate for providing the various
> necessities; where corner bars usually run by "outsiders"
> not only took more than their share of the neighborhood
> income but frequently created the setting for arguments,
> fights, and other criminal activity.
>
> Our neighborhood, moreover, was where the police (all
> white during my boyhood) frequently were considered a
> dictatorial and unchallengeable source of power and
> authority who walked into houses at will, who saw no need
> to display any courtesy in speech, who often brought frivo-
> lous charges and committed physical violence on helpless
> and frequently innocent citizens. Almost everyone in our
> neighborhood believed that any person accused by the
> police was automatically convicted and that the courts and
> the police were practically one and the same. I can person-
> ally recall numerous killings of black citizens by police
> officers. Some were teenage boys. Some were even shot in
> the back. All of the officers involved were either not prose-
> cuted at all or were dismissed by magistrates (political
> appointees who were assigned to sit in specific police sta-
> tions) at preliminary hearings. The first time I laid eyes on

a black uniformed police officer, I was twenty years old,
and that was in New York.

Judge Baylor's reminiscence is the essence of black judicial
activism. Coupled with firsthand knowledge of the judicial
system, it accounts for the growing determination among
black jurists to serve as the catalyst for genuine judicial reform
that, in Judge Crockett's words, will help make that system
function "as democratically for the have-nots as it does for the
haves."[30] "What chance have we poor against a powerful rich?"
That question, put to Jerome E. Carlin by a black man,[31]
reverberates along the halls of so-called justice, demanding an
answer very much different from the one that has been inescapable: "None."

One of the many areas in which a different answer is
demanded is employment. During slavery, whites feared and
repressed black competitors for jobs.[32] They still do, and that
is why the story of job discrimination against blacks is a sordid
account of unemployment twice or higher among them than
among whites. For example, in 1971 the national unemployment rates, black and white, were 9.9 and 5.4 percent respectively.[33] The rate among black ghetto youth in the summer of
that year soared above 51 percent.[34] In September, 1974,
blacks outnumbered whites about two to one among out-of-
school teenagers (sixteen to nineteen) who were searching in
vain for jobs.[35] Each leap forward in technology darkens the
future of many blacks who are concentrated in jobs that
technology is wiping out. "It is as if racism, having put the
Negro in *his economic 'place,' stepped aside to watch technology
destroy that place,*" Tom Kahn writes.[36] The point is made more
forcefully and ominously by Samuel F. Yette. Blacks are
vulnerable to oppression and even genocide because the
whites who control America consider them an economic liability.

   . . . Black Americans have outlived their usefulness. Their
   raison d'être to this society has ceased to be a compelling

issue. Once an economic asset, they are now considered an economic drag. The wood is all hewn, the water all drawn, the cotton all picked, and the rails reach from coast to coast. The ditches are all dug, the dishes are put away, and only a few shoes remain to be shined.

Thanks to old black backs and newfangled machines, the sweat chores of the nation are done. Now the some 25 million Blacks face a society that is brutally pragmatic, technologically accomplished, deeply racist, increasingly overcrowded, and surly. In such a society, the absence of social and economic value is a crucial factor in anyone's fight for a future.[37]

Yette's pessimism is not shared by those who see Title VII of the Civil Rights Act of 1964 as a potentially powerful antibias weapon. Title VII was overdue. Long years of involvement in the struggle for equal job opportunity led Herbert Hill to conclude that until its enactment "the law was no more than an exercise in hypocrisy intended not to eliminate racial discrimination but to deceive and confuse the black worker."[38] The hypocrisy consisted of the enactment but not the enforcement of a host of state laws, executive orders, and court decisions against discrimination. The failure of enforcement was assured in part when administrative civil rights agencies were given a strategic role in the fight against discrimination, because these agencies acted as though mediation, not enforcement, were their mission; as though fair play were a matter of negotiation, not of legal right; as though the interests of their administrators, not those of clientele, were paramount; and as though in employment instances of job discrimination were the exception, not the rule. Title VII replaces administrative agencies with federal district courts in the key enforcement role. It permits one person to file suit on behalf of another, and the suit is treated as a class action. Any matter of employment or union membership or affiliation is subject to court action, which can be pressed free of administrative restraints. With the battle against job bias being pressed in the courts by private litigants and on other fronts by the Equal Employment Opportunity Commission (EEOC), which Title VII created, an unprecedented possibility of effective enforcement of antidiscrimination law exists. This possibility is directly related to the existence of genuine risk, financial or ote, for employer or labor union defendants. The risk, however, is not as real as it would be if court orders were self-enforcing, if private litigants were likely to monitor compliance with them, if the EEOC were likely to provide that service on a comprehensive basis, or if other federal agencies were dependable in this regard. Since these conditions of effective enforcement do not hold, court orders must be considered but part of the elusive answer to job discrimination.[39]

A number of appropriate court decisions have been obtained,[40] but much more needs to be done. There remains, for example, the task of prodding the National Labor Relations Board into action againtjob bias. Successful coaxing of the agency would provide civil rights advocates and their clientele with valuable leverage against labor union discrimination.[41] So would vigorous application of the ban on bias on construction projects that involve federal assistance. Executive Order 11246, which contains that prohibition, not only commands affirmative action to correct past inequities, as does Title VII, but differs significantly from Title VII in requiring federal contractors to determine through self-evaluation the need for affirmative action, without reliance on judicial ascertainment. All possible remedies must be tried, because neither federal courts nor administrative tribunals can make more than a small dent in the mass of job discrimination.[42]

The persistence of the racism that runs rampant in employment is attributable largely to organized labor's antipathy toward black workers.[43] Victimizing black workers, labor unions exclude them from membership, force them into segregated locals, subject them to the unfairness of racially separate seniority and promotional policies that relegate them to menial or unskilled work, and refuse them the benefits of union hiring halls and other job referral services. These and other racist practices not only minimize black competition with white unionized workers but also maximize subsidization of the whites through exploitation of the blacks. This is the assessment of the situation by one expert:

> Although some isolated progress has occurred, patterns of discriminatory employment practices have not been eliminated. Thus, the broad patterns of racial discrimination remain intact. But two new phenomena have emerged: where once they were openly racist and acknowledged to be such, these practices have now become covert and subtle. . . .
>
> The second new development is to be found in the way many labor unions have responded to the requirements of the new body of law prohibiting discriminatory racial practices, in the use of what has become known as "tokenism"; that is, a device to preserve old patterns and as a tactic to evade genuine compliance with the law. Thus, at best, there has been minimal strategic accommodation by labor organizations to the entire body of federal and state anti-discrimination laws and executive orders.[44]

Some unions are active against discrimination, but organized labor's general reputation as a perpetuator of discrimination is well deserved by virtue of its official national policies as well as its more publicized rank-and-file local resistance to equal opportunity. Hardships for black workers are not the doing of unions alone; employers also create them, especially in industries (*e.g.*, electric power) in which technological advancement reduces their need for labor and thus weakens unions. Still, unions remain a dominant force for discrimination, using collective bargaining to undermine black workers, keeping their executive boards lily-white with few major exceptions, and resisting voluntary settlement of disputes concerning discrimination.[45]

The fruits of job discrimination against blacks include racially disparate family income. In 1971, for example, the median family income for whites ($10,672) was well above that ($6,440) for nonwhites, mainly blacks.[46] This bears directly on a second vital area—that is, housing. Housing adequacy is discussed in terms of condition, crowding, and cost, but regarding blacks, it must be understood in light of two additional terms: "freedom of locational choice" and "turn-over." The first of these additional terms refers, really, to discrimination that sharply curtails choice. The second refers to the fundamental process by which urban low-income families gain better housing—namely, by moving into units as they are vacated by whites who very likely are suburbia bound. The determinants of successful operation of this process—an abundance of new housing, a dearth of destruction of existing units, and satisfactory conservation of older units—characterized the 1950's but not the 1960's, and the outlook beyond then is bleak. One consequence of this is the growing urban racial friction that occurs as some whites flee the city, leaving behind others whose inability to join the exodus puts them in stiff housing competition with blacks.[47]

"As long as they remained in the cities, the better-off groups constituted a 'middle ground' between the blacks and the immobile 'ethnics,' " Samuel Lubell writes. "But as the exodus to the suburbs continued the 'middle ground' has narrowed steadily, and our cities have moved from coalition politics toward the politics of confrontation."[48]

Confrontation is an inevitable result of urban growth and its attendant depletion of the supply of housing through clearance and redevelopment, which at first were private activities but have become mixed public and private efforts. The term "urban renewal" came into common usage after the enactment of the Housing Act of 1954 broadened the redevelopment concept of the Housing Act of 1949. It was coined to suggest a more enlightened approach to the task of dealing with blights, one that provided not only for redevelopment, but also for rehabilitation or for both. Since 1954, amendments have provided for plans to be drawn to cover projects of increasing scope and duration; for payment of individual, family, and business moving and direct property-loss costs; and for larger federal grants and greater local discretion.[49] Relocation of families and businesses is a perennial controversy in urban renewal. Federal law requires the provision of decent, safe, and sanitary housing to families that are uprooted by renewal; the housing must be in existence or preparation.[50]

But relocation has been decidedly detrimental to relocatees. Many of them cannot find housing; others cannot afford what they find, much of it being luxury housing whose construction motivated area clearance in the first place. So long as it is a means of wiping out slums to "renew" the city rather than a program of proper rehousing, urban renewal will be tragically inadequate. To transform it from the former into the latter, we must first construct low- and moderate-cost city, suburban, and new town housing and make it possible for people to move from slum dwellings to this housing, and after, not before, that move has been partially made, renew slum areas through clearance and rehabilitation. Public housing will be needed because private housing can never solve our housing crisis: urban renewal as we know it is much too profitable for private enterprise for that to happen.[51] An area may be chosen for renewal because it has high potential for sale and advantageous reuse or because there is a need for public facilities, for a model of renewal results, or for keeping renewal time and monetary costs at a minimum.[52] Or an area may be chosen to force blacks out of it and even out of town. In other words, urban renewal is Negro removal all too often. As Gans writes:

> . . . Renewal sometimes even created new slums by pushing relocatees into areas and buildings which then became overcrowded and deteriorated rapidly. This has principally been the case with Negroes who, both for economic and racial reasons, have been forced to double up in other ghettos. Indeed, because almost two-thirds of the cleared

slum units have been occupied by Negroes, the urban renewal program has often been characterized as Negro clearance, and in too many cities, this has been its intent.[53]

It is not that other groups have not suffered; it is, he says, that blacks, who "lack a stable family life and have trouble finding neighbors, shopkeepers, and institutions they can trust," have suffered more, dramatizing the emotional as well as financial and social costs victims of renewal endure.

The Kerner Commission documented the housing problem of blacks, pointing out that in each of the fourteen largest cities in the nation a larger percentage of black than white-occupied homes were classified as deteriorating, dilapidated, or lacked plumbing; that the vast majority of slum dwellers were black; that, on the average, black-occupied housing was much older than white-occupied housing and was almost invariably more overcrowded; and that blacks pay more and get less or, at best, the same accommodations.[54] Too few of us understand indecent housing. Anthony Downs protrays it for us:

. . . Thousands of infants are attacked by rats each year; hundreds die or become mentally retarded from eating lead paint that falls off cracked walls; thousands more are ill because of unsanitary conditions resulting from jamming large families into a single room, continuing failure of landlords to repair plumbing or provide proper heat, and pitifully inadequate storage space. Until you have actually stumbled through the ill-lit and decaying rooms of a slum dwelling, smelled the stench of sewage and garbage and dead rats behind the walls, seen the roaches and crumbling plaster and incredibly filthy bathrooms, and recoiled from exposed wiring and rotting floorboards and staircases, you have no real idea of what bad housing is like. These miserable conditions are not true of all inadequate housing units, but enough Americans are trapped in the hopeless desolation of such surroundings to constitute

both a scandal and a serious economic and social drag in
our affluent society.[55]

Who stands to benefit from racial fairness in housing and
renewal? To be sure, blacks, other minorities, and poor
people would be the immediate beneficiaries—but not the
only beneficiaries. One federal report states:

> . . . But fair housing is of vital importance to us all. The
> dual housing market has bred a variety of ills from which
> our whole society is suffering: the physical decay and finan-
> cial insolvency of our cities; the irrational proliferation of
> jurisdictions in metropolitan areas separated from each
> other by race and income; and the racial alienation and
> distrust that make us strangers to each other. This is the
> legacy that the present generation has inherited from the
> past. It is we who will determine which legacy we leave our
> children.[56]

The problem of racism in housing has confronted the federal government since it entered that industry in the 1930's.
The principal federal response has been to aggravate the
problem through subsidization of the white flight to suburbia,
failure to enforce its own fair housing laws and executive
orders, and effectuation of development programs that
reduce rather than increase the supply of housing accessible
to blacks. The perpetrators of discrimination include private
homeowners, real estate brokers, financial institutions, and
private builders. But government at all levels is a special
villain, "for it supports and indeed to a great extent it created
the machinery through which housing discrimination operates."[57]

Government—federal, state, and local—also created the
machinery through which discrimination in another important area, education, works. Some progress has been made
against school discrimination, notably in the South rather
than in the North or West. For example, the percentage of
black students in elementary and secondary schools in 1970

was 27.2 in the eleven Southern states, 17.3 in the six border states and the District of Columbia, and 9.8 in the 32 Northern and Western states. The number of black students in the South (3,150,192) exceeded the number in the border states and the District of Columbia (667,362) and in the North and West (2,889,858). Between 1968 and 1970 the percentage of black students in majority schools increased in the South from 18.4 to 39.1, barely increased in the six border states from 28.4 to 29.8, and actually decreased in the North and West from 27.6 to 27.5; nationally it rose from 23.4 to 33.1.[58]

School integration progress has resulted mainly from the reduction of minority student isolation in the South, which makes the suburbanization of the South a point of concern. In the 1960's American suburbs attracted 12,500,000 whites but only 800,000 blacks, while the central cities gained 2,500,000 blacks and lost 3,000,000 whites. The pattern is developing in the South: Between 1960 and 1970, Atlanta's central city population changed from 38.3 percent black to 51.3 percent black; its suburbs, from 91.3 percent white to 93.6 percent white. The white percentages of Houston's and New Orleans' suburbs are 90.7 and 87.2 percent respectively. Increases in the black population in central cities have been accompanied by greater isolation of black students.

What is to be done? Senator Abraham A. Ribicoff argues that integration in housing, welfare, transportation, and other areas in addition to education must be achieved, with the latter emphasis expanded beyond individual schools, school districts, or even cities, outside as well as inside the South. Responsibility for this achievement must be placed squarely on all branches of government, not the judiciary alone, and penalties must be accompanied by positive incentives for compliance with integration policies. Because school districts "are part of the racial isolation problem, not its solution," we must search for "mechanisms which transcend existing school districts."[59]

To negate the Supreme Court's ruling that school segregation is unconstitutional, whites have resorted to violence against blacks, drawn school boundary lines to confine them to separate and unequal schools, adopted freedom-of-choice plans that deterred whites and blacks alike from pursuing integrated education, championed legislation and constitutional amendments to sabotage the ruling, and shrieked in outrage against it.[60] Laws that empowered local school boards to promulgate pupil assignment criteria, forbade the use of state funds for desegregation, sanctioned the use of public school property by segregated private schools, and diluted compulsory attendance requirements were designed to thwart enforcement of the *Brown* decision. So were the tampering with teacher tenure regulations, bills closing schools, interposition resolutions, and attacks on the NAACP, the warrior of black children.[61]

The racists' repertoire included violence, just as it does now. Their outrage centers on busing to facilitate school integration, which is one way of making school integration a red herring that diverts the attention of blacks and whites from the genuine gut issues: "taxes, utility bills, consumer protection, government services, environmental preservation, and other problems," according to Governor Reubin O'D. Askew of Florida. Mention those needs, he adds, and up pops the race issue. Busing is a proper means to a proper end—that is, putting "the divisive and self-defeating issue of race behind us once and for all. It is a goal worthy of vigorous pursuit by anyone who believes that all people should live together in peace, justice and harmony."[62]

But not in President Gerald R. Ford's opinion. Busing is not "the best solution to quality education" in Boston, he declared during the peak of violent resistance by whites to a federal court order. This, said Mayor Kevin H. White, "fanned the flames of resistance" in his city in the North in 1974, twenty years after the Supreme Court's decision against segregated schooling.[63] And not in the opinion of Ford's predecessor, Richard M. Nixon, whose administration in effect virtually repealed the authorization (under Title VI of the Civil Rights Act of 1964) to deny funds to federally assisted schools, sided with Mississippi officials in court action to prevent desegregation, attempted to tilt the Supreme Court against desegregation, and led the campaign for antibusing constitutional amendments and to postpone busing orders.[64]

More than half the nation's students travel to and from school by some means other than on foot or by bicycle; busing at public expense is but one of those means, and its long history was unmarred by racial controversy until some recent federal court decisions were made. In the first of these, the Fifth Circuit Court of Appeals in 1966 ordered the conversion of dual systems into nonsegregated single systems; in the second decision, the Supreme Court in 1968 notified school districts of their duty to establish the latter systems. Often reluctantly, school authorities have used busing to surmount housing segregation that otherwise makes the right to unsegregated schooling meaningless.[65]

Two later federal court decisions contained the promise of far-reaching impact on metropolitan school and housing segregation. The decisons were made in Richmond by Federal District Judge Robert H. Merhige (who received the Judicial Council's [NBA] Special Award in 1972) and in Detroit by Federal District Judge Stephen Roth: by encompassing areas larger than the cities themselves, they offered the possibility of integration even in school districts that were predominantly black. Moreover, the decisions were based on nationally applicable legal principles and factual findings—namely, that the responsibility of providing equal educational opportunity for all students rests with the state; that school districts are created by the state and must be changed as necessary to protect constitutional rights; that a showing that pupil assignment policies are determined by segregated housing policies establishes de jure school segregation; and that in a single biracial metropolitan community there is no compelling state interest in the maintenance of racially separate school systems. A former staff director of the U.S. Commission on Civil Rights, William L. Taylor, identifies as "the core" of these decisions "heavy government involvement in housing discrimination which contained blacks within the central cities." Approvingly, he quotes Judge Merhige: "When a school board operating in any area where segregated housing patterns prevail and are continuing, builds its facilities and arranges its zones so that school attendance is governed by housing segregation, it is operating in violation of the constitution."[66]

No one has made the point of all this more clearly than has federal District Court judge Damon J. Keith:

> . . . When the power to act is available, failure to take the necessary steps so as to negate or alleviate a situation which is harmful is as wrong as is the taking of affirmative steps to advance that situation. Sins of omission can be as serious as sins of commission. . . .
>
> . . . For a School Board to acquiesce in a housing development pattern and then to disclaim liability for the eventual segregated characteristic that such pattern creates in the schools is for the Board to abrogate and ignore all power, control and responsibility. A Board of Education simply cannot permit a segregated situation to come about and then blithely announce that for a Negro student to gain attendance at a given school all he must do is live within the school's attendance area. To rationalize thusly is to be blinded to the realities of adult life with its prejudices and opposition to integrated housing.
>
> . . . The harm to another generation of Black children while awaiting implementation of "long-range plans" to integrate simply cannot be tolerated; and no degree of expense is unbearable when placed alongside of the unbearable situation which exists for those Black children. . . .

That declaration made, Judge Keith ordered busing in Pontiac, Michigan.[67]

"I dissent." Those words were to be expected from Mr. Justice Marshall when the U.S. Supreme Court overturned a district court's order and an appeals court affirmation of it as the only feasible means of achieving school integration in the Detroit public schools. The district court had concluded that the state, by virtue of the action of the city school board, was responsible for creating and perpetuating segregation. Rejecting a city-only desegregation plan as impractical, the court appointed a panel to draw up a plan that involved fifty-three suburban school districts that were not accused of segregation and ordered the city school board to buy 295 buses to transport students under an interim plan to be prepared for the 1972-73 school year. The court of appeals upheld the core of the order but remanded to give the suburban school districts a chance to be heard, and vacated the bus purchase requirement subject to appropriate reimposition. The Supreme Court, however, held that interschool district busing could be required only if all affected districts were found to have engaged in segregation. "After 20 years of small, often difficult steps toward that great end [school desegregation], the Court today takes a giant step backwards," wrote Justice Thurgood Marshall, who had launched the nation on the road to that goal while leading the NAACP's legal battle against school segregation. A graduate of Lincoln University and Howard University Law School, Mr. Justice Marshall objected to what many informed observers consider the prevailing tone of the current Supreme Court.

METROPOLITAN SCHOOL DESEGREGATION

(*Milliken* v. *Bradley*
41 L Ed 2nd 1069)

Thurgood Marshall

. . . MR. JUSTICE MARSHALL, with whom Mr. Justice Douglas, Mr. Justice Brennan, and Mr. Justice White join, dissenting.

In Brown v Board of Education, 347 US 483, 98 L Ed 873, 74 S Ct 686, 38 ALR2d 1180 (1954), this Court held that segregation of children in public schools on the basis of race deprives minority group children of equal educational opportunities and therefore denies them the equal protection of the laws under the Fourteenth Amendment. This Court recognized then that remedying decades of segregation in public education would not be an easy task. Subsequent events, unfortunately, have seen that prediction bear bitter fruit. But however imbedded old ways, however ingrained old prejudices, this Court has not been diverted from its appointed task of making "a living truth" of our constitutional ideal of equal justice under law. Cooper v. Aaron, 358 US 1, 20, 3 L Ed 2d 5, 78 S Ct 1401 (1958).

After 20 years of small, often difficult steps toward that great end, the Court today takes a giant step backwards. Notwithstanding a record showing widespread and pervasive racial segregation in the educational system provided by the State of Michigan for children in Detroit, this Court holds that the District Court was powerless to require the State to remedy its constitutional violation in any meaningful fashion. Ironically purporting to base its result on the principle that the scope of the remedy in a desegregation case should be determined by the nature and the extent of the constitutional violation, the Court's answer is to provide no remedy at all for the violation proved in this case, thereby guaranteeing that Negro children in Detroit will receive the same separate and inherently unequal education in the future as they have been unconstitutionally afforded in the past.

I cannot subscribe to this emasculation of our constitutional guarantee of equal protection of the laws and must respectfully dissent. Our precedents, in my view, firmly establish that where, as here, state-imposed segregation has been demonstrated, it becomes the duty of the State to eliminate root and branch all vestiges of racial discrimination and to achieve the greatest possible degree of actual desegregation. I agree with both the District Court and the Court of Appeals that, under the facts of this case, this duty cannot be fulfilled unless the State of Michigan involves outlying metropolitan area school districts in its desegregation remedy. Furthermore, I perceive no basis either in law or in the practicalities of the situation justifying the State's interposition of school district boundaries as absolute barriers to the implementation of an effecive desegregation remedy. Under established and frequently used Michigan procedures, school district lines are both flexible and permeable for a wide variety of purposes, and there is no reason why they must now stand in the way of meaningful desegregation relief.

. . . The great irony of the Court's opinion and, in my view, its most serious analytical flaw may be gleaned from its concluding sentence, in which the Court remands for "prompt formulation of a decree directed to eliminating the segregation found to exist in Detroit city schools, a remedy which has been delayed since 1970." Ante, at—, 41 L Ed 2d at 1096. The majority, however, seems to have forgotten the District Court's explicit finding that a Detroit-only decree, the only remedy permitted under today's decision, "would not accomplish desegregation."

Nowhere in the Court's opinion does the majority confront, let alone respond to, the District Court's conclusion that a remedy limited to the city of Detroit would not effectively desegregate the Detroit city schools. I, for one, find the District Court's conclusion well supported by the record and its analysis compelled by our prior cases. Before turning to these questions, however, it is best to begin by laying to rest some mischaracterizations in the Court's opinion with respect to the basis for the District Court's decision to impose a metropolitan remedy.

The Court maintains that while the initial focus of this lawsuit was the condition of segregation within the Detroit city schools, the District Court abruptly shifted focus in midcourse and altered its theory of the case. This new theory, in the majority's words, was "equating racial imbalance with a constitutional violation calling for a remedy." Ante, at—n 19, 41 L Ed 2d at 1089. As the following review of the District Court's handling of the case demonstrates, however, the majority's characterization is totally inaccurate. Nowhere did the District Court indicate that racial imbalance between school districts in the Detroit metropolitan area or within the Detroit school district constituted a constitutional violation calling for inter-district relief. The focus of this case was from the beginning, and has remained, the segregated system of education in the Detroit city schools and the steps necessary to cure that condition which offends the Fourteenth Amendment.

The District Court's consideration of this case began with its finding, which the majority accepts, that the State of Michigan, through its instrumentality, the Detroit Board of Education, engaged in widespread purposeful acts of racial segregation in the Detroit school district. Without belaboring the details, it is sufficient to note that the various techniques used in Detroit were typical of methods employed to segregate students by race in areas where no statutory dual system of education has existed. See, e.g., Keyes v School District No. 1, 413 US 189, 37 L Ed 2d 548, 93 S Ct 2686 (1973). Exacerbating the effects of extensive residential segregation between Negroes and whites, the school board consciously drew attendance zones along lines which maximized the segregation of the races in schools as well. Optional attendance zones were created for neighborhoods undergoing racial transition so as to allow white [sic] in these areas to escape integration. Negro students in areas with over-crowded schools were transported past or away from closer white schools with available space to more distant Negro schools. Grade structures and feeder school patterns were created and maintained in a manner which had the foreseeable and actual effect of keeping Negro and white pupils in separate schools. Schools were also constructed in locations and in sizes which ensured that they would open with predominantly one-race student bodies. In sum, the evidence adduced below showed that Negro children had been intentionally confined to an expanding core of virtually all-Negro schools immediately surrounded by a receding band of all-white schools.

. . . Having found a de jure segregated public school system in operation in the city of Detroit, the District Court turned next to consider which officials and agencies should be assigned the affirmative obligation to cure the constitutional violation. The court concluded that responsibility for the segregation in the Detroit city schools rested not only with the Detroit Board of Education, but belonged to the State of Michigan itself and the state defendants in this case—that is, the Governor of Michigan, the Attorney General, the State Board of Education, and the State Superintendent of Public Instruction. While the validity of this conclusion will merit more extensive analysis below, suffice it for now to say that it was based on three considerations. First, the evidence at trial showed that the State itself had taken actions contributing to the segregation within the Detroit schools. Second, since the Detroit Board of Education was an agency of the State of Michigan, its acts of racial discrimination were acts of the State for purposes of the Fourteenth Amendment. Finally, the District Court found that under Michigan law and practice, the system of education was in fact a *state* school system, characterized by relatively little local control and a large degree of centralized state regulation, with respect to both educational policy and the structure and operation of school districts.

Having concluded, then, that the school system in the city of Detroit was a de jure segregated system and that the State of Michigan had the affirmative duty to remedy that condition of segregation, the District Court then turned to the difficult task of devising an effective remedy. It bears repeating that the District Court's focus at this stage of the litigation remained what it had been at the beginning—the condition of segregation within the Detroit city schools. . . .

The District Court first considered three desegregation plans limited to the geographical boundaries of the city of Detroit. All were rejected as ineffective to desegregate the Detroit city schools. Specifically, the District Court determined that the racial composition of the Detroit student body is such that implementation of any Detroit-only plan "would clearly make the entire Detroit public school system racially identifiable as Black" and would "leave many of its schools 75 to 90 percent Black." The District Court also found that a Detroit-only plan "would change a school system which is now Black and White to one that would be perceived as Black, thereby increasing the flight of Whites from the city and the system, thereby increasing the Black student population." Based on these findings, the District Court reasoned that "relief of segregation in the public schools of the City of Detroit cannot be accomplished within the corporate geographical limits of the city" because a Detroit-only decree "would accentuate the racial identifiability of the district as a Black school system, and would not accomplish desegregation." The District Court therefore concluded that it "must look beyond the limits of the Detroit school district for a solution to the problem of segregation in the Detroit public schools. . . ."

. . . There is simply no foundation in the record, then, for the majority's accusation that the only basis for the District Court's order was some desire to achieve a racial balance in the Detroit metropolitan area. In fact, just the contrary is the case. In considering proposed desegregation areas, the District Court had occasion to criticize one of the State's proposals specifically because it had no basis other than its "particular racial ratio" and did not focus on "relevant factors, like eliminating racially identifiable schools [and] accomplishing maximum actual desegregation of the Detroit public schools.". . .

. . . The Court also misstates the basis for the District Court's order by suggesting that since the only segregation proved at trial was within the Detroit school district, any relief which extended beyond the jurisdiction of the Detroit Board of Education would be inappropriate because it would impose a remedy on outlying districts "not shown to have committed any constitutional violation." Ante, at—, 41 L Ed 2d at 1091. The essential foundation of inter-district relief in this case was not to correct conditions within outlying districts who themselves engaged in purposeful segregation. Instead, inter-district relief was seen as a necessary part of any meaningful effort by the State of Michigan to remedy the state-caused segregation within the city of Detroit.

Rather than consider the propriety of inter-district relief on this basis, however, the Court has conjured up a largely fictional account of what the District Court was attempting to accomplish. With all due respect, the Court, in my view, does a great disservice to the District Judge who labored long and hard with this complex litigation by accusing him of changing horses in mid-stream and shifting the focus of this case from the pursuit of a remedy for the condition of segregation within the Detroit school district to some unprincipled attempt to impose his own philosophy of racial balance on the entire Detroit metropolitan area. See ante, at—, 41 L Ed 2d at 1087-1088. The focus of this case has always been the segregated system of education in the city of Detroit. The District Court determined that inter-district relief was necessary and appropriate only because it found that the condition of segregation within the Detroit school district could not be cured with a Detroit-only remedy. It is on this theory that the inter-district relief must stand or fall. Unlike the Court, I perceive my task to be to review the District Court's order for what it is, rather than to criticize it for what it manifestly is not.

As the foregoing demonstrates, the District Court's decision to expand its desegregation decree beyond the geographical limits of the city of Detroit rested in large part on its conclusions (A) that the State of Michigan was ultimately responsible for curing the condition of segregation within the Detroit city schools, and (B) that a Detroit-only remedy would not accomplish this task. In my view, both of these conclusions are well supported by the facts of this case and by this Court's precedents.

. . . We recognized only last Term in Keyes that it was the State itself which was ultimately responsible for de jure acts of segregation committed by a local school board. A deliberate policy of segregation by the local board, we held, amounted to "state-imposed segregation." 413 US, at 200, 37 L Ed 2d 548.

Wherever a dual school system exists, whether compelled by state statute or created by a local board's systematic program of segregation, "the *State* automatically assumes an affirmative duty 'to effectuate a transition to a racially nondiscriminatory school system' [and] to eliminate from the public schools within their school system 'all vestiges of state-imposed segregation.' " Keyes, supra, 413 US, at 200, 37 L Ed 2d 548 (emphasis added).

Vesting responsibility with the State of Michigan for Detroit's segregated schools is particularly appropriate as Michigan, unlike some other States, operates a single state-wide system of education rather than several separate and independent local school systems. The majority's emphasis on local governmental control and local autonomy of school districts in Michigan will come as a surprise to those with any familiarity with that State's system of education. School districts are not separate and distinct sovereign entities under Michigan law, but rather are "auxiliaries of the State," subject to its "absolute power." Attorney General v Lowrey, 199 US 233, 240, 50 L Ed 167, 26 S Ct 27 (1905). The courts of the State have repeatedly emphasized that education in Michigan is not a local governmental concern, but a state function.

. . . Centralized state control manifests itself in practice as well as in theory. The state controls the financing of education in several ways. The legislature contributes a substantial portion of most school districts' operating budgets with funds appropriated from the State's General Fund revenues raised through statewide taxation. The State's power over the purse can be and is in fact used to enforce the State's powers over local districts. In addition, although local districts obtain funds through local property taxation, the State has assumed the responsibility to ensure equalized property valuations throughout the State. The State also establishes standards for teacher certification and teacher tenure; determines part of the required curriculum; sets the minimum school term; approves bus routes, equipment, and drivers; approves textbooks; and establishes procedures for student discipline. The

State Superintendent of Public Instruction and the State Board of Education have the power to remove local school board members from office for neglect of their duties.

Most significantly for present purposes, the State has wide-ranging powers to consolidate and merge school districts, even without the consent of the districts themselves or of the local citizenry. . . .

. . . In sum, several factors in this case coalesce to support the District Court's ruling that it was the State of Michigan itself, not simply the Detroit Board of Education, which bore the obligation of curing the condition of segregation within the Detroit city schools. . . .

. . . Negro students are not only entitled to neutral nondiscriminatory treatment in the future. They must receive "what Brown II promised them: a school system in which all vestiges of enforced racial segregation have been eliminated." . . .

After examining three plans limited to the city of Detroit, the District Court correctly concluded that none would eliminate root and branch the vestiges of unconstitutional segregation. The plans' effectiveness, of course, had to be evaluated in the context of the District Court's findings as to the extent of segregation in the Detroit city schools. As indicated earlier, the most essential finding was that Negro children in Detroit had been confined by intentional acts of segregation to a growing core of Negro schools surrounded by a receding ring of white schools. Thus, in 1960, of Detroit's 251 schools, 100 were 90% or more white and 71 were 90% or more Negro. In 1970, of Detroit's 282 schools, 69 were 90% or more white and 133 were 90% or more Negro. While in 1960, 68% of all schools were 90% or more one race, by 1970, 71.6% of the schools fell into that category. The growing core of all-Negro schools was further evidenced in total school district population figures. In 1960 the Detroit district had 46% Negro students and 54% white students, but by 1970, 64% of the students were Negro and only 36% were white. This increase in the proportion of Negro students was the highest of any major northern city.

It was with these figures in the background that the District Court evaluated the adequacy of the three Detroit-only plans submitted by the parties. . . .

. . . Under our decisions, it was clearly proper for the District Court to take into account the so-called "white flight" from the city schools which would be forthcoming from any Detroit-only decree. . . . One cannot ignore the white-flight problem, for where legally imposed segregation has been established, the District Court has the responsibility to see to it not only that the dual system is terminated at once but also that future events do not serve to perpetuate or re-establish segregation. . . .

We held in Swann that where de jure segregation is shown, school authorities must make "every effort to achieve the greatest possible degree of actual desegregation." 402 US, at 26, 28 L Ed 2d 554. This is the operative standard re-emphasized in Davis v Board of School Commissioners, 402 US 33, 37, 28 L Ed 2d 577, 91 S Ct 1289 (1971). If these words have any meaning at all, surely it is that school authorities must, to the extent possible, take all practicable steps to ensure that Negro and white children in fact go to school together. This is, in the final analysis, what desegregation of the public schools is all about.

. . . The continued racial identifiability of the Detroit schools under a Detroit-only remedy is not simply a reflection of their high percentage of Negro students. What is or is not a racially identifiable vestige of de jure segregation must necessarily depend on several factors. Cf. Keyes, supra, 413 US, at 196, 37 L Ed 2d 548. Foremost among these should be the relationship between the schools in question and the neighboring community. For these purposes the city of Detroit and its surrounding suburbs must be viewed as a single community. Detroit is closely connected to its suburbs in many ways, and the metropolitan area is viewed as a single cohesive unit by its residents. About 40% of the residents of the two suburban counties included in the desegregation plan work in Wayne County, in which Detroit is situated. Many residents of the city work in the suburbs. The three counties participate in a wide variety of cooperative governmental ventures on a metropolitan-wide basis, including a metropolitan transit system, park authority, water and sewer system, and council of governments. The Federal Government has classified the tri-county area as a Standard Metropolitan Statistical Area, indicating that it is an area of "economic and social integration." United States v Connecticut Nat'l Bank—,US—,—, 41 L Ed 2d 1016, 94 S Ct—(June 26, 1974).

Under a Detroit-only decree, Detroit's schools will clearly remain racially identifiable in comparison with neighboring schools in the metropolitan community. Schools with 65% and more Negro students will stand in sharp and obvious contrast to schools in neighboring districts with less than 2% Negro enrollment. Negro students will continue to perceive their schools as segregated educational facilities and this perception will only be increased when whites react to a Detroit-only decree by fleeing to the suburbs to avoid integration. School district lines, however innocently drawn, will surely be perceived as fences to separate the races when, under a Detroit-only decree, white parents withdraw their children from the Detroit city schools and move to the suburbs in order to continue them in all-white schools. . . .

. . . The majority asserts, however, that involvement of outlying districts would do violence to the accepted principle that "the nature of the violation determines the scope of the remedy." 402 US, at 16, 28 L Ed 2d 554. See ante, at 25, 41 L Ed 2d at 1091. Not only is the majority's attempt to find in this single phrase the answer to the complex and difficult questions presented in this case hopelessly simplistic, but more importantly [sic], the Court reads these words in a manner which perverts their obvious meaning. The nature of a violation determines the scope of the remedy simply because the function of any remedy is to cure the violation to which it is addressed. In school segregation cases, as in other equitable causes, a remedy which effectively cures the violation is what is required. See Green, supra, 391 US, at 439, 20 L Ed 2d 716;

Davis, supra, 402 US, at 37, 28 L Ed 2d 577. No more is necessary, but we can tolerate no less. To read this principle as barring a District Court from imposing the only effective remedy for past segregation and remitting the court to a patently ineffective alternative is, in my view, to turn a simple commonsense rule into a cruel and meaningless paradox. Ironically, by ruling out an inter-district remedy, the only relief which promises to cure segregation in the Detroit public schools, the majority flouts the very principle on which it purports to rely.

Nor should it be of any significance that the suburban school districts were not shown to have themselves taken any direct action to promote segregation of the races. Given the State's broad powers over local school districts, it was well within the State's powers to require those districts surrounding the Detroit school district to participate in a metropolitan remedy. The State's duty should be no different here than in cases where it is shown that certain of a State's voting districts are malapportioned in violation of the Fourteenth Amendment. See Reynolds v Sims, 377 US 533, 12 L Ed 2d 506, 84 S Ct 1362 (1964). Overrepresented electoral districts are required to participate in reapportionment although their only "participation" in the violation was to do nothing about it. Similarly, electoral districts which themselves meet representation standards must frequently be redrawn as part of a remedy for other over- and under-inclusive districts. No finding of fault on the part of each electoral district and no finding of a discriminatory effect on each district is a prerequisite to its involvement in the constitutionally required remedy. By the same logic, no finding of fault on the part of the suburban school districts in this case and no finding of a discriminatory effect on each district should be a prerequisite to their involvement in the constitutionally required remedy.

It is the State, after all, which bears the responsibility under Brown of affording a nondiscriminatory system of education. . . .

. . . To suggest, as does the majority, that a Detroit-only

plan somehow remedies the effects of de jure segregation of the races is, in my view, to make a solemn mockery of Brown I's holding that separate educational facilities are inherently unequal and of Swann's unequivocal mandate that the answer to de jure segregation is the greatest possible degree of actual desegregation.

. . . Our cases, of course, make clear that the initial responsibility for devising an adequate desegregation plan belongs with school authorities, not with the District Court. The court's primary role is to review the adequacy of the school authorities' efforts and to substitute its own plan only if and to the extent they default. See Swann, supra, 402 US, at 16, 28 L Ed 2d 554; Green, supra, 391 US, at 439, 20 L Ed 2d 716. Contrary to the majority's suggestions, the District Judge in this case has consistently adhered to these procedures and there is every indication that he would continue to do so. After finding de jure segregation the Court ordered the parties to submit proposed Detroit-only plans. The state defendants were also ordered to submit a proposed metropolitan plan extending beyond Detroit's boundaries. As the District Court stated, "the State defendants . . . bear the initial burden of coming forward with a proposal that promises to work." The state defendants defaulted in this obligation, however. Rather than submit a complete plan, the State Board of Education submitted six proposals, none of which was in fact a desegregation plan. It was only upon this default that the District Court began to take steps to develop its own plan. Even then the District Court maximized school authority participation by appointing a panel representing both plaintiffs and defendants to develop a plan. App 99a—100a. Furthermore, the District Court still left the state defendants the initial responsibility for developing both interim and final financial and administrative arrangements to implement inter-district relief. App 104a—105a. The Court of Appeals further protected the interests of local school authorities by ensuring that the outlying suburban districts could fully participate in the proceedings to develop a metropolitan remedy.

These processes have not been allowed to run their course.
No final desegregation plan has been proposed by the panel
of experts, let alone approved by the District Court. We do not
know in any detail how many students will be transported to
effect a metropolitan remedy, and we do not know how long
or how far they will have to travel. No recommendations have
yet been submitted by the state defendants on financial and
administrative arrangements. In sum, the practicality of a
final metropolitan plan is simply not before us at the present
time. Since the State and the panel of experts have not yet had
an opportunity to come up with a workable remedy, there is
no foundation for the majority's suggestion of the impracti-
cality of inter-district relief. Furthermore, there is no basis
whatever for assuming that the District Court will inevitably
be forced to assume the role of legislature or school superintendent. Were we to hold that it was its constitutional duty to
do so, there is every indication that the State of Michigan
would fulfill its obligation and develop a plan which is workable, administrable, financially sound and, most important, in
the best interest of quality education for all of the children in
the Detroit metropolitan area.

Since the Court chooses, however, to speculate on the feasi-
bility of a metropolitan plan, I feel constrained to comment on
the problem areas it has targeted. To begin with, the majority's questions concerning the practicality of consolidation of
school districts need not give us pause. The State clearly has
the power, under existing law, to effect a consolidation if it is
ultimately determined that this offers the best prospect for a
workable and stable desegregation plan. See ante, at 16-17, 41
L Ed 2d at 1086. And given the 1,000 or so consolidations of
school districts which have taken place in the past, it is hard to
believe that the State has not already devised means of solving
most, if not all, of the practical problems which the Court
suggests consolidation would entail.

Furthermore, the majority ignores long-established Michigan procedures under which school districts may enter into
contractual agreements to educate their pupils in other dis-

tricts using state or local funds to finance non-resident education. Such agreements could form an easily administrable framework for inter-district relief short of outright consolidation of the school districts. The District Court found that inter-district procedures like these were frequently used to provide special educational services for handicapped children, and extensive statutory provision is also made for their use in vocational education. Surely if school districts are willing to engage in inter-district programs to help those unfortunate children crippled by physical or mental handicaps, school districts can be required to participate in an inter-district program to help those children in the city of Detroit whose educations and very futures have been crippled by purposeful state segregation.

Although the majority gives this last matter only fleeting reference, it is plain that one of the basic emotional and legal issues underlying these cases concerns the propriety of transportation of students to achieve desegregation. While others may have retreated from its standards, see, e.g., Keyes, supra, 413 US, at 217, 37 L Ed 2d 548 (Powell, J., concurring in part and dissenting in part), I continue to adhere to the guidelines set forth in Swann on this issue. See 402 US, at 29—31, 28 L Ed 2d 554. And though no final desegregation plan is presently before us, to the extent the outline of such a plan is now visible, it is clear that the transportation it would entail will be fully consistent with these guidelines.

First of all, the metropolitan plan would not involve the busing of substantially more students than already ride buses. The District Court found that statewide, 35-40 percent of all students already arrive at school on a bus. In those school districts in the tri-county Detroit metropolitan area eligible for state reimbursement of transportation costs, 42-52 percent of all students rode buses to school. In the tri-county areas [sic] as a whole, approximately 300,000 pupils arrived at school on some type of bus, with about 60,000 of these apparently using regular public transit. In comparison, the desegregation plan, according to its present rough outline, would involve the transportation of 310,000 students, about 40% of the population within the desegregation area.

With respect to distance and amount of time travelled, 17 of the outlying school districts involved in the plan are contiguous to the Detroit district. The rest are all within 8 miles of the Detroit city limits. The trial court, in defining the desegregation area, placed a ceiling of 40 minutes one way on the amount of travel time, and many students will obviously travel for far shorter periods. At [*sic*] to distance, the average statewide bus trip is 81/2 miles one way, and in some parts of the tri-county area, students already travel for one and a quarter hours or more each way. In sum, with regard to both the number of students transported and the time and distances involved, the outlined desegregation plan "compares favorably with the transportation plan previously operated. . . ." Swann, supra, 402 US, at 30, 28 L Ed 2d 554.

As far as economics are concerned, a metropolitan remedy would actually be more sensible than a Detroit-only remedy. Because of prior transportation aid restrictions, see ante, at 11-12, 41 L Ed 2d at 1117—1118, Detroit largely relied on public transport, at student expense, for those students who lived too far away to walk to school. Since no inventory of school buses existed, a Detroit-only plan was estimated to require the purchase of 900 buses to effectuate the necessary transportation. The tri-county area, in contrast, already has an inventory of 1,800 buses, many of which are now underutilized. Since increased utilization of the existing inventory can take up much of the increase in transportation involved in the inter-district remedy, the District Court found that only 350 additional buses would probably be needed, almost two-thirds fewer than a Detroit-only remedy. Other features of an inter-district remedy bespeak its practicality, such as the possibility of pairing up Negro schools near Detroit's boundary with nearby white schools on the other side of the present school district line.

Some disruption, of course, is the inevitable product of any desegregation decree, whether it operates within one district or on an inter-district basis. . . .

Desegregation is not and was never expected to be an easy task. Racial attitudes ingrained in our Nation's childhood and adolescence are not quickly thrown aside in its middle years. But just as the inconvenience of some cannot be allowed to stand in the way of the rights of others, so public opposition, no matter how strident, cannot be permitted to divert this Court from the enforcement of the constitutional principles at issue in this case. Today's holding, I fear, is more a reflection of a perceived public mood that we have gone far enough in enforcing the Constitution's guarantee of equal justice than it is the product of neutral principles of law. In the short run, it may seem to be the easier course to allow our great metropolitan areas to be divided up each into two cities—one white, the other black—but it is a course, I predict, our people will ultimately regret. I dissent.

Black workers have had a hard time of it in an important industry that receives little attention—namely, the railroads. Charles Hamilton Houston's article, which is reprinted with the permission of *The Crisis* magazine, is a reminder that job discrimination long has permeated all facets of employment and that black resistance to it has been equally widespread and persistent. Those were essential observations he made in his address to the Fortieth Anniversary NAACP Conference in Los Angeles, California, on July 14, 1949. Adapting the article from that address, Houston wrote with the authority born of deep involvement in the controversy and contribution so excellent that it established him as the grand architect of legal protest against bigotry. Houston was educated at Amherst, Harvard University, and the University of Madrid.

FOUL EMPLOYMENT PRACTICE ON THE RAILS

Charles H. Houston

THIS IS the story of the fight for economic survival by two groups of Negro workers on American railroads. I am not talking about the shop craft men who help keep the rolling stock in repair and running condition. I am not talking about the maintenance of way men who look after the tracks and the roadbed. I am not talking about the cooks and waiters, the Red Caps [*sic*] or the Pullman Porters. I am talking about the men out on the mainline who help speed the traffic from terminal to terminal, and the men in the yards who switch the engines and cars about and make up the trains to go on the road. I am talking about the Negro firemen and brakemen and switchmen who used to be all over the South and Southwest forty years ago, but who are vanishing now thru [*sic*] the organized prejudice and discriminations imposed on them by the national white operating railroad unions.

The Bureau of the Census did not make a separate breakdown on Negro and white firemen, brakemen and switchmen until 1920. The 14th Census in 1920 showed 6,505 Negro firemen in that year. By the 1940 Census the Negro firemen had dwindled to 2,263. The 1920 Census showed a total of 8,275 Negro brakemen, switchmen, flagmen and yardmen. The 1940 Census gave the total of Negro brakemen, switchmen, flagmen and yardmen as 2,739.

Figures are not available showing the number of Negro firemen, brakemen, switchmen, flagmen and yardmen as of 1919: but if we had them they would show figures much lower than those for 1940 due to deaths, retirement, discharge and other reasons. There were no Negro replacements by way of new hiring. The big-four operating brotherhoods (Brotherhood of Locomotive Engineers, Brotherhood of Locomotive Firemen & Enginemen, Brotherhood of Railroad Trainmen and Order of Railway Conductors) presented a solid front against the hiring of Negroes even during the manpower emergency shortage in World War II.

It is reasonably safe to say that practically no Negro firemen, brakemen, switchmen, flagmen or yardmen have been hired on Class I American railroads since 1928.

On many railroads hiring of Negroes in train and engine service stopped before that. On the Norfolk & Western Railroad, as the result of a secret agreement between the railroad and the Brotherhood of Locomotive Firemen and Enginemen and the Brotherhood of Railroad Trainmen in 1909, not a single Negro fireman or brakeman has been hired in the last forty years, and the last Negro fireman on the Norfolk & Western has now retired. There are a few Negro brakemen still left, but they too will soon be gone. For the past fifty years the Big-four Brotherhoods have been using every means in their power to drive the Negro train and engine service worker out of employment and create a "racially closed shop" among the firemen, brakemen, switchmen, flagmen, and yardmen. They have just about succeeded on the Norfolk & Western and will soon succeed on all the other railroads in the

South and Southwest unless they are checked by judicial decision and the force of public opinion.

Key Workers

White collar or professional workers often look down on the Negro firemen and brakemen without realizing the strategic role they play in the struggle to democratize the industrial structure of the United States. Transportation workers are always key workers in the industrial structure. A major transportation strike can paralyze the country; and the Government always steps in and seizes the railroad on which such a strike is threatened in order to avoid this economic paralysis.

The transportation workers are usually the most favored industrial workers so far as rates of pay and working conditions are concerned. Hour for hour of service the firemen and brakemen make more money than most white collar and professional workers. The average brakeman earns from $350.00 to $400.00 a month; the average fireman from $400.00 to $500.00—with vacation with pay, and liberal compensation laws. On a fast passenger or fast freight the fireman or brakeman makes his run in from 90 minutes to three hours and is then thru [sic] for the day. He works on an average of from 20 to 25 days a month. Unless something goes wrong, a fireman or brakeman does less than thirty minutes physical work on a road trip; the rest of the time he is sitting still watching the road and his train. The next time you go to a station or pass by a railroad switching yard, or ride a fast streamliner, watch and see just how much physical work the fireman or brakeman is actually doing.

That is part of the secret; the jobs are too soft and the pay too good for these Big-four Brotherhoods to permit these jobs to be held by Negroes.

Negroes are not the only minority that these Big-four Brotherhoods fight. Get railroad conscious and ask yourselves how many Latin-American firemen or brakemen have you seen; how many Japanese-American or Jewish or Italian? These Big-four Brotherhoods have the railroad train and engine service tied up tight for a white monopoly, for a "Nordic closed shop." Every race, color, and creed has to use the railroads. Every race, color, and creed has to pay taxes to help support the railroads; but the Big-four Brotherhoods have the train and engine service reserved for 100 percent pure Gentile firemen and brakemen. The census figures for 1940 show the whites have 99.9 percent of the railroad conductors, 99.4 percent of the locomotive engineers, 94.8 percent of the locomotive fireman, and 97.4 percent of the brakemen, switchmen, flagmen and yardmen. This sounds like an advertisement for "Ivory Soap"—99.4 percent pure.

The Big-four Brotherhoods are rich and powerful. President Whitney of the Brotherhood of Railroad Trainmen threatened to spend one million dollars in 1948 to defeat President Truman. He could afford to do this. The Brotherhood of Railroad Trainmen has over 200,000 members. The Brotherhood of Locomotive Firemen & Enginemen has over 100,000 members; the Brotherhood of Locomotive Engineers about 80,000 members and the Order of Railway Conductors some 60,000 members. The four brotherhoods maintain an independent legislative lobby in Washington. In fact theirs is the oldest labor lobby in Washington. They helped write the 1934 Railway Labor Act, and each one of the four brotherhoods has its representative sitting on the First Division of the National Railroad Adjustment Board which has jurisdiction over all grievances affecting train and engine service employees, including firemen, brakemen, switchmen, flagmen, and yardmen.

Shocking Testimony

During World War II the President's Committee on Fair Employment Practice was able to integrate minority workers in many industries, but it was not able to budge the Big-four Brotherhoods one inch. The FEPC in 1943 cited the four brotherhoods because all of them have clauses in their constitution excluding Negroes from membership and because of their hostile and discriminatory acts against Negro train and engine service workers. The Big-four Brotherhoods ignored the charges. The FEPC held a four-day hearing in Washington in September, 1943, on discriminations against minority railroad workers as impeding the war effort. The Big-four Brotherhoods refused to attend the hearings, send representatives, or to submit any evidence. The FEPC issued its directives against the carriers and the railroad unions. Neither obeyed the directives, but instead both the carriers and the unions preferred charges against the FEPC before the Smith Committee of the House of Representatives. The lawyer for the Railway Labor Executives Association stated to the Smith Committee that if the directives of the FEPC ordering elimination of the color bar in the brotherhood constitutions and of the discriminatory working conditions were carried out the organizations would not be responsible for what their membership might do.

The Big-four Brotherhoods never felt the necessity of defending their acts of discrimination, any place, except in court, until this spring. Then they were called before a subcommittee of the House Committee on Education and Labor presided over by Congressman Adam C. Powell of New York, who was holding hearings on his FEPC Bill H.R. 4453.

Congressman Powell was so shocked by the testimony of discrimination put in the record against the Big-four Brotherhoods that he issued telegrams to the heads of the four organizations requesting them to appear. He dropped a hint that if they did not appear he was going to issue subpoenas, that he wanted them to know they were dealing with a committee of the Congress and not with a war-time FEPC. The four brotherhoods appeared on schedule. The presidents did not come. Even when they were licked they wanted to make a last show of defiance. But the vice-presidents came, and if you ever read their testimony before the Powell committee you will see how the most powerful can squirm when they are finally exposed in the floodlight of public opinion.

This article might sound anti-labor or anti-union; but basically we are not fighting the brotherhoods as such. What we are fighting is discrimination and jim-crow in the brotherhoods. Nobody recognizes more than the Negro firemen and brakemen how much the Big-four Brotherhoods have done generally to raise wages and improve working conditions on the railroads. What the Negro firemen and brakemen complain about is that the Big-four Brotherhoods raise wages and improve working conditions, then just as soon as the wages are raised and working conditions improved, they set about to limit or to completely eliminate the Negro from the road.

Origin of Brotherhood

The history of aggression of the Big-four Brotherhoods against the Negro firemen and brakemen goes way back. In every major war the United States has fought since railroading began the unions have put their prejudices over and above the national safety. The Brotherhood of Locomotive Engineers is the oldest of the big-four. It started under the name of the Brotherhood of the Footboard on the Michigan Central in 1863. Part of the reason was resentment against the Michigan Central's proposing to hire some Negro firemen during the manpower shortage caused by the Civil War.

In World War I the Baltimore & Ohio and the New York, New Haven & Hartford, which up to that time had hired only white firemen, proposed to hire some Negro firemen to tide them over the war emergency. Both the Grand Chief Engineer of the Brotherhood of Locomotive Engineers and the President of the Brotherhood of Locomotive Firemen & Enginemen instructed their members to refuse to work with Negro firemen on any railroad which up to the War had had a pure white firing force. The Brotherhood of Railroad Trainmen in its official journal in October, 1917, announced that its organization was in full accord with the Engineers and Firemen, and advised its membership to notify the President of the Brotherhood of Railroad Trainmen as soon as they received an intimation that any railroad was contemplating hiring Negroes for freight, yard or passenger service on jobs, theretofore held by white men.

In World War II the Brotherhood of Locomotive Firemen & Enginemen put out a strike ballot to prevent the hiring of additional Negro firemen on the Atlantic Coast Line where Negroes had been working as firemen ever since there had been an Atlantic Coast Line. Hundreds of white firemen had been hired by the Coast Line during World War II. But not a single Negro fireman had been hired by the Coast Line since 1929. Yet the Firemen's Brotherhood was willing to strike, without regard to its effect on the war effort, rather than let a single new Negro fireman be hired.

On the St. Louis-San Francisco Railroad not a Negro fireman or brakeman had been hired since 1928 due to a blanket agreement the four brotherhoods had forced the Frisco to sign under strike threat not to hire any more Negro firemen or brakemen. In 1944 after the Battle of the Bulge, when the United States was straining every nerve and sinew against Germany and Japan, the Frisco management approached the four brotherhoods to get their consent to hiring some Negro firemen and brakemen during the war emergency on the Southern Division from Memphis to Birmingham, where Negro firemen and brakemen had been working since 1894. All four brotherhoods replied that they were unalterably opposed to the hiring of a single Negro fireman or brakeman.

Negroes Not Wanted

Inch by inch, and yard by yard, down thru [sic] the years, the brotherhoods have been choking off the employment rights of Negro train and engine service employees. In 1890 the Trainmen, Conductors, Firemen and Switchmen's Mutual Aid Association demanded that all Negroes in the train, yard, and locomotive service of the Houston & Texas Central Railway System be removed and white men employed in their places. In 1898 the Trainmen tried to get all the Negro brakemen removed from the Missouri Pacific System. In 1899 the four brotherhoods had all the colored porters on the Gulf, Colorado and Santa Fe Railway passenger trains removed and replaced by white brakemen.

In 1908 the Brotherhood of Locomotive Engineers voted to organize the railway engineers in South America and sent a vice-president down for that purpose. In 1910 that officer reported back to the Engineers' convention that the reason he did not attempt to organize the railway engineers in Cuba was because there was no way of telling the "nigger" from the white man.

In 1909 the Firemen's Brotherhood staged a bitter and violent strike against Negro firemen on the Georgia Railroad, demanding white supremacy and the replacement of Negro firemen by whites. In 1910 the Trainmen and the Conductors negotiated what is called the Washington Agreement with most of the Southwest railroads providing that no more Negroes were to be employed as baggageman, flagman, or yard foreman; they followed up in 1911 by negotiating a similar agreement with some of the railroads in the Mississippi Valley.

In 1914 the four brotherhoods joined in a letter to Colonel Goethals of the Panama Canal demanding the removal of Negro engineers, firemen, conductors and brakemen from the railroads at the Panama Canal, stating that it was the policy of the four brotherhoods in the United States to oppose the use of Negroes as engineers, firemen, conductors, or brakemen on the railroads in the United States.

In 1919 while the railroads were under Federal Control in World War I the Brotherhood of Railroad Trainmen demanded of the United States Director General of Railroads that he guarantee the brotherhood a majority of men employed, so that contracts made by the brotherhood could be protected by the brotherhood. The Trainmen further notified the United States Southern Regional Director, Mr. Winchell, that it desired to negotiate an agreement which would thereafter prevent the employment of Negroes in train and yard service.

The list is too long for all the acts of aggression to be pointed out. We have already pointed out the attitudes of the brotherhoods in putting their prejudices above the national safety in World Wars I and II. We close this part of our survey by noting that in 1940 the Firemen's Brotherhood served a notice on the Southeastern carriers which if adopted would have driven every Negro fireman out of service within a year. Also in the 1940's the Brotherhood of Railroad Trainmen, facing losses of job for their members because of streamlined trains, diesel engines, and competition of bus and air lines, began raiding or trying to drive off all the Negro train porters who are really passenger brakemen on the head-end of the passenger trains and have them replaced by white brotherhood members. They have tried this on the Santa Fe, the M-K-T, the Frisco, the Missouri Pacific and other roads.

Negro Trainporter (Brakeman)

The story of the Negro trainporter is a story in itself and illustrates how the Negro has been exploited by railroad management as well as persecuted by white railroad labor which has refused to recognize the essential economic unity of interest between white and black workers in the same craft.

The Negro trainporter on the head-end of the passenger trains does all the braking work, and in addition handles mail, baggage, takes care of the passengers and sweeps out the coaches en route: but because he is black, the railroads classify him as a "porter" and refuse to pay him even a brakeman's pay. During World War I while the railroads were under federal control the Negro trainporter was actually classed as a passenger brakeman and paid standard brakeman's pay. But when the railroads were turned back to private ownership, the private management reclassified the Negro as a trainporter and cut his pay in half. The Negro is the only American railroad worker who the more he does the less he is paid.

Most people are familiar with the subterfuge the Pullman Company used to employ of sending a Pullman car out in charge of a Pullman porter, calling him "Porter-in-charge" in order to keep from recognizing him as a Pullman conductor and paying him a conductor's pay altho [sic] he did everything a Pullman conductor did.

Equally familiar is the subterfuge of the railroad companies in sending out dining cars in charge of waiters who do everything a steward does, but to keep from recognizing the waiter-in-charge as a steward and paying him steward's pay, the railroads call him "waiter-in-charge" and give him a pat on the head and a few pence in his palm. During the War the FEPC tried to find out the difference between a steward and a waiter-in-charge, and finally came to the conclusion that outside of recognition and pay the only difference was that the steward had a white face and black coat, while the waiter-in-charge had a black face and a white coat.

Hat in Hand

For a long time the Negro railway workers did not know their rights, did not know how to fight. They depended on making friends and being humble to management, as in the pitiful tragic letter of April 7, 1928, which the Negro brakemen wrote to the president and vice-president of the Frisco lines in 1928 when the four brotherhoods clubbed the Frisco into agreeing never to hire any more Negro firemen or brakemen:

Dear Sir:
   We the undersigned colored (freight) brakemen of the Tupelo and Birmingham Sub. Div. wish to petition your sovereignty by asking you farther privilige to meet you in a personal conference which is of a very serious nature and vital interest to us. Dear Mr. Kurn, we feel with all due respect to our superior officials that you are our only

refuge in this most (terrible) calamity that has happened in the history of this your magnificent rail road. Hoping you will give this your earliest attention. Yours truly.

> Limit Brown, Gen. Chr (man) 17 yrs. service
> Jim Judge, Local " (man) 13 yrs. service
> Abe Smith, Local " (man) 14 yrs. service

or in this follow-up letter of April, 1928:

Mr. J. E. Hutchinson. Vice President of St. L. and S.F. RR

Dear Sir:

We the undersigned colored freight brakemen are the humble and submissive voices of the colored brakemen of the Tupelo and Birmingham Sub. Div. wish to petition your *majesty* to meet you in a conference to ascertain why and what accusations you have against us and our posterity to cast us off in old age after serving you most faithfully for over a decade and almost half our lives.

Dear Mr. Hutchinson. If it be possible for us to remedy such an accusation we are more than willing to do all there is in our power to remove the obstacles which hinder the free and embarrassed actions of those about us, thanking you in advance for consideration you may give us, we beg to remain your servants for ever.

> Limit Brown, Gen. Chr., 17 yrs. service
> Abe Smith

Of course, Mr. Kurn and Mr. Hutchinson did absolutely nothing.

To bring the story to a close, about ten years ago two small Negro organizations of firemen and brakemen started to fight. It probably sounds like David and Goliath when one realizes that the Trainmen alone had 200,000 members while there were just 2,739 Negro brakemen, switchmen, and yardmen both in and out the two Negro organizations: 100,000 members in the Brotherhood of Locomotive Firemen & Enginemen while there were only 2,263 Negro firemen in the entire railroad industry: most of them unorganized.

There was no use in the Negro workers going to Congress and asking for remedial legislation. Congress, unfortunately, on most occasions shows itself more concerned with votes than principle. In addition the Negro firemen and brakemen were all in Southern states, and *Smith* v. *Allwright* had not been handed down ten years ago to crack the white primary. The only place the organizations could wage their fight was in the courts.

In Court

So the Association of Colored Railway Trainmen & Locomotive Firemen with headquarters in Roanoke, Virginia, and the International Association of Railway Employees with headquarters in Memphis started out. They have been joined by the Colored Trainmen of America from Kingsville, Texas. And recently five Negro railway labor unions: the Association of Colored Railway Employees, the Colored Trainmen of America, the Southern Association of Colored Railway Trainmen and Firemen from North Carolina, and the Dining Car and Railroad Food Workers Union of New York have joined hands and formed the Negro Railway Labor Executives Committee, which issues its own bimonthly bulletin to educate the Negro railroad workers as to their rights and to keep them advised of the cases which are being carried thru [*sic*] the courts.

In their first bulletin issued June, 1948 they stated:

> We Negro workers are no strangers, no newcomers to the industry. We were at work, firing and laying tracks, when the going was real rough, when railroading was still in its infancy.
>   . . . the first steam locomotive to run on U.S. tracks . . . was called the "Best Friend of Charleston" and in December 1830 first ran the six-mile stretch of the Charleston & Hamburg R.R. *The firemen on that first engine was a Negro fireman.* . . .

> Our fathers and grandfathers pioneered the industry.
> We will not be driven out more than 100 years later.

The Associaton of Colored Railway Trainmen & Locomotive Firemen and the International Association of Railway
Employees carried the Steele and Tunstall cases to the Supreme Court of the United States, which established the basic
principle that a majority union under the Railway Labor Act
cannot make contracts which discriminate against the non-
member minority workers (323 U.S. 192, 210). They are now
working on cases in the United States District Courts in the
District of Columbia, Louisville, Kentucky, and St. Louis,
Missouri, which, if won, will establish the principle that a
railroad union has no right to represent a non-member
minority worker unless it gives him the chance to elect the
officials who conduct the collective bargaining process, to
censure and remove them, as possessed by the union members. If these cases are won the jim-crow union membership
will be nothing but an empty shell.

In the federal courts in the District of Columbia and Louisville, Kentucky, the International Association of Railway
Employees has obtained injunctions against the Firemen's
Brotherhood putting forth proposals affecting Negro firemen's working conditions without first calling in the Negro
firemen and giving them an opportunity to be heard and to
vote on the propositions. Then, even if outvoted, we can still
fall back on the Steele and Tunstall cases which establish the
principle that the majority union cannot make a contract
which unfairly discriminates against the non-member minority workers.

In the federal court in St. Louis the Association of Colored
Railway Trainmen & Locomotive Firemen is conducting the
Tillman case against the four brotherhoods and the Frisco in
one lump trying to obtain a ruling that it violates the Railway
Labor Act, the Federal Civil Rights Act and the Constitution
of the United States for a railroad and a union to make a
contract not to hire any qualified worker on the irrelevant and

invidious distinctions of race, color, creed or national origin. That case is not over, but we are happy to report that on April 25, 1949, the Association forced the four brotherhoods to come into court and cancel the iniquitous contract of March 14, 1928, wherein they had forced the Frisco to agree never to hire any more Negro firemen or brakemen.

In Chicago the International is striking at the packed National Railroad Adjustment Board which has its First Division packed with representatives from the big-four brotherhoods, all of which exclude Negroes from membership. And credit is due to Richard R. Westbrooks of Chicago, representing the trainporters on the Santa Fe, who saved their jobs by an injunction against the Santa Fe and the Brotherhood of Railroad Trainmen against a decision of the packed First Division of the Adjustment Board giving the Santa Fe trainporters' jobs away to the white brotherhood brakemen.

The Negro railway labor organizations have now been battling ten years. They are prepared to battle ten or twenty years more, because what they are doing is basic to the whole concept of economic democracy. Every principle which they establish for railroads can be applied to every other public utility: gas, electricity, telephone and telegraph, bus lines and air lines, every industry affected with a public interest. As the Negro Railway Labor Executives Association announced: "Other [*sic*] fathers and grandfathers pioneered the railway industry, and we intend to hold this employment and broaden its base until every vestige of segregation and discrimination, and every limitation on a man's right to hold a job on the railroad based on race, creed, color or national origin, is wiped out. When we do this we shall have gained a victory not only for ourselves but we shall have gained a victory for the white railroad workers by freeing them from their prejudice and their fears: because they are imprisoned just as much as we are."

The ubiquitous governmental practice of using urban renewal programs to force blacks out of communities resulted in a reduction of the black percentage of the population in Hamtramck, Michigan, from 14.5 in 1960 to 8.5 in 1966. Appearing before Judge Damon J. Keith in the U.S. District Court for the Eastern District of Michigan, city and federal officials were ordered to cease that practice. Moreover, Judge Keith took the unprecedented step of ordering them to provide housing choices not only for persons who would be displaced in the future but also for those who had been displaced in the past. Judge Keith was educated at West Virginia State College and Howard University Law School.

URBAN RENEWAL/
NEGRO REMOVAL

(*Sarah Sims Garrett et al.* v. *City of Hamtramck* 355 F. Supp 16 [1971])

Damon J. Keith

... THE EXODUS of black residents from Hamtramck resulted primarily from urban renewal projects but had many supporting factors. Testimony at the trial reveals that strong racial prejudices exist within the defendant City making relocation of displaced blacks in the community a difficult if not sometimes impossible task. City officials had long been aware that, especially in urban renewal areas, if displaced blacks were to relocate within the City's boundary, they would find themselves living in slums or substandard housing. As a majority of the persons displaced by governmental projects was black, and in view of the discriminatory practices of residents within defendant City, it is readily apparent that the high proportion of blacks displaced by such projects would be forced to relocate outside the City's boundary. Few if any plans were made or implemented by city officials to correct a known unfair practice of discrimination by the white citizens toward the black citizens of the community.

To the contrary, it would appear that ever since the advent of renewal programs, defendant City has relied on a "planned program of population loss" and has had every reason to know and observe that the loss experienced was primarily in the number of black residents. Such a program was to be, and in part has been, accomplished through the demolition without replacement of low and moderate income dwelling units and the eventual conversion of land from residential to non-residential use. Throughout it all, federal urban renewal funds were utilized toward fulfillment of the City's program. Dwelling units serving the low-income citizens were demolished while there existed no scheduled replacement of new low-income dwellings. Considering that the areas of the City intended for renewal contained a majority of low-income black citizens, it appears that the population which the City planned to reduce was its Black population.

. . . Defendant City does not challenge the testimony that the condition of the houses occupied by black citizens in the area was not significantly different than [sic] that of houses occupied by the white citizens. Many, if not all, of the buildings in the area were deemed by the City to be structurally substandard to a degree requiring clearance. Nevertheless, the uncontradicted evidence is that the City proceeded to destroy the houses in which the black families were living before doing anything to the houses occupied by white persons in the area. Not only was there no relocation assistance afforded these black individuals, but in addition they were persuaded and even harassed to vacate their homes speedily and find other dwellings. Because of the discriminatory housing practices in the City, and the consistent failure and refusal by the City to afford adequate relocation assistance, the majority of black citizens relocated outside the City. Testimony shows that Hamtramck officials were well aware of the difficulties in relocating encountered by these black citizens, but ignored their requests for assistance, failed to investigate complaints and in no way compensated such displacees for the loss suffered. The evidence is that many displaced black citizens relocated in dwellings that were unsafe, unsanitary and for the most part uninhabitable.

To a large extent, then, the City has, by virtue of the "Smith-Clay Project," the Chrysler Expressway and the "Wyandotte Project" successfully implemented its planned population loss of black citizens. In those low-income areas still awaiting renewal, i.e., portions of the "Grand Haven-Dyar-Dequindre Area" and the "Denton-Miller Area," the City has knowingly permitted a decrease in City services and has actively encouraged the deterioration of the vicinity by dissuading citizens from making any improvements, by encouraging people to vacate the premises, by actively promoting industrialization of the area and by demolition of homes through strict enforcement of Building Code Regulations. Widespread oral and written notice from the City concerning the scheduled industrialization of the area has discouraged new small community type business in both of the areas mentioned and has accelerated the growing blighted condition of the vicinity to such an extent that rehabilitation of residential dwelling is now almost, if not totally, impossible. Slowly, the black inhabitants are finding it necessary to move out of the areas scheduled for renewal and because of the shortage of low-income housing within the boundaries of defendant City, coupled with the undenied racial discrimination in housing practices, those black persons who must move find themselves forced to relocate outside of the Hamtramck city limits.

. . . The evidence at the trial clearly indicated that as early as April, 1959, before the "Smith-Clay Area Project" was initiated, federal defendants had available to them reports from the defendant City which reports apprised that Hamtramck intended to reduce its population by massive elimination of residential structures; the reports further indicated that the elimination was to take place in predominately black areas of the City, and that the land vacated thereby was to be changed from residential to industrial uses without any planned replacement of the dwellings eliminated. It would seem, therefore, that federal defendants knew or should have known very early in the planning stage of the program that a substantial majority of the population removed by urban renewal activities would be black. Despite this information and knowledge and irrespective of the statutory obligations under which they function, the Department of Housing and Urban Development, through its officers, made no effort to prevent the "Negro removal" which the plans indicated would obviously result from the program. To the contrary, by the very funding of the "Smith-Clay Area Project" and the "Wyandotte Area Project" and by failure to insist upon and enforce adequate relocation of those black persons displaced, the Department of Housing and Urban Development, by its omissions, acquiesced in the City's program.

. . . Urban renewal is accomplished through federal means, and the federal government must take responsibility for the direction which the program takes. . . . If what has occurred in Hamtramck is ever to be stopped, responsibility must be placed at the source, that is, the Department of Housing and Urban Development which funds and administers the programs. . . .

. . . THEREFORE, IT IS ORDERED that the defendant City of Hamtramck and the defendant Department of Housing and Urban Development, in cooperation with the plaintiffs, present to this court within ninety (90) days from the date of this order a program designed to remedy the wrongs suffered by virtue of defendants' conduct. It is essential to this order that the remedy devised include an increase of low and moderate income housing for those black persons who have been and are scheduled to be displaced by renewal projects. Such a plan should encompass construction of new housing as well as a profound, meaningful, comprehensive and enforceable program to eliminate the existing discrimination in housing within the City so as to make available to black citizens those existing dwellings geared for low-income individuals. The plan should also provide for a sufficient number of units, either through construction of new homes or through the elimination of discriminatory real estate practices, so as to accomodate all those displaced, past and future. Along with the scheduled increase in housing, the plan should also provide a specific and scheduled program for the relocation of any additional persons displaced through code enforcement, renewal projects, or encroaching industry. Finally the plan must contain an acceptable time schedule in which all of the above is to be accomplished.

Although the plan to be submitted will pertain primarily to the land contained in the "Amended Wyandotte Area Project," it is not of necessity limited thereto. . . .

A classic case of labor-management collusion against black workers occurred at the Detroit Edison Company whose 10,630 employees in April, 1973, included 832 blacks. Statistics gathered a year earlier disclosed that in supervisory positions whites outnumbered blacks 1,099 to 12; in professional and technical jobs, 1,785 to 73. In 1970, blacks formed about 44 percent of Detroit's population and 18.2 percent of the metropolitan area population. The company and the unions, Local 17 of the International Brotherhood of Electrical Workers, AFL-CIO, and Local 223 of the Utility Workers of America, AFL-CIO, shared a reputation for discriminating against blacks. Their discriminatory practices involved exclusion of blacks from the collective bargaining process, reliance on nonjob-related tests as a condition of granting employment, word-of-mouth referrals to keep blacks uninformed about job openings, and use of subjective criteria to disqualify them in job interviews. The case came before Judge Damon J. Keith in the U.S. District Court for the Eastern District of Michigan. Judge Keith holds degrees from West Virginia State College and Howard University Law School.

LABOR-MANAGEMENT COLLUSION AGAINST BLACKS

(*Stamps* v. *Detroit Edison Co.*,
365 F. Supp 87 [1973])

Damon J. Keith

. . . IT IS unfortunate in the view of the Court, that the Company has consistently refused to admit, much less seek to remedy, that its employment practices perpetrate racial discrimination. Indeed, the Company at trial simply denied that it has ever engaged in racial discrimination in employment. . . .

. . . It is the conclusion of the Court, in light of the evidence adduced, that the Company is refusing to acknowledge the obvious and has therefore adopted an intractable position. Its denials of culpability only serve to indicate the myopia in the history of the Company with regard to its recognition and treatment of the ignoble disease of racial discrimination. . . .

. . . The long and short of the evidence with respect to the Defendant Unions is simply that the Unions have promoted the interests of its [sic] white members without regard to the interests of its [sic] black members, and have ignored the plight of the black members in gaining the equal employment opportunity that is their due under the Constitution and laws of the United States. Tragically, the Unions, which one would look to for leadership in improving the lot of this sector of the population, have instead become an obstacle to human progress to the point where the Court has reluctantly concluded that they are justifiably made defendants in this law suit.

The Constitutional provisions and statutes enacted by Congress on the subject of equal employment opportunity all find their objective in the brief and eloquent phrase of Thomas Jefferson in the Declaration of Independence:

> "We hold these truths to be self-evident, that all men are created equal, that they are endowed by their Creator with certain unalienable Rights, that among these are Life, Liberty and the Pursuit of Happiness."

In the modern industrial society which is the United States, and certainly in the modern industrial urban society which is Detroit, to be denied an equal chance at decent employment, and an equal chance at advancement within one's employment, is to be denied that equality so nobly articulated by Jefferson. It is in this context unthinkable that a person would be denied equal employment opportunities at the Detroit Edison Company when employment to a man means earning a living which will enable him to provide adequately for his family and provide a good education for his children. Being denied a job is demeaning to a person and strips him of his dignity and assurance. A person has a right to extend his God-given working abilities to their fullest without being encumbered by artificial, irrelevant, insignificant and superficial barriers, and reasons such as the color of his skin.

The Company and the Unions by their individual and collective actions are guilty of denying this fundamental equality to the members of the class who are the plaintiffs in this law suit, and the Court will accordingly move on to consider and put into effect suitable remedies.

. . . Therefore, it is hereby ordered, adjudged and decreed, as follows:

. . . The affected class for the purposes of the hiring and transfer provisions of this decree shall be deemed to consist of all black individuals who applied for employment with defendant Detroit Edison Company subsequent to July 2, 1965, and were rejected and black employees who would have applied but for defendant's discriminatory hiring policy and/or black employees who were hired prior to the date of the decree and who were actively employed at any time after July 2, 1965, and who were at any time regular employees in the job classifications referred to above as low opportunity jobs.

. . . All members of the affected class who were refused hire [*sic*] or who would have been refused hire [*sic*] at Detroit Edison Company between July 2, 1965, and the date of the decree shall be put on notice through newspaper and radio advertisements in the black media (which shall include but not be limited to the *Michigan Chronicle* and 1 black radio station and 1 black television station), the *Detroit News* and/or the *Detroit Free Press* regarding the content of this decree. Such notices shall run for at least 60 days. . . .

. . . At each location and in each department where a member of affected class is employed, the Company shall post vacancies for all jobs in all departments at least 20 days before such vacancies are to be filled. The Company shall also establish a procedure by which it shall receive bids for posted jobs in writing. No affected class member shall be required to hold a labor or helper job which does not provide training for craft jobs in a line of progression as a condition of progress into such a line of progression.

A member of the affected class may effectuate a single transfer with carry-over seniority rights and earnings retention to a new department within five years after the effective date of this decree unless the period is extended by the court. In the event that an affected class member who transfers chooses to return to his former department, or fails to perform the duties of his new department, within 90 days after his transfer, he may return to his former department without loss of seniority or benefits. . . .

. . . All members of the affected class shall be credited with their Company seniority as if it were that department or unit seniority in the department or unit to which they transfer pursuant to this decree or in departments or units to which they previousy transferred.

. . . At no time shall a member of the affected class who is transferred under this decree be paid a lower rate than the rate for the job for which he transferred.

. . . Subject to the availability of qualified applicants, the Company shall recruit and endeavor to hire black applicants for all positions within the Company on an accelerated basis with the goal of having a number of blacks employed by the Company at 30% of its total work force.

. . . In order to insure that the Company's policy of non-discriminatory hiring is communicated to minority groups, the Company shall establish contacts with high schools, technical schools and vocational schools and organizations which specialize in minority employment in the Detroit area and inform them of the employment opportunities available at Detroit Edison and of the Company's non-discriminatory hiring policy. . . .

. . . A committee will be established which will report to the Court on a bi-monthly basis for the duration of this decree which shall be six years. The committee shall be composed of representatives of defendants, the Association for the Betterment of Black Edison Employees and the Justice Department and a chairman to be appointed by the Court. . . .

. . . Defendants Detroit Edison Company and Local 223 shall pay plaintiffs punitive damages. Since those defendants have been extremely obdurate and intransigent their determination to implement and perpetuate racial discrimination in employment at Detroit Edison, the awarding of punitive damages is appropriate and necessary. The trial record indicates that these two defendants repeatedly and callously disregarded or rejected the numerous appeals of blacks who asked that Edison's hiring and promotion practices be reformed and that blacks be afforded fair representation by the unions. It is both commendable and remarkable that black workers at Detroit Edison so long persisted in seeking justice by means of persuasion in the face of the defendants' unwillingness to respond to reasonable expressions of concern by black workers, before resorting to this law suit. When a defendant's behavior is so extremely unreasonable and violative of the law as has been the behavior of two of the defendants in this case, one can only infer that the defendants have acted with malice. Therefore, this Court hereby orders defendant Detroit Edison Company to forthwith pay plaintiffs, including both those individually named as plaintiffs and those comprising the class represented by the named plaintiffs but excluding the United States, Four Million Dollars ($4,000,000.00). This Court hereby orders defendant Local 223 to forthwith pay plaintiffs, including both those individually named as plaintiffs and those comprising the class represented by the named plaintiffs but excluding the United States, Two Hundred Fifty Thousand Dollars ($250,000.00). The Court finds that although Local 17 has engaged in racial discrimination against blacks at Detroit Edison in its collective bargaining agreement, it has not acted with the requisite malice of the Company or Local 223; this Court will therefore not award punitive damages against Local 17. The punitive damages awarded in this case shall be paid to the Clerk of the U.S. District Court, and this Court shall issue a subsequent Order providing for the manner in which the money is to be disbursed to plaintiffs. . . .

At the hiring hall of local 542 of the International Union of Operating Engineers, AFL-CIO, in Philadelphia, white union members ganged up on two blacks, Marion J. Eaddy and John Dent, and the white union dispatcher and business agent, William Ciavaglia, made no attempt to prevent their beating the two men. Just over a week later, Eaddy, Dent, and Cleveland Allen, another black who was at the hiring hall, were set upon by a group of whites. Why the violence? Eaddy was a plaintiff in a suit that a group of blacks and the State of Pennsylvania had filed seven months earlier, accusing the union of having spent $1,200,000 in state and federal funds to train blacks as operators of heavy construction equipment and then having refused to place them on jobs. Judge A. Leon Higginbotham, Jr., concluded that union members had conspired to beat the blacks in order to convince them to drop the earlier suit. He heard the case in the U.S. District Court for the Eastern District of Pennsylvania. Judge Higginbotham was educated at Antioch College and Yale Law School.

LABOR UNION RACIAL VIOLENCE

(Commonwealth of Pennsylvania et al.
v. *Local Union No. 542, International*
Union of Operating Engineers et al.)

A. Leon Higginbotham, Jr.

. . . THE INSTANT petition for an injunction *pendente lite* and a protective order is directly related to the expansion of rights which were assured by Congress in Title VII (Equal Employment Opportunity) of the Civil Rights Act of 1964. . . . So far as the present emergency motion for an injunction *pendente lite*, the instant case is also a tragic reflection of a partial failure in the twentieth century to make real for all Americans the elusive rhetoric in the Declaration of Independence and the more precise rights guaranteed by the Civil Rights Acts of 1964 and 1972.

. . . As in most litigation, the instant case cannot be simplistically cast by a finding that only angels dwell on one side and only villains on the other. The reality and complexity of human affairs usually encompass a broader spectrum and mixture of characters who at various times ambivalently display qualities of good or evil. Thus, necessarily, several singular events must be broadly probed to ascertain their interrelationship with prior and subsequent acts. Through the testimony of witnesses, the panorama of this case is not one of only blacks on one side and whites on the other. This case has less of the continuous, brutal, racist conduct which was so often legendary in many of the classic southern civil rights cases of the 1960's. Instead, this matter has a northern syndrome where individuals have professed commitment to civil rights, but some (though by no means all) of their actions repudiate their rhetoric for equality.

. . . Thus, in the presence of the union's business agent, his assistant, a "C" branch agent, and twelve to fifteen union members, Dent and Eaddy were physically attacked and assaulted. . . . Dent also testified, and I find, that fifteen minutes prior to the assaults ". . . the guy who hit Eaddy with a chair [had been] inside Ciavaglia's office with another agent, business agent George Holland." . . . Mr. Ciavaglia denies that he knew or could identify the assailants; . . . he testified that he was shoved aside by someone "white" as Eaddy was hit with a chair. I do not find Ciavaglia's testimony credible that he did not know the assailant with whom he and Holland had been previously talking. Moreover, Ciavaglia testified that his office was usually locked and he did not allow anyone in the office except on "rare occasions." . . . I find that the men who attacked Eaddy and Dent were white operating engineers . . . and that the attack was not attributable to any improper or provoking conduct by either Eaddy or Dent. . . .

. . . The record conclusively establishes, and I find, that

Ciavaglia and Sautter (union officials) and other union members present rendered no assistance, aid, or help to Dent or Eaddy while they were being assaulted by white operating engineers. I find that Ciavaglia's and Sautter's refusal to render assistance to Eaddy and Dent was part of a conspiracy and plan to permit Eaddy to be attacked because he is a named plaintiff in [an earlier suit charging union discrimination] and to permit other blacks to be attacked when the latter support the named or class plaintiffs.

. . . Both Allen and Eaddy corroborate Dent's testimony. As Allen said, he was too far away to hear the conversation with Dent but "this white fellow, he hit Eaddy first. He attempted to but Eaddy blocked the punch.". . . The testimony of record is unchallenged that Dent, Eaddy and Allen were attacked without provocation by groups of white operating engineers . . . . Officer Felton Morrison of the Philadelphia Police Labor Unit also corroborated the testimony of Allen, Dent and Eaddy. . . .

. . . The major strategy of the Union's defense appears to be (1) the branding of Marion Eaddy as a black who hates whites and as one who constantly uses four-letter curse words, and (2) to argue that the violence was insignificant or almost nothing more than the fact that boys will be boys. . . .

. . . From some black union members who were called as defense witnesses, there is evidence that Mr. Eaddy has spoken to blacks about his antagonism for whites. But there is no evidence that Mr. Eaddy had expressed these racial invectives to whites. Of course, it is regrettable if, by the nature of his experience in life, Mr. Eaddy has developed a hatred for whites. But if, as Mr. Justice Frankfurter so often observed, ". . . there comes a point where this Court should not be ignorant as judges what we know as men," I must observe that regrettably there is much hatred in America, some Negroes hating whites and some whites hating Negroes. The history of the labor movement reveals that at various times racism was so institutionalized that Negroes were excluded from many unions. The history of the labor movement also shows that some unions have made major efforts to eradicate discrimination.

Racism and hatred of blacks has [*sic*] been pervasive in our national history. . . .

. . . As recently as 1968, a Presidential Commission, the National Advisory Commission on Civil Disorders, said:

> Discrimination and segregation have long permeated much of American life; they now threaten the future of every American.
>
> Segregation and poverty have created in the racial ghetto a destructive environment totally unknown to most white Americans.
>
> What white Americans have never fully understood— but what the Negro can never forget—is that white society is deeply implicated in the ghetto. White institutions created it, white institutions maintain it, and white society condones it.

. . . Since such a representative commission found that there was substantial division, polarization and racial hatred in America in 1968, I am not shocked if some men like Marion Eaddy in 1972 have some residuum of hatred. I deplore the hatred. . . . All of us—black and white—must join together to eradicate our legacy of yesterday's hatred to build a tomorrow of mutual dignity, respect and total justice. But on today's present record whether Eaddy has hatred for whites or whether some whites have hatred for blacks, the hatred *per se* is no basis for judicial intervention. It is only when, as here, that the hatred has been catapulted into actual repressive actions and violence that judicial intervention is required. Eaddy never took any repressive actions, provocative or physical, against any whites. He was blameless on June 19th and 20th. I find that the Union's defense as to Eaddy's hatred and vulgarity is irrelevant and specious. . . .

. . . According to the Union, these 40 or 50 white operating engineers suddenly arrived as a group at the request of a

Business Agent of Local 542, Mr. O'Donoghue, to receive assignments as marshals. . . .

It is not significant whether the men came originally to merely receive assignments as marshals or whether they came originally for the sole purpose of attacking black named and class plaintiffs. The relevant fact which I find is that at least after they arrived at the hiring hall, and probably before they arrived at the hiring hall, they had a "meeting of the minds" and an agreement to conspire to attack black named and class plaintiffs. The attack was a direct follow-up of the events which occurred on June 19, 1972; the attacks and conspiracy took place for the purpose to further intimidate Eaddy and any other blacks associated with or supportive of Eaddy in the litigation in issue.

. . . In a nation which has been so often rocked with violence, our challenge is to develop alternatives to violence. The most appropriate alternative is evolving rules of law where disputants seek to resolve their differences in court rather than to riot on the streets. Fortunately and appropriately, the black plaintiffs have chosen the non-violent method by pursuing their disputes in a federal court. However, if defendants' violence is not precluded by federal law, certainly some blacks who are named or class plaintiffs might feel uncertain about their future physical security if the federal courts are remediless [sic] to thwart that violence which is directed against federal litigants.

The issue cannot be relegated to the simplistic conclusion, in counsel's argument, that some blacks have confidence in the Union and that therefore there is no animosity against blacks. . . . From the time of slavery to the present, there have always been some blacks on each side of every racial issue, in fact, some blacks even owned slaves. Thus a judgment must be made on the totality of facts rather than whether some blacks are friends of the Union's distinguished counsel, or friends of the business agent.

. . . Every thoughtful study emphasizes our nation's burden to check that hate which is escalated to violence. Tragically here the Union not only failed to take an affirmative position to preclude the violence, but it was a part of the conspiracy to perpetuate it. As to the events of June 19th and 20th, "The mind of justice, not merely its eyes, would have to be blind to attribute such an occurrence to mere fortuity."

. . . During the last four decades the rights of labor and the power of the labor movement have been appropriately broadened beyond the restrictive parameters of earlier generations. By the laws and the Constitution of the United States the defendant union is not permitted to be a divisive and coercive force to retard blacks from also seeking an open society with the equal rights of other men.

The purposes of the early civil rights statutes and the Thirteenth, Fourteenth and Fifteenth Amendments to the Constitution were to make real to blacks the earlier "self evident truths" uttered in the Declaration of Independence. In the 1860's and early 1870's, Congress made indubitably clear their intent [sic] to eradicate racial injustice from the American scene. It is not too late in the corridors of history for a court to sanction defendant-labor union's attempt to turn back the swelling tides for that equal racial justice which the federal law demands.

. . . It is hereby ORDERED that the defendant, Local Union 542, its officers, agents, members, and others acting on its behalf or in concert with the foregoing are hereby ENJOINED and RESTRAINED, *pendente lite*, from at any place (whether on job sites, the union hall, public streets, or anywhere else) doing each and all of the following:

1. Threatening, intimidating, harassing, assaulting, injuring or otherwise interfering in any manner with the named and class plaintiffs' federal statutory and Constitutional rights to be free from retaliation because of their instituting and processing the instant employment discrimination lawsuit; and

2. Doing any and all other acts which in any manner interfere with named and class plaintiffs' federal statutory and

Constitutional rights to institute and process the instant employment discrimination lawsuit.

Note: The defendant union and the employers' associations in the above case filed motions with the district court asking that Judge Higginbotham be disqualified to sit as judge on the grounds that he is black, that on Friday, October 25, 1974, he addressed a meeting in Philadelphia of the Association for the Study of Afro-American Life and History, and that he has "a personal bias . . . in favor of the plaintiff class in the instant action." On December 4, 1974, Judge Higginbotham rejected the contention that he refrain from further participation in this case because of his race and color and in his opinion stated that the arguments for his disqualification were "as a matter of law, insufficient to justify my disqualification as judge in the instant action." On December 30, 1974, the U.S. Court of Appeals declined to modify Judge Higginbotham's opinion, and on June 2, 1975, the U.S. Supreme Court refused to grant certiorari for an appeal.

William H. Brown III, as chairman of the Equal Employment Opportunity Commission, gained experience that enables him to write authoritatively about genuine and false attempts to wipe out bias against minority groups and women in employment. As he sees it, the costs of bias include considerable waste of manpower and unnecessary stress on an economy that is already overburdened. In the context of job discrimination in general, he explains the events that culminated in the historic agreement that required the American Telephone and Telegraph Company to spend millions of dollars to compensate for past discrimination. Mr. Brown believes further progress will be made, provided business, labor, and the private bar help enforce the law against discrimination—and obey it themselves. An alumnus of Temple University and the University of Pennsylvania Law School, Mr. Brown is a partner in the law firm of Schnader, Harrison, Segal and Lewis in Philadelphia.

RITUAL AND REALITY IN EQUAL EMPLOYMENT

William H. Brown III

IT IS WELL KNOWN to everyone who has lived, or is living, in a ghetto or barrio and to every black, Spanish-surnamed individual, and other minority group member, no matter where they live, that regardless of how well qualified or well prepared they are, when they apply for a job or seek a promotion, there is a high possibility that they will confront racial discrimination. Sometimes it may not be overt—discrimination can be subtle and often not intentional—but it is discrimination nonetheless. And it is racial and sexual discrimination that is denying a basic right to millions of Americans—the right to earn a decent living. It is racial and sexual discrimination that is permitting a large reservoir of human resources to lie fallow and untapped. We are wasting a tremendous manpower pool and thus placing an unnecessary strain on an already-overtaxed economy.

The problem is circular because the same people who face discrimination and thus cannot earn a decent living are the very ones disadvantaged by inadequate education, filthy streets that never see a sanitation truck, and crime and drug addiction that are not just problems but everyday living conditions. These people, the minority groups of our cities, have nowhere to turn. Inside their community, there is poverty, disease, hopelessness. Outside, there are promises and pledges repeatedly broken.

To deal with problems of discrimination in employment, Title VII of the Civil Rights Acts of 1964 established the Equal Employment Opportunity Commission. The commission was empowered to accept charges of discrimination in employment based on race, color, religion, sex, or national origin, to investigate those charges, and, if discrimination had occurred, to attempt to reach an equitable conciliation between the charging party and the respondent. Until March, 1972, when the act was amended, if these efforts of conciliation failed—and they often did—all that could be done was for the commission to recommend a suit be filed by the Attorney General or to have the charging party institute suit on his own. The latter course placed the burden on the person least able to bear it—namely, the person who had been discriminated against. All this has been changed by the 1972 amendment. The effect of the change and what course of action the Equal Employment Opportunity Commission will take now that it has the right to go directly into federal court in the event conciliation fails will be discussed later.

In its very first year of operation the Equal Employment Opportunity Commission received more than 8,500 complaints of discrimination. It is expected that in the fiscal year ending June 30, 1974, the number of new incoming charges of discrimination will exceed 60,000. Since 1965 the commission has investigated and decided almost 100,000 charges and found discrimination to exist in 65 percent of those charges. There can only be one conclusion from these figures—that discrimination in employment is a reality—not a remote topic of some report to the President, but an everyday reality to tens of thousands of Americans. Discrimination is widespread; it is not confined to any geographic area. Discrimination is entrenched, enmeshed in the traditional functioning of our society. It permeates every class of employment, and no industry is exempt from responsibility. The great industries of this nation—the same corporations that developed the extraordinary technology that has taken man to the moon— the same industries are practicing discrimination, systematic, often unintentional discrimination 365 days a year.

We have stood by indolently and watched this happen far too long. We have dawdled and engaged in tokenism while a vast segment of our society wallowed in poverty and lost faith in our system. We watched horrified as some of those on whom we turned our backs dealt with the inequity in their own, often violent way.

We have already waited too long to end discrimination, waited too long to correct the mistakes of the past. And if we do not act now, we are going to find ourselves split into two separate and hateful societies—one white and one nonwhite.

Ending discrimination and providing equal employment opportunity—that is, the chance for all people to earn a decent living and work to their full abilities—are the keys to achieving a prosperous and truly democratic society. When the minority group members of our cities have decent jobs, they will also have the money to pay their full share of taxes, taxes that will go for better schools, for efficient mass transportation, for cleaner streets, for decent housing. More important, the sincere practice of equal opportunity in employment is needed to persuade the victims of past discrimination that the white community is now truly prepared to work toward and create an integrated society. Not integration on paper or in the lawbooks, but integration and equality in the streets, on the job, everywhere we live and work—in short, our entire environment.

Indeed, there has been a great deal of talk about the environment within the past few years. Talk about environment and ecology, the balance of living things in the environment. Although three or four years ago ecology was almost an unknown word to most Americans, it will probably be one of the keynotes of the seventies. Concern for the environment has centered on pollution of the air and water, mainly pollution by American industry, which has for years ignored warnings of the growing crisis.

Ecology, however, does not refer solely to our physical surroundings; it applies also to the balance of our social environment—how the benefits and opportunities of society are distributed among people. This ecology, the ecology of humanity, shows great imbalance indeed. Just as pollution of the air and water has upset the balance in nature and threatened man with disease, so too, does the imbalance in society threaten the welfare and safety of all Americans.

Daniel P. Moynihan, ambassador to India and former chief of the President's Council for Urban Affairs, has declared: "Poverty and social isolation of minority groups in central cities is the single most serious problem of the American city today." Minority group people—blacks, Spanish-surnamed Americans, Orientals, and native Americans (American Indians)—live in a separate America, isolated socially and economically from the general well-being of the nation. All too familiar statistics tell the story: The black unemployment rate is twice that of the rate for whites, and even higher in slum areas. The unemployment rate for black teenagers (sixteen to nineteen) in both poverty and urban neighborhoods was more than double the rate for whites. The median family income for blacks is lessthan two-thirds the corresponding amount for whites.

Contrary to popular belief, the gap is not narrowing; in many ways it is widening. The same forces of technology and industry which have created economic prosperity are at the same time responsible for driving deeper social and economic wedges among different groups in our society.

The same great American industries which have polluted our air and water and endangered our physical environment have also polluted our social environment by exacerbating the gulf between the disadvantaged and the rest of America. When left unchecked, this form of social imbalance tends to intensify, rather than seek an equilibrium. As Moynihan phrased it, "Economic and social forces in urban areas are not self-balancing. Imbalances in industry, transportation, housing , social services and similar elements of urban life tend to become more rather than less pronounced."

EEOC

In March 1972, the Equal Employment Opportunity Commission was granted the right to go into the federal district courts with its own attorneys in the event discrimination was found and conciliation efforts failed. The greatest deficiency in the original act was a lack of enforcement powers. The battle to secure enforcement powers for EEOC was waged each session of the Congress with the bill passed in the Second Session of the Ninety-second Congress and signed into law by President Nixon on March 24, 1972. By the 1972 amendment the Congress heartily reaffirmed the commission's responsibility to eliminate employment discrimination in this country. More important, it finally placed in the hands of the commission the mechanism to compel compliance. Five years on the commission have taught me voluntary compliance does not work.

The amendments of 1972 greatly expanded and broadened the coverage and authority of Title VII of the 1964 Civil Rights Act. As with any new law, there was, and to some extent continues to be, an initial period during which many questions needed to be resolved. During the past two years, several specific questions have been put to the commission regarding what the law says and particularly where it and the courts intend to go.

I, of course, cannot speak for the federal bench, but there is one thing that should be made clear—namely, that these amendments in no way alter the substantive law of Title VII which has been developed by the courts and by the commission over the last several years. Indeed, the new law clearly represented Congressional reaffirmation of the law as it had been developed. Given this Congressional support, the Equal Employment Opportunity Commission has used, and will continue to use, its new enforcement authority to its fullest and most effective extent. Because we have labored so long under the handicap of no real enforcement authority, there is a lot of catching up to do.

Since the passage of the amendments more than two years ago, many people have wondered what can be expected of the EEOC over the next several years. Because we now appreciate that discrimination is less an isolated event than business systems reinforcing a history of unequal opportunity, the agency will be directing its efforts toward altering those systems. This means that it will be concentrating on class actions, which almost all employment discrimination complaints are by their very nature, and on pattern or practice suits. It means that EEOC will be initiating inquiry where it has reason to believe there are problems, as well as investigating the many complaints which it receives. It also means that the remedies sought will be those sufficient to compensate for past injury as well as to avoid future damage.

Since the date of the amendment, the commission has authorized the filing of more than 275 lawsuits in every geographic area of the country against employers large and small, against labor unions on each of the proscribed bases of discrimination. The full staffing of the Office of General Counsel was undertaken immediately after the passage of the new legislation. During fiscal year 1973, which ended on June 30, 1973, the size of the General Counsel staff increased from about 50 to more than 450 people. The number of attorneys rose from 30 to more than 240, with an additional 40 to 50 to be added in the current year. Litigating centers were established in Philadelphia, Atlanta, Chicago, Denver, and San Francisco. Extensive training was immediately begun for new lawyers as well as paralegals. Restructuring of both the General Counsel Office and the compliance arm of the commission was quickly completed. New procedures were designed, tested, and adopted.

No one can reasonably expect that discrimination will now miraculously disappear simply because the EEOC will bring the full weight of the federal courts to bear on the issue. Business and labor leaders, state and local governments, and educational institutions, as well as the private bar, have to make themselves aware of the law and commit themselves to obeying and enforcing it in their own activities. The demise of employment discrimination in this country will be neither easy nor graceful. The one great void in our society today is that men know what is right but fail to show the necessary courage in pursuing that which is right.

Remedial Treatment

For many years, discrimination has been the norm of American life. The continuation of this norm is found in an assertion prevalent among employers, labor leaders, state and local officials, and educators. The assertion is that qualified minorities and women cannot be found. One of my primary missions as chairman of the EEOC was to put to rest once and for all the myth that qualified workers from minority groups and women are in short supply. There are more than 25,000,000 blacks alone in the United States. This is more than the total population of many European countries— countries that have armies, air forces, school systems, and even representation in the United Nations. Who would dare say that these countries lack qualified people to carry out all the substantial tasks necessary for the running of a gov-

ernment and the production of goods and services necessary
to maintain the economy of those countries?

Qualified minority applicants are being found and hired
every day—from predominantly black campuses and from
urban universities with high concentrations of minority students, from urban high schools and community centers, from
state and local governments. They are being found and hired
at all job levels by those firms truly committed to equal opportunity. They are being ignored or screened out or underutilized by hundreds, indeed, thousands of other firms
because of bias, inefficiency, ignorance, and lack of concern
and initiative.

The concern of the commission, while acknowledging good
intentions, is oriented toward results. The federal courts have
also indicated that it is the consequences of the employer's act
that is important. The United States Supreme Court, speaking through Mr. Chief Justice Burger, in the case of *Griggs* v.
Duke Power Company, 401 U.S. 424 (1971), affirmed this. It
should be noted that the decision was unanimous with Mr.
Justice Brennan not participating. The Court said:

> . . . What is required by Congress is the removal of artifi-
> cial, arbitrary and unnecessary barriers to employment
> when those barriers operate invidiously to discriminate on
> the basis of racial or other impermissible classifications.
> . . . The Act proscribes not only overt discrimination but
> also practices that are fair in form, but discriminatory in
> operation. The touchstone is business necessity. If an em-
> ployment practice which operates to exclude Negroes can-
> not be shown to be related to job performance, the practice
> is prohibited.
> . . . good intent or absence of discriminatory intent does
> not redeem employment procedures or testing mech-
> anisms that operate as "built-in headwinds" for minority
> groups and are unrelated to measuring job capability.
> The company's lack of discriminatory intent is suggested
> by special efforts to help the undereducated employees

through Company financing of two-thirds the cost of tui-
tion for high school training. But Congress directed the
thrust of the Act to the *consequences* of employment practices, not simply the motivation. . . . [Emphasis by the
Court.]

The Fifth Circuit Court of Appeals states it even stronger.
In the case of *Rowe* v. *General Motors Corporation*, 457 F. 2d 348
(1972), the court found that the defendant had an affirmative
policy of nondiscrimination which the court found "commendable." Still the court explained:

> . . . the problem is not whether the employer has willing-
> ly—yea, even enthusiastically—taken steps to eliminate
> what it recognizes to be traces or consequences of its prior
> pre-Act segregation practices. Rather, the question is
> whether on this record—and despite the efforts towards
> conscientious fulfillment—the employer still has practices
> which violate the Act. In this sense, the question is whether
> the employer has done enough.

It seems to me that the courts are saying the test is what are
the objective social consequences of what you, Mr. Employer,
are doing. What is being seen today is a new judicial perception of race and sex discrimination—a judicial perception
which says you can't substitute the ritual for the reality. In
effect, Title VII of the Civil Rights Act of 1964 has transferred
a negative duty—*i.e.,* thou shall not discriminate—into an
affirmative obligation—thou shall take whatever steps necessary to achieve the intent of Congress.

In dealing with the question of remedies for discriminatory
conduct, much has been said about quotas, preferential hiring, and reverse discrimination. If discrimination is found to
exist, what will the unions, universities, and private employers
be required to do? The answer is to eliminate it, all of it, make
certain it won't return, and develop a remedy for those who
have been victims. Race-conscious injuries require race-
conscious remedies. This has been clearly spelled out by the

United States District Court for the Western District of
Pennsylvania in the case of *Erie Human Relations Commission* v.
Tullio, 6 FEP Cases 733 (W.D. Pa. 1973) in which the court
stated:

> The quota system has been called "reverse discrimina-
> tion" and it may be properly so labeled. Like the infections
> in the human body which are cured by injections of the
> same poison, the antitoxin of reverse discrimination is a
> recognized judicial remedy for the toxin of discrimination.
>
> There is a compelling public interest in preventing the
> perpetration of discrimination or undoing the effects of
> past discrimination. . . the consideration of a racial quota
> in making appointments to the Police Department is not a
> form of invidious discrimination since the goal of this pol-
> icy is not to promote segregation but rather to achieve
> integration.

In the Alabama highway patrol case, the court ordered that
50 percent of those hired be black until such time as 25
percent of those in the training course were black. The court
required aggregating existing registers and waiting lists, if
necessary, to reach this remedial goal and further ordered
affirmative recruitment efforts, including "regular recruitment visits to predominantly Negro schools." A similar
decision requiring numerical remedies has been required by
the courts in dealing with the Minneapolis Fire Department
and a number of other employers.

Many newspaper stories concerning statements of government officials and others have led some public commentators
to ask whether there has been a change in the policy of the
federal government or the EEOC in requiring this type of
remedy for employment discrimination. Regardless of any
interpretation which may have been placed on certain
developments by the press and others, there is no change in
the policy of the federal government or the EEOC concerning
appropriate remedies for the elimination of discrimination in
employment. These remedies are based on the statutory duty

of the EEOC to identify and eliminate discrimination in employment. We are not concerned with "quotas" or "preferential treatment" in the abstract where there is no discrimination.

What does concern those at EEOC and throughout the federal government is the legal obligation to eliminate all discrimination. Sometimes the action taken to eliminate discrimination may be voluntary, if an employer conducts a comprehensive self-audit and determines that certain action is necessary to bring its operations into compliance with the law. For example, many employers have made such audits, concluded that certain practices had a discriminatory effect, and developed good remedial programs. More often, such action is necessary in the context of an enforcement or compliance procedure before an administrative agency such as EEOC. In either case, the standard of remedy must be consistent with those required by the courts.

The Supreme Court has given us a great deal of guidance regarding a standard of remedy, and has made clear the distinction between preferential treatment, as some might call it, and remedial treatment which is necessary to eliminate discrimination. In the case of *Swann* v. *Charlotte-Mecklenberg Board of Education*, 402 U.S. 1 (1971), the Court spoke directly to the issue in pointing out that if all things were equal, certain remedial practices might not be necessary or appropriate. All things, however, are not equal where segregation or discrimination has existed. The remedy for such discrimination may be "awkward, inconvenient, and even bizarre in some situations and may impose burdens on some; but all awkwardness and inconvenience cannot be avoided in the interim period when remedial adjustments are being made to eliminate the [discrimination or segregation]."

Among the cases which the Supreme Court discussed was the case of *United States* v. *The Montgomery Board of Education*, 395 U.S. 225 (1970), in which the district court had set a remedy requiring a specific racial ratio in faculty assignments and the court of appeals had changed this part of the remedy. The Supreme Court reversed the court of appeals' decision and reinstituted the numerical remedy. It specifically permitted the use of a mathematical ratio as a starting point in the process of shaping a remedy. The Supreme Court pointed out: "Awareness of the racial composition of the whole school system is likely to be a useful starting point in shaping a remedy to correct past . . . 'discriminatory practice.' "

Careful reading of the Supreme Court decision makes it clear that where discrimination exists, it must be entirely eliminated and the remedy adopted must be appropriate to such elimination.

The use of what, I believe, may appropriately be called numerical remedies was clearly endorsed by the Supreme Court in this case. Such terms as "quotas" and "preferential treatment" and "discrimination in reverse" have had many meanings to many different people and have unfortunate connotations. The important thing to the EEOC and the federal courts is that where discrimination exists it must be eliminated and where such elimination requires the numerical remedy, it is part of the policy of the commission to obtain the remedy that has been approved by the Supreme Court.

Many well-meaning people believe that what is required under Title VII is a color-blind application of the act. This obviously means that even where discrimination is found to exist, we could not correct the past unlawful practices. An employer found to have violated Title VII by not employing blacks in other than laboring jobs would not be required consciously to recruit blacks as professionals, sales workers, managers, etc.

Much public controversy has developed in this area because most people are not aware of current legal definitions of discrimination established by the courts and followed by the EEOC in its case-processing activity. Thus, much of the action, including the requirement of a "numerical remedy" necessary to eliminate discrimination in employment, appears harsh to those who do not understand the law or who do not realize that discrimination is defined as more than just plain evil intent or unequal treatment. But even if they do not understand the legal definition of discrimination, they certainly can understand the words of the Supreme Court that "all things are not equal" where discrimination exists.

AT&T Case

In the past three years, the EEOC has taken new bold steps to resolve complaints of discrimination in employment. The plan of the commission was to achieve two basic goals:

1. To obtain adequate relief for all parties filing meritorious charges under Title VII.

2. To identify and eliminate systematic discriminatory practices from the manpower systems of private employers, unions and employment agencies, and, now under the 1972 amendment, state and local governments as well as educational institutions.

For these reasons, the EEOC in December, 1970, embarked on its most ambitious undertaking. In a petition filed with the Federal Communications Commission (FCC), it asked that the American Telephone and Telegraph Company's request for a rate increase in the long lines division be denied on the grounds that the company had discriminated against women and minorities. Preliminary studies conducted by the EEOC had shown that a substantial number of charges backlogged in the EEOC were against the Bell System and its twenty-two operating companies. These charges represented 6 to 7 percent of all charges pending before the EEOC at that time.

It was apparent that the EEOC could not handle this burgeoning workload with its limited resources unless a new approach was taken. What we were attempting to do, of course, was to develop a resource allocation strategy in this matter which would improve the EEOC's effectiveness. In business terms, we aimed to increase our return on investment by concentrating resources where there was the most potential for payoff. The plan also hoped to achieve one added objective: to serve as a warning light to other major employers with a large number of unresolved charges. It was hoped that this case would cause other employers to begin a critical self-audit and take steps on their own to correct deficiencies leading to discriminatory employment practices.

Utilities by their nature tend to be monopolies, and they are therefore required to operate in the "public interest." Operating in the "public interest," reasoned the EEOC, meant obeying all the laws of the United States, of which Title VII was certainly an important one.

After the initial filing, the FCC decided that it was not proper for the question of discrimination to be raised in the rate hearings since there was no relationship shown between the alleged discriminatory practices and the rate structure. It was decided, however, that the EEOC did raise substantial questions of whether or not the phone company had violated the FCC's own regulations against discrimination in employment. The FCC ordered a separate hearing before an administrative trial judge on the issue of discrimination within the Bell System. The EEOC then demanded and, beginning in the spring of 1971, received from the company various documents, letters, rules, and regulations for the Bell System. In all, the company provided 100,000 pages of information.

A task force was established reporting directly to the chairman of the commission. This group's sole responsibility was to receive, make copies of all documents, analyze, index, and prepare summaries of all the information secured as a result of the demand. The EEOC prepared and submitted to the hearing examiner a very comprehensive statement of the case which clearly substantiated the charges of discrimination against the headquarters unit of AT&T and the twenty-two operating companies.

The actual hearing on this matter began in January, 1972, before an administrative trial judge assigned by the FCC. The EEOC's complete case was presented to the administrative judge, in the form of both written documents and direct testimony by the many witnesses called on behalf of the commission. At the conclusion of the commission's case, the company was given an opportunity to summarize the evidence it intended to present. It became obvious to the representatives of EEOC and the Bell System that the total process would be very time-consuming and, of course, quite expensive. Because of this, negotiations were quietly begun between myself as chairman of the EEOC and Mr. Robert Lilly, president of AT&T, during the summer of 1972.

Throughout these negotiations the commission and the company sincerely explored every possible avenue of agreement. Hundreds of hours of negotiations were spent trying to resolve on an amicable basis the differences between the parties. During the course of these negotiations, the General Services Administration of the federal government accepted an affirmative action plan proposed by the company but rejected by the EEOC. Because of the possible conflict between two federal agencies on this matter, the Office of Federal Contract Compliance of the Department of Labor required that the negotiations, which had been taking place between the GSA and the company, be transferred to the Department of Labor. And so it was that late in the negotiations the Department of Labor began to participate in the settlement discussions. Throughout all the legal proceedings, as well as the negotiations, substantial support and aid were rendered by the FCC. It was because of this aid and support, as well as the conscious attempt to resolve the matter on an amicable basis, that on January 18, 1973, a historic agreement was signed between AT&T, EEOC, and the Department of Labor. It should also be noted that the Department of Justice was a party to this agreement since it represented the Department of Labor at the consent hearing, the EEOC by this time having the authority to represent itself in court.

The consent agreement provided for some $15,000,000 in back pay to minorities and women found to have been denied employment or promotional opportunities owing to their race, sex, or national origin. In addition thereto, it was estimated that some $23,000,000 additional would be required in the form of higher pay after the minorities and women had secured promotions or had been permitted into lines of progression previously denied to them. This latter figure has proved to be a substantial underestimation since the figure supplied by the company and verified by the commission indicates that the new salary scales will represent an increase of some $35,000,000 or $36,000,000. Moreover, during the balance of the agreement, which covers a four-year period, it is estimated that minorities and women will be receiving some $30,000,000 to $35,000,000 additional salary.

In addition to the very substantial back pay awards, as well as the other increases in salary benefits to minorities and women, the agreement changes many of the systemic problems within the Bell System. New procedures were designed and are presently in effect for the hiring of employees, the promotion of employees, and the assignment of employees to various jobs. It is my sincere belief that the company showed tremendous corporate responsibility in agreeing to the terms and conditions of the settlement.

After the actual signing of the agreement, of course, the hard work really began. AT&T and the EEOC established a task force to work together to make certain that the agreement was in fact implemented. This task force traveled around the country visiting all the various operating Bell companies, explaining the terms and conditions of the settlement as well as identifying those people who were to receive back pay, and discussing the new opportunities for promotion with minorities and women. Having had the opportunity to review the effectiveness of the agreement for over a year, I believe that not only was this a landmark agreement, but the implementation of this agreement has far exceeded even the most optimistic expectations.

The most significant concept of the agreement was the concept of delayed restitution. In the attempt to determine who was entitled to back pay, a major stumbling block was encountered. It was extremely difficult to determine who would be entitled to back pay awards or promotions since a significant number of those people covered under the agreement had never applied for other positions and had been turned down. The feeling on the part of many women and minorities was that the act of applying for other positions would be a futile one since the history of the company had shown women and minorities were basically congregated in only certain job classifications. The company and the commission, therefore, agreed to the concept of delayed restitution. It was agreed that notice would be given to all the affected Bell employees, who would then be afforded an opportunity to bid on jobs they felt were previously denied to them. Any employee having two years of service with the Bell System would be eligible to bid into new lines of progression and job categories. If they remained on the new job for a period of six months, they then would be entitled to the back awards, as well as continue with the higher salaries afforded them in the new position. This system has appeared to work much better than anticipated; thus, the increase of payments made to people transferring under the agreement from an estimated total in the first year of $23,000,000 to $36,000,000.

Goals and timetables were established for the headquarters units, as well as all the twenty-two operating Bell companies. While the agreement did not require the company to eliminate the various tests which had been in use, it did provide that the company could not use as an excuse for failure to meet their goals and timetables the failure on the part of minorities to pass the various examinations. The agreement, of course, also provided that any employee who had filed a charge of discrimination against the company could opt not to be bound by the terms and conditions of this agreement, in which case he or she was at liberty to press his or her own complaints through the commission and, indeed, into the federal courts. The desire on the part of the company to make certain that this agreement does in fact work has been outstanding.

Perhaps the greatest fallout benefit of this agreement has been the ripple effect on other major employers and labor unions—ripples which have gradually built into giant waves.

Major employers quickly began to recognize that the EEOC was indeed a force to be reckoned with. The shock waves from this agreement reverberated throughout the business communities of the country. The EEOC, which just a few short years before had been treated with disdain by the major employers and labor unions of this country, had truly come into its own. The paper tiger now had flesh and blood, sinew and muscle. The quiet meow was now transformed into a powerful roar by the substantial enforcement powers granted to the commission in March, 1972. No longer could the respondents ignore the commission's request to conciliate after finding that discrimination in fact existed.

The commission was flooded with requests for copies of the AT&T agreement. The requests for officials of the commission, as well as officials of the phone company, to discuss this settlement and implications of the settlement were almost overwhelming. Employers began to review their responsibilities under Title VII in a different light—a light made uncompromisingly harsh by the threat of substantial back pay awards being demanded by the commission and, indeed, enforced by the courts. Even now, it is too early to realize the total effect of the AT&T settlement on the economy of this country. Indeed, it may be even impossible for us to measure with precision the thousands, even millions, of minorities and women who are now being promoted and hired into positions previously denied them because of this one settlement.

By reason of this settlement, a sense of pride seemed to swell in the hearts of every employee of the EEOC—a sense of pride based on the realization that this commission had indeed come of age, a sense of pride which seemed, at least for the moment, to wipe away the years of frustration and disappointment at seeing so little being done to really achieve equal employment opportunity for all persons.

Conclusion

I believe that there is going to be real progress against

discrimination in the next few years. But government can't do the job alone. *As noted above, business and labor leaders, and the private bar, have to make themselves aware of the law and commit themselves to obeying and enforcing it in their own activities.* Our cities are entrapped in a quagmire of disease, corruption, filth, second-rate education and transportation, and every one of these tragedies is partly the result of and reinforced by the specter of discrimination.

The problem we face today is fundamentally unchanged from the one we faced twenty or thirty years ago. Discrimination comes in different forms today and wears different disguises, but it remains as humanly denigrating and economically costly as ever.

In 1944, after studying the problems of the blacks in America, sociologist Gunnar Myrdal set out for this country the same goal we are seeking today. In his treatise, *The American Dilemma*, Myrdal declared:

> The Negro problem is not only America's greatest failure, but is also America's incomparably great opportunity for the future. If America should follow its now deepest convictions, its well being at home would be increased directly. At the same time, America's prestige and power abroad would rise immensely. The century old dream of American patriots, that America should give to the entire world its own freedom and its own faith, would come true. America can demonstrate that justice, equality, and cooperation are possible between white and colored people.

Our attempts at resolving these problems cannot stop at attending luncheons and dinners or applauding speakers or reading articles about discrimination. We cannot—particularly those of you who are white cannot—sit in the exclusive environment of our offices and homes contemplating the abstract concept of "equal employment opportunity" and in good conscience believe that we are doing anything effective.

All of us have a vital role to play: in providing to companies impetus where prodding seems necessary; ideas where these are lacking; and special insights wherever these will help.

A company that really wants to do something to improve its employment of minorities and women faces the fact that the goal, after all, is to end up with a substantial number of minority-group people and women on the payroll, not just a record of trying.

Judge Howard E. Bell's article about landlord-tenant conflict in New York City points up the unfairness of the enforcement of law in a critical aspect of urban life—and misery. Lawyers and laymen alike will profit by his cogent explanation of proceedings that, ostensibly at least, are intended to resolve disputes that bring people daily in droves into court. Judge Bell, who holds degrees from Virginia Union University and Brooklyn Law School, is assigned to the Civil Court of the City of New York.

LANDLORDS AND TENANTS IN NEW YORK CITY

Howard E. Bell

Introduction

ANY DOGMATIC answer given to the logical question of what causes tensions to run so high between landlord and tenant litigants would be pure speculation on my part. There are those who contend that there is a "desperate shortage of housing" in the City of New York and that the landlords have taken advantage of it by refusing to provide the tenants, in many instances, with the minimum services required for the habitation of a dwelling unit, while demanding maximum rentals for those units. Thus, they claim, the tenant looks upon the landlord with suspicion and hostility. On the other hand, there are those who assert that rent control has been a noose around the neck of the New York City property owner and has been the direct cause of the deterioration and abandonment of tens of thousands of apartments.

Commenting on the effects of rent control on housing in the City of New York, Dr. Frank Kristof, director, Division of Economics and Housing Finance of the Urban Development Corporation (a New York State Agency), states:

The economic arithmetic of rent control is simple. It has provided the greatest transfer of income in American economic history to rent control tenants from landlords, from tenants in the free markets, and from the city. The political arithmetic of rent control is even simpler. Two thirds of the city's renters live in rent control housing—a fact that no individual in public life who values his political existence can ignore. The irrationality of housing policy decisions that have emerged from the political facts of rent control have their counterparts in other areas of economic policy influenced by public intervention—for example, national agricultural policy where benefit payments every year are aiding fewer and fewer needy small farmers and more and more profitable corporate entities. But public intervention on behalf of a majority of the population seldom has had such a long-run adverse influence on the welfare of the entire community as rent control seems to be having on the city's housing stock. Only after a quarter of a century are we able to begin to measure the extent of deterioration and housing loss attributable to this phenomenon. Even though rent control today provides predominantly reasonable-cost housing to the elderly, poor and low-income Negro and Puerto Rican families of the city, the price being paid in the form of deterioration and abandonment clearly is proving too high.

Dr. Kristof also argues that the exodus of between 100,000 to 120,000 whites annually from the city has made available 30,000 to 35,000 standard rent-controlled apartments to blacks and Puerto Ricans and permitted them to shift out of overcrowded rooming houses and single-room-occupancy-type units into apartments all over the city. Since Dr. Kristof's article was written, the law has been amended for the purpose of decontrolling all housing accommodations which became vacant on or after June 30, 1971, as the result of the tenant's voluntarily surrendering the premises. Thereafter the property owner is permitted to charge the incoming tenant any amount that he chooses for the accommodations.
Since the enactment of the Vacancy De-control Law many

tenants have complained about harassment by their landlords who want to force them to move from their apartments. The city's rent and housing maintenance commissioner recently levied what he called a "record package of fines" totaling $39,600 on seven landlords in four separate cases of alleged tenant harassment. He also indicated that he would turn the matter over to the district attorneys of New York and Kings Counties for possible further prosecution.

RENT CONTROL IN NEW YORK CITY

Rent control of one form or another of housing accommodations as compared to commercial properties (which have been decontrolled and will not be discussed) has been in effect continuously since the 1940's. It began under federal controls. When these were lifted, state controls were imposed and on May 1, 1962, city controls became effective under the City Rent and Rehabilitation Law.

During the latter part of 1968 there appeared to be a rising public indignation over the excessive rent increases demanded by owners of decontrolled housing accommodations. These were generally housing accommodations that were not subject to the provisions of the City Rent and Rehabilitation Law because they had been constructed since February 1, 1947, or were decontrolled because of monthly rental on April 1, 1960, of $250 or more, or for other reasons. Responding to the public indignation, the mayor appointed a committee to investigate the spiraling rent increases. After having received the committee's report, the mayor called a press conference on February 8, 1969. He said that he had given the real estate industry the option of rolling back the excessive rent increases and producing a plan of self-control within twenty-one days or having that accomplished by law (there was an extension of the twenty-one-day period). He also asked the industry to freeze rents during the twenty-one-day period. From this background emerged the Rent Stabilization

Law of 1969, which became effective on April 6 of that year. The law provides that it shall expire on April 1, 1974, unless rent control shall sooner terminate under the City Rent and Rehabilitation Law.

Approximately 1,000,000 housing accommodations in the city are subject to control under the provisions of the New York City Rent and Rehabilitation Law, and approximately 300,000 housing accommodations are subject to control under the provisions of the Rent Stabilization Law. Basically, so long as a tenant whose accommodations are subject to control under either of the programs pays the prescribed rent he cannot be evicted. There are a number of exceptions, which need not be enumerated here. The housing accommodations that are subject to control under the Rent Stabilization Law generally are in buildings that were constructed between five and twenty-five years ago. The owners of these accommodations do not have the severe maintenance problems that confront the owners of the much older accommodations that are subject to control under the City Rent and Rehabilitation Law. Many of the latter buildings are between seventy-five and one hundred years old and they are probably best described in a recent commercial that was on the air. A man was asked if he lived on 125th Street, which is in the heart of Harlem, and he answered yes. He was then asked when was the building in which he lived built. His response was: "It was built when you had to swim across the Hudson River to get to New Jersey."

Tenants of the latter buildings will complain to the supervising agency of broken plaster in their apartments through which rats enter, while tenants of the former buildings will complain to the agency that the doorman was not on duty at a certain hour or that there is something wrong with the swimming pool, air conditioners, or elevators.

Most of the housing accommodations that are covered by the City Rent and Rehabilitation Law are occupied by blacks, Puerto Ricans, and poor whites, whereas most of the housing accommodations that are subject to control under the Rent Stabilization Law are occupied by whites who are considered in the middle- or lower-upper-income status.

There comes a time when these rent control laws, as well as all other laws relating to landlord and tenant relationship, must be judicially interpreted and enforced. The responsibility falls mainly on the shoulders of the 120 judges of the Civil Court of the City of New York, twelve of whom are black. This court is referred to as the busiest court in the world. According to the 18th Annual Report of the Judicial Conference of the State of New York, for the judicial year July 1, 1971, through June 30, 1972, a total of 333,281 cases appeared on the calendar of this court. *About a third (102,707) of those cases were summary proceedings or what is commonly called landlord and tenant cases.*

New York State by statute (Article 7 of the Real Property Action and Proceedings Law) has provided a simple, expeditious, and inexpensive means for the recovery of real property as a substitute for ejectment, which was described by the court of appeals in *Reich* v. *Cochran* (201 NY 450, 453-54) as "an expensive and dilatory proceeding which in many instances amounted to a denial of justice."

Nonpayment Proceeding

Most of the summary proceedings (landlord and tenant actions) in the Civil Court are for nonpayment of rent and are commenced by the service of petition and notice of petition. The notice of petition is returnable before the clerk within five days after its service. If the respondent answers, the clerk will fix a date for trial or hearing not less than three or more than eight days after joinder of issue and will immediately notify by mail the parties or their attorneys. If the determination is for the petitioner, the warrant of eviction cannot be stayed for more than five days from such determination without his consent. If the respondent fails to answer within five days from the date of service, the court must render judgment in favor of the petitioner and may stay the issuance of the warrant for a period not to exceed ten days from the date of service. It is not necessary to indicate, here, all the allegations that must be included in the petition. However, it should be pointed out that if the accommodations are subject to rent control under the provision of the City Rent and Rehabilitation Law, the petition must allege that the rent demanded is not greater than the maximum rent established and fixed by the City Rent and Rehabilitation Administration. If the premises are not subject to rent control under that law, the petition must contain the following allegations as needed:

1. The property is not subject to rent control by reason of. . . .
2. The property is subject to the Rent Stabilization Law of 1969.
3. The property is not subject to the Rent Stabilization Law of 1969 by reason of. . . .

A summary proceeding is a special proceeding governed entirely by statute and there must be strict compliance with the statutory requirements to give the court jurisdiction. Many petitions that have been prepared by attorneys not experienced in the procedure of summary proceedings are dismissed without prejudice at the beginning of the trial because they do not conform to the statutory requirements. A few lawyers have become specialists in the field. Most of them represent landlords, and they usually have fifteen to twenty cases on the calendar each day.

Many of the tenants who appear in court are not represented by counsel. A number of them have appeared so often that they are more familiar with the rights of tenants in the City of New York than many of the lawyers who have had only limited experience in that branch of the law. Most of the tenants who appear with counsel are represented by the Legal

Aid Society, MFY Legal Services, Inc., and the Harlem Assertion of Rights, Inc. The two latter organizations are financed by the federal government.

Long before the Legal Aid Society was known to accept landlord and tenant actions, and before the birth of MFY Legal Services, Inc., and the Harlem Assertion of Rights, Inc., another organization was giving aid to the black tenants of Harlem. Organized in September, 1934, and still in existence, though not as potent as it was years ago, it is the Consolidated Tenants League. Donelan J. Phillips has been president of the league since it was organized. The league's original attorneys were two black lawyers, Lucius L. Delaney and Vernon J. Williams who volunteered their services. They are now deceased. Tenants who became members of the league paid a membership dues of .25 cents per month back in 1934 (today, $1). The league ironed out its members' problems with the landlord and furnished free legal services to them.

I can recall sitting in the old Municipal Court of the City of New York Tenth District as a young lawyer in the late 1940's and early 1950's, watching numerous legal battles between Thomas C. Murray, a black lawyer representing tenants who were members of the Consolidated Tenants League, and Nathaniel Borah, a white lawyer, representing landlords. Both specialized in the field of landlord and tenant law. It may be of interest to the reader to know that Mr. Murray still represents tenants and Mr. Borah still represents landlords, and they are still fighting legal battles in the landlord and tenant part of the Civil Court.

In most instances where a tenant has refused to pay his rent his defense to the nonpayment summary proceeding is that the landlord has failed to furnish the essential services or make the necessary repairs to the accommodations as required by law. This is particularly true with respect to those accommodations that are occupied by blacks and Puerto Ricans who have been compelled to live in those areas in the city which have the majority of the substandard housing. Where such a defense is interposed, the court *may*, pursuant to Section 755 of the Real Property Actions and Proceedings Law, stay the nonpayment proceedings or any action for rent if it finds the condition is such as to constructively evict the tenant from a portion of the premises occupied by him or is likely to become dangerous to life, health, or safety.

The usual procedure is that an inspection of the premises is made by a representative of the municipal department that is charged with enforcing the local housing code. If the condition as alleged by the tenant exists, a violation is placed on the record with respect to the premises. The records of that department may be introduced into evidence at the trial and are prima-facie evidence of the existence of the condition of the premises. The tenant is not limited to this manner of proof and may show the condition in any way that he can. In such proceedings the burden of disproving the condition of the premises as described in the violation is upon the landlord. The court may not stay the proceedings where it appears that the condition of the premises was created by acts of the tenant. The stay remains in effect until an order of the court is entered vacating it, but no order vacating the stay may be made except on three days' notice to the tenant and upon proof that the repairs have been made.

The tenant is not entitled to a stay, however, unless he deposits with the clerk of the court the rent due. The stay may be vacated on three days' notice upon the failure of the tenant to deposit with the clerk the rent within five days after it is due, during the pendency of the proceeding or action. During the stay the court may direct, upon three days' notice to all parties, the release to a contractor or materialmen of all or part of the money on deposit as shall be sufficient to pay the bills for maintenance of and necessary repairs to the building.

I have found in most cases where the tenant has refused to pay his rent because he claims the landlord has failed to supply essential services or make certain repairs, the evidence has supported the claim. But I have also found that many tenants attempt to use that defense as an excuse to avoid or at least delay the payment of rent. For example, a tenant once

appeared in a nonpayment summary proceeding in the landlord and tenant part of the court in which I was presiding and
admitted that the rent was due but said she had not paid the
rent because the landlord had promised to make certain
repairs in her apartment and had failed to do so. I then asked
her to list for the record all the repairs that were required.
The landlord stated for the record that all the repairs listed
had been made. The tenant insisted that they had not been
made. I asked the attorneys for the parties if they would have
any objection to my secretary taking the list prepared by the
tenant and inspecting the apartment. They not only con-
sented but indicated that they would have no objection to
being bound by whatever facts he ascertained from the
inspection. My secretary made an inspection and found that
all the repairs that were on the list had been made and that the
tenant sought to find other items that were not included on
the list that she claimed should have been made.

Many of the landlords who appear in court are also not
without sin. On one occasion an elderly black tenant who
appeared to be in his middle eighties appeared in a nonpayment summary proceeding wherein the landlord was claim-
ing that the tenant owed three months' rent. When the tenant
was asked if he owed the rent, he replied that he owed no rent
at all. The landlord, of course, insisted that he had not been
paid for the three months in question. I called the elderly
gentleman to the bench and asked if he had any proof of
payment. He handed me a dirty brown paper bag filled with
receipts for rents for the past five years. After spending nearly
half an hour examining the receipts, I finally found three
receipts covering payment of the rent for the period in question. When they were shown to the landlord, he admitted the
receipts contained his signature. The proceedings were dis-
continued. When the tenant left the courtroom, he was smil-
ing and said to me, "I told you I didn't owe no rent."

Holdover Proceeding

In addition to the nonpayment summary proceeding in which the landlord usually seeks only to obtain rent, there are holdover summary proceedings, in which he seeks to recover actual possession of the premises, not just the rent. Holdover proceedings are a summary method by which a tenant who remains in the accommodations without permission of the landlord after the expiration of his term of occupancy may be evicted. In this proceeding, if the court decides in favor of the respondent (tenant), the petition is naturally dismissed. If it decides in favor of the petitioner (landlord), the court may in its discretion, on application of the occupant, grant a stay of the execution of the warrant of eviction for a period not in excess of six months, if it appears that the premises are used for dwelling purposes; that the application is made in good faith; that the applicant, after reasonable effort, has not secured in the neighborhood suitable premises similar to those he occupies; or that by reason of other facts it would occasion extreme hardship to him or his family if the stay were not granted. Such a stay can be granted only on the condition that the person against whom the judgment was entered deposits with the clerk of the court an amount, for the occupation of the premises for the period of the stay, at the rate for which he was liable as rent for the month immediately prior to the expiration of his term or tenancy, plus such additional amount, if any, as the court may determine to be the difference between such rent and the reasonable rent or value of the use and occupation of the premises.

The stay may not be granted where the petitioner seeks to recover the premises for the purposes of demolishing them with the intent of constructing a new building. Nor may it be granted in a proceeding where the petitioner seeks to recover possession upon the ground that the occupant is holding over and is objectionable, if the petitioner satisfies the court that the occupant is objectionable.

Numerous holdover summary proceedings are commenced each year by owners of properties to recover apartments that are occupied by janitors or superintendents. In New York, whenever there are thirteen or more families occupying a multiple dwelling and the owner does not reside on the premises, he must provide "a janitor, housekeeper or some other person responsible" on his behalf, who must reside on the premises or within a dwelling located within 200 feet of the premises, rent free, as an incident to his employment. There is usually no written agreement between the parties or lease for the apartment. Whenever the owner decides to discharge the janitor or superintendent, he simply writes him a letter informing him that his services will be terminated on a certain day and he is to move from the apartment.

In most cases the janitor or superintendent has moved his family into the apartment and has no other place to move. Since his occupancy of the apartment is an incident of his employment, his status is that of a servant and not that of a tenant under the New York law and the apartment is not subject to the controls that are explained above. Inasmuch as he is not a tenant, the court does not have the discretion previously mentioned to grant a stay of the issuance of the warrant of eviction up to a period not in excess of six months. At the trial of these proceedings the landlord usually insists that he has hired a new janitor or superintendent for whom he needs the apartment immediately. The employee, in most instances not knowing his legal rights to the occupancy of the apartment when he accepts the job, is caught in a tragic situation. When I granted one discharged superintendent a stay of the issuance of the warrant of eviction for a period of five weeks over the strenuous objection of the landlord and his attorney, I was informed by the attorney that most of the judges granted stays no greater than ten to fifteen days. The argument was most unimpressive.

In a summary proceeding the court directs that a final judgment be entered determining the rights of the parties. Upon the rendering of a final judgment in favor of the petitioner (landlord), the court must issue a warrant to the city marshal commanding him to remove all people from the premises and put the petitioner into full possession. The officer to whom the warrant is delivered must give at least seventy-two hours' notice in writing to the person or persons to be evicted or dispossessed, and it can be executed only between the hours of sunrise and sunset.

Many final judgments are entered on default each year in favor of landlords owing to what we call sewer services—that is, the tenant is never served with a copy of the process even though the process server signs an affidavit, which is filed in the clerk's office, indicating that he has served the tenant. Recently, a number of process servers were prosecuted for engaging in this practice. The administrative judge of the Civil Court issued an order forbidding the entry of any default judgment without a hearing on the issue of service, where the affidavit of service is signed by certain process servers. In a case where the practice has occurred, the tenant learns for the first time that a summary proceeding has been commenced against him when he receives the seventy-two-hour notice from the city marshal. As one would probably suspect, the practice has occurred quite often in the past in the ghetto areas where blacks and Puerto Ricans live.

When tenants are faced with a possible eviction within seventy-two hours and no place to move, they naturally become frantic. Since most of them appear to be without sufficient funds with which to retain private counsel, they immediately consult one of the free legal services agencies previously mentioned. A motion is usually made to vacate the default final judgment and to set aside the warrant of eviction and to permit the tenant to serve and file an answer to the proceeding. These motions are generally granted by the court. In some cases the tenants' counsel asks that the matter be set down for a traverse (hearing to determine whether the tenant has been properly served). After traverse, if the court finds that the tenant has been properly served, it may let the final judgment stand. Because of the desire of most judges to let tenants have their day in court, final judgment entered on default in most cases are vacated, and the tenants are directed to serve and file their answers, even though it has been found that they have been properly served with process. If it is found that the tenant has not been properly served with process, the final judgment entered on default is vacated, the warrant is set aside, and the petition is dismissed.

Squatter Proceeding

Occasionally a landlord will find that he has an occupant of one of his apartments whom he did not place therein. This occurred quite often during World War II, when the housing shortage in the City of New York was more acute than it is today. The situation usually resulted from the tenant's turning the apartment over to a relative or some other person without the landlord's knowledge or consent. One would often hear a tenant say that he "sold his apartment." What he actually sold was the furniture that he owned in the apartment and turned the key over to the new occupant. In such a case, if the landlord does not want the new occupant as a tenant, he refuses the rent and has the occupant served with a ten-day notice to quit the premises. If the occupant fails to obey the notice, a squatter proceeding is usually commenced to remove him.

To succeed in a squatter's proceeding, he must prove that the occupant squatted upon the premises, in the first instance, without the permission of the owner *or one entitled to possession of the premises.* Many of these proceedings are dismissed after trial for failure of the owner to prove that the occupants' entrance upon the premises was without the permission of one entitled to possession of the premises at that time, since in most instances they were placed there by tenants who were entitled to possession at that time.

The New Housing Court

Prior to October 1, 1973, the judicial enforcement of the state and local laws "for the establishment and maintenance of proper housing standards" in the City of New York, was dispersed among a number of criminal and civil courts. No single court was able to deal consistently with all the factual and legal problems presented by the continued existence of housing violations in any one building. On October 1, 1973, the new housing part of the Civil Court of the City of New York (established pursuant to Chapter 982 of the laws of 1972 of the State of New York) was opened, which, *inter alia,* is to be "devoted to actions and proceedings involving the enforcement of state and local laws for the establishment and maintenance of housing standards." It has jurisdiction of sufficient scope to consolidate all actions related to building maintenance and operation and to recommend or employ any and all of the remedies, programs, and procedures authorized by the federal, state, or local laws for the enforcement of housing standards, regardless of the relief originally sought by the plaintiff, if it believes those procedures will be more effective to accomplish and protect the public interest and compliance. It also has the right to retain continuing jurisdiction of any action or proceeding relating to a building until all violations of state and local laws for the establishment and maintenance of proper housing standards have been removed.

Since the new housing part of the Civil Court has just been established, it is too early to determine what effect it will have on the "maintenance of housing standards" in the City of New York. It is being closely observed by both landlord and tenant organizations.

Conclusion

If one were to check the landlord and tenant part of the Civil Court, on any day, he would find more blacks and Puerto

Ricans in that part of the court than in any other part. This is not surprising, since most of the landlord and tenant litigation seems to involve substandard housing and, as previously indicated, it is in this type of housing that most blacks and Puerto Ricans live. It is the first appearance in a courtroom for many of the tenants. As for whether or not they or their landlords feel that justice has been done when they depart from that courtroom, is a question that remains unanswered.

In a firsthand account of proceedings in a special court that was created to handle landlord-tenant disputes in Baltimore, Judge Solomon Baylor explains the criticalness of participation by the community, legislators, and other government officials in the search for solutions. He reports the usefulness of having landlords and tenants attend special training projects as a condition of probation resulting from their transgressions. A graduate of Coppin State College and the University of Maryland Law School, Judge Baylor is assigned to the District Court of Maryland in Baltimore.

SPECIAL COURTS FOR LANDLORDS AND TENANTS

Solomon Baylor

ENVIRONMENT is of utmost importance in the influence and control of human behavior. Of all the environmental factors, the house and the neighborhood in which one lives are perhaps the most significant. I conceive the first duty of government and of society in general is continually to cause the creation and maintenance of conditions which will guarantee safe and peaceful neighborhoods and structurally sound and sanitary housing for everyone. Failure to do this is tantamount to sowing those seeds which will ripen in the form of negative attitudes, insecurity, and destructive activities, which will ultimately spell doom for the overall community.

Many of the housing evils would not have developed in our city but for the fact that segregated housing has for so many years been a fact of life. The slumlords of past years invested heavily in Negro areas because there they found no formidable resistance to their system of "milking" the properties. For example, they could intimidate and verbally abuse the tenants without fear of reprisals; it was relatively easy to get permission to cut up single family dwellings (formerly used by

and in many instances run down by whites) into several apartments (to be inhabited by blacks); needed repairs could rather
easily be ignored; and dwellings or portions thereof could be
easily changed to commercial. Some of the real estate interests
which now complain that legislation or the public attitude is
slanted too heavily in favor of tenants and that property taxes,
nonpayment of rents, vandalism, etc. prevent the realization
of a fair return on real estate investments have, either directly
or indirectly, been instrumental in the creation of the present-
day monster. I agree that such problems are presently with us
and that it is incumbent on all to see that investors get a fair
return from their investments, as well as to see that tenants are
reasonably well protected. I do emphasize, however, that for
too many years the pendulum has swung too far in the other
direction. Thus the widespread indifference toward the general well-being and healthful development of poorer (and
particularly black) neighborhoods have in previous years
made the exploitation of such neighborhoods profitable.
Such activity is criminal in nature.

Criminal-like activity is seldom, if ever, excusable. It is
equally true that those who directly or indirectly contribute to
the degradation of other human beings, whether done for
personal gain or to fan the inner flames of prejudice, are no
less criminal than the person who robs another or burglarizes
his home. I must heartily add that this is by no means a
condemnation of investors or landlords in general, for my
own experiences convince me that those individuals who have
been chronic violators are in the minority although the number of properties they control are numerous.

The housing picture in Baltimore since World War II has
been one of slow (far too slow) but continuous progress.
About the only bright spot at that time was the existence of the
Poe House and the McCulloh House—two public housing
projects under the auspices and control of the Housing
Authority, a private corporation created under federal laws
and financed jointly by the federal and city governments.

By the early 1950's the city had virtually completed the

enforcement of its ordinance which banned the existence of outdoor hoppers (toilets) and the "high board" fences which enclosed so many of the inner-city backyards. This was definitely a giant step toward the elimination of health hazards and some of the conditions which accentuated blight. Among the physical and mental health problems created by the existence of the outdoor hoppers were the facts that: (1) they were difficult to keep clean, (2) the shelters enclosing them were often leaky and dilapidated, (3) they were extremely cold in the winter and hot in the summer, with flies and odors emanating therefrom, (4) it was necessary to return to the house for washing after using them, (5) they had no inside lights, (6) one could not feel a real sense of privacy while using them, and (7) they were often breeding places for rats.

As for the fences, they were definitely rat harbors, were usually dilapidated, and often served to hide unsightly and unsanitary conditions in a yard from one's neighbors. In spite of the overwhelming benefits inherent in the enforcement of this local ordinance, there were those who vehemently argued the enforcement was an invasion of property rights and that it imposed undue financial burden on the property owners. However, approximately twenty-five years have passed, and no one can now honestly contend that these arguments were well founded. Nor would anyone, including the most recalcitrant slumlord, prefer a return to those horrors.

By 1951 a Housing Bureau headed by Yates Cook had been set up within the Health Department. The Health Department, pursuant to the Baltimore City Code, adopted a set of regulations relative to housing and dealing with such matters as sanitation, structural maintenance, density, light and ventiliation, and electrical and plumbing standards. Yates Cook soon became nationally known and respected for the vitality, enthusiasm, resourcefulness, aggressiveness, and general interest that he continuously displayed in connection with his work. It was he who instituted the pilot program, also known at that time as the Baltimore Plan, under which housing inspectors, for the first time, concentrated on inspecting every structure in a designated geographical area and issued notices on any condition which was not in conformity with code requirements. Prior to the installation of this plan the inspectors had acted only on complaints and spot checks. The new approach, it was theorized, by simultaneously eliminating blight from all structures in a given area, would, in addition to protecting the health and welfare of the community, create a sense of pride and encourage the occupants and the owners to keep their properties in a clean and healthful condition and in a state of good repair. It was hoped, moreover, that this approach would halt or prevent blight in neighborhoods which were on the verge of blight or were already partially blighted. A single deteriorated or poorly kept house has the unavoidable effect of lowering the property values of remaining houses in the block, of destroying the motivation of owners and occupants of adjoining houses, of lowering the morale of those living nearby, and of lowering neighborhood property values.

Although diligently opposed by many owners, the pilot program was widely publicized and enthusiastically embarked upon by the very limited staff of the Housing Bureau. The approach was excellent. A combination of factors, however, combined to lessen its effectiveness. These included but were not limited to an insufficient number of housing inspectors, the absence of a systematic follow-up program, the failure of city officials and citizens in general to recognize the importance of the movement, the hard-core resistance of many professional landlords, and the high degree of racism which negatively affected the lives of most inhabitants of the blighted areas. Little or no hope can be generated in persons whose houses are repaired but who are constant victims of a racially segregated society, job discrimination, inferior educational facilities, police brutality, and discourteous treatment in public or official places.

The pilot program also suffered because there was no full-time housing court. In 1947 Governor William Preston Lane appointed the late Harry S. Kruger as a magistrate to preside part time over the trial of housing violations in Baltimore City, thereby making Baltimore perhaps the first major city in the nation to establish a housing court. In 1967 the city prevailed on the state legislature to extend the trial date in cases of alleged nonpayment of rent from two days after filing to one week after filing. What is perhaps the most progressive single piece of legislation relative to housing in Baltimore City was passed in 1968. It is known as the Rent Escrow Law. Prior to its passage, the tenant's obligation to pay rent to the landlord continued regardless of the condition of the rented property. The fact that the property was in a state of disrepair was no defense in an action of summary ejectment for arrearages in rent. It was not an unusual practice, moreover, for landlords to eject tenants who made complaints to municipal authorities about the conditions on the rented property. This law, however, authorized the court to order rental payments made into court if the court found as a fact that conditions which were detrimental to life, health, or safety or which constituted a fire hazard were present on the property. The payments into court would continue until the conditions were corrected. The 1968 law was seriously limited, primarily in that it could be invoked only by way of defense in summary ejectment proceedings for nonpayment of rent. Thus the amended Escrow Law passed in 1971 was a welcome piece of legislation. Under it, a tenant may file an affirmative action requesting the right to pay his rent into escrow.

In September, 1971, Baltimore City established its first full-time Housing Court as another step in its battle against the numerous housing-related problems. I was assigned to preside over that court from its inception to July 1, 1973. The court held two sessions daily. The morning session dealt with the landlord-tenant cases, and in the afternoon criminal cases were heard. The bulk of afternoon cases involved the failure to comply with violation notices from city officials. These notices covered such items as zoning violations, exterior painting of residences, sanitation, structural repairs, electrical and plumbing violations, and tenant violations. (The city code

makes it illegal for a tenant to move out of the premises
without giving prior notice to the landlord, adequately cleaning the premises and securing them, and returning the key to
the landlord or his agent.)

Although the Housing Court is a gigantic task for a single
judge, it is definitely an instrumentality through which new
plateaus of success in the area of housing might be reached.
The judge involved must have a sense of dedication toward
civic improvement in general and toward housing in particular. He must be willing to work long hours in and out of the
courtroom. Needless to say, however, this must be done
within the framework of the spirit and letter of our laws and
constitutions.

One of my earliest "extracurricular" activities in connection
with my tenure as Housing Court judge was to prevail upon
the mayor to activate a Citizens Advisory Committee on
Housing Law Enforcement. Such a group is valuable not only
because it suggests meaningful changes in laws and regulations relative to living conditions, but also (and perhaps more
so) because it brings together citizens of various backgrounds
and diversified interests in an effort to solve some of their
common problems. Even before the committee was organized, I personally called informal meetings of persons
representing different segments of the community. This
approach, if cautiously used and if exercised through reasonably intelligent and open-minded people, can serve as an
important wedge in the opening of doors of understanding,
thereby diminishing some of the erroneous concepts and
unfortunate attitudes which some groups or individuals may
have concerning others, be they landlords or tenants, educated or uneducated, black or white, business or professional, Jew or Gentile, rich or poor.

I held meetings with the officials of the Citizens Planning
and Housing Association, the Property Owners Association,
the Real Estate Broker Association, and the Department of
Housing Community Development. I also conferred with
legal aid authorities. In a further effort to acquire a general

knowledge, to gather opinion from experts in the housing field, and to sense some of the prevailing community attitudes, I called together a group of citizens shortly after my tenure began. Some of the people included in that group were the Reverend Sidney Daniels; Delegate Troy Brailey; William E. Koons; Reverend Frank Downing; Kenneth Wilson, member of the Zoning Board and executive of the *Afro-American* newspaper; William R. Smith, who at that time was an executive with the Community Relations Commission; Lee Seabolt, assistant state attorney handling Housing Court cases; Charles Noon, an assistant to the commissioner of Housing Community Development; Kenneth Pillar, attorney with Legal Aid; and Ms. Bailey Fine, who at that time was representing the Citizens Planning and Housing Association, but is now a member of the mayor's staff.

From time to time among the landlord-tenant cases a Housing Court judge is faced with parties who are bitter and hostile toward each other. In many instances, the situation is hopeless. Not infrequently, however, I have assigned myself the task of bringing about a reconciliation. In many of such efforts the results have been gratifying. Such efforts will sometimes necessitate conference in chambers or visits to the property involved. The fact that this might require personal time and expense is far outweighed by the knowledge that the flame of a single source of controversy and discontent has been extinguished. Very often tenants are guilty of nonpayment of rent because the financial means, through no fault of that tenant, were simply not available. With reasonable diligence on the part of the judge, some financial aid can often be found.

On the other side of the coin, there are some instances where tenants are destructive, negligent, poor housekeepers, and deliberate in their nonpayment of rent. In such instances it is the duty of the court to afford appropriate relief to the landlord.

In an effort to enlighten some of the more chronic violators of sanitation violations, I encouraged the reactivation of a tenants clinic. This was a system whereby a tenant who was convicted of violations involving sanitation was put on probation for a specified period. The primary condition of probation was that the defendant attend a series of classes called the Tenants Clinic. These classes were headed by a professional psychiatrist and social worker who was paid through city funds.

Shortly after the establishment of the Tenants Clinic the idea of a training session for property owners was conceived. We were successful in getting key members of the Property Owners Association to organize this class. They, in turn, solicited the aid of other key people. Defendants who were guilty of not complying with violation notices, but who lacked the experience and expertise to enable them to be good landlords, were granted probation (except, of course, where the defendant's prior conduct or the facts of the case would not justify same) and were required to attend the series of classes known as the Owners' Management Workshop.

When the new Housing Court began, the vast majority of the cases tried involved violation dates from six to eighteen months preceding trial. This delay was due in part to the numerous cases which had been remanded from the Supreme Bench and also the high postponement rate. I believe that the multitude of delays would be avoided if people other than the police were authorized to serve summons. The postponement rates were curtailed partly due to the newly instituted system of initial appearances before the commissioner, at which time firm trial dates are set.

The Rent Escrow Law has been very effective, and many problem cases have been resolved without escrow orders, either by brief postponements or by negotiations between the parties. I understand from Legal Aid that in many instances conditions are corrected upon writing the owner, and that this was not the case two years ago. There are definitely fewer escrow cases now than there were a year ago. The majority of the citizens, however, do not know how the Rent Escrow Law functions, and in many instances when they learn of the law, it is too late to take advantage of it. Legislation should be sought to liberalize the Rent Escrow Law. For instance, the tenant may not have sent the owner a registered letter but may have told him personally about the conditions. Also, forms for affirmative escrow might be printed and made available to the public upon request. The court should be empowered to institute rent escrow on its own motion.

It is readily apparent that the number of chronic housing code violators has been appreciably curtailed. On the other hand, it appears that many of the cases brought would be more appropriately and more effectively resolved at the administrative level. This is particularly true in the numerous cases where owner occupants are desperately lacking the funds needed to comply with the notice.

I have seen many confrontations in rent court which could have been avoided if the landlord had provided the tenant with a rent book or an adequate receipt. I have seen other instances where certain landlords who did give books or receipts required the tenant to furnish a stamped address envelope in order to have the book returned. The court, of course, is powerless, in the absence of legislation, to remedy such conditions. I would suggest legislation which would create a presumption of correctness of the tenant's version of the rental account, where the landlord had failed to supply the tenant with the continuing record of payments or balances.

Some of my own experiences in Housing Court led me to believe that a housing court judge could be more efficient and effective if he had at his disposal an additional court official to function in the role of investigative social worker. This official should be directly responsible to the judge and should be given some of the duties which I have heretofore performed on a somewhat limited scale. These would consist of, but would not be limited to, determining the mathematical accuracy of rent claims by examining books and records, inspecting properties, holding joint conferences with landlords and tenants to resolve minor misunderstandings, arranging for tenants to obtain financial and other aid from other agencies, counseling tenants about budgeting, evaluating requests for extension in Housing Court cases and rent cases, and dispensing to the public information about housing matters.

One seemingly insurmountable problem confronting Baltimoreans is that of vacant houses, many of which are owned by the city. It seems that the largest single ingredient of the problem is vandalism. It is common knowledge that houses are frequently vandalized during the course of rehabilitation. I recommend a concentrated drive by the city to reduce the number of vacant houses and that reasonably small areas of the city be worked one at a time with a special detail of police (special or regular) patrolling that area around the clock. I suggest further that diligent effort be made to interest more people to become homeowners and that they be permitted to take over some of the vacant properties without cost where appropriate and where necessary with some assistance in financing of repairs.

It is the inescapable duty of local, state, and federal government not only to institute and enforce laws to accomplish these aims, but to assume such moral leadership as would result in the lessening of suspicion and mistrust between individuals and groups from different areas of society. Such leadership, moreover, would necessarily have the effect of destroying some of the roots of crime, such as prolonged poverty, despondent and rebellious attitudes, greed, and the general lack of concern so frequently displayed by and between citizens. I fear, however, that such idealistic leadership will not be forthcoming until such time as it is seriously demanded by a larger percentage of the citizens.

May God hasten that day—lest we *all* perish in the process of waiting.

Quasi-judicial agencies determine much of the quality of justice and, accordingly, are crucial to the improvement of life chances for blacks. Their vast powers make it imperative for black lawyers to get involved in their work. This is the thrust of remarks made by Robert E. Millender, Sr., at the Judicial Council's meeting in Miami Beach, Florida, on August 3, 1972. Educated at the Detroit Institute of Technology and the Detroit College of Law, Mr. Millender is a senior partner in the law firm of Goodman, Eden, Millender, Goodman, and Bedrosian in Detroit.

QUASI-JUDICIAL AGENCIES: CRUCIAL BUT IGNORED

Robert L. Millender, Sr.

MEANINGFUL access to the judicial decision making process is instrumental in improving the life conditions of minority groups. That channel of access is being emphasized, as it should be. But there is another which I want to highlight because it is at our peril that we continue to overlook it. This channel has been instrumental in the development of law in this country since the middle of the nineteenth century and thus instrumental in shaping and effecting this nation's social, economic, and political posture, including its response to the needs, aspirations, rights, and privileges of blacks.

I am speaking of the administrative and quasi-judicial bodies, often mentioned, seldom understood. They have as much impact upon the individual and collective lives of members of this society as any of our courts. The practical reason for this is that, in most cases, the laws creating these bodies gave them exclusive jurisdiction in their field with only the right of appeal to the court. This right of appeal was limited in many instances to those issues involving questions of law. The limitation on the right of appeal, coupled with the cost and

time-consuming method involved, make [sic] the decisions of
these agencies' final decisions. For most claimants, these are
the courts of last resort.

The Interstate Commerce Commission is perhaps the prototype of these federal agencies. Established in 1887, it has the
exclusive jurisdiction over the flow of all goods in commerce
among the states. Each of its eleven members draws an annual
salary of more than $26,000. Its Washington office has a full
staff of six attorneys whose expertise in interstate commerce
law is matched by a precious few. It has numerous regional
offices and deputy commissioners who function much as do
hearing examiners or referees. Their duties are to inquire
into and ascertain the existence of certain facts as these relate
to provisions and interpretation of the Interstate Commerce
Code, thereafter, to render recommendation as a basis for
official—yes, legal—action. In other words, they exercise discretion of a quasi-judicial nature.

The ICC is but one of several exceedingly important quasi-
judicial agencies. Others are the Federal Aviation Administration, controlling and regulating civil air transportation;
the Federal Trade Commission, regulating trade product,
drug and medicine sale, and advertising in this country; the
Federal Power Commission, overseeing the supply, service,
installation, transportation, and *cost* of fuels in interstate
trade; the Securities & Exchange Commission, regulating the
sale and trade of securities, bonds, stocks, and financial papers in our nation; the Federal Communications Commission,
controlling the establishment and maintenance of radio, television, telephone, and telegraph systems in America; the Federal Housing Administration, responsible for the building
standards, financing rates, and establishments of fair housing
patterns in the various communities; the Equal Employment
Opportunities Commission, policing fair employment practices; the National Labor Relations Board, administering and
supervising the rights and obligations of organized labor; the
Veterans Administration, governing the interest and benefits
to those who have served in the armed forces; state Work-

men's Compensation Bureaus, Power Commissions, Tax Services, and Civil Rights panels.

The list is seemingly endless, but the message is clear. The length of the list, which includes only a few state and local agencies, should serve to highlight the crucial roles which these boards and commissions occupy in the community and in our American system of jurisprudence. But what does all of this have to do with you and the black community? The black community, disproportionally speaking, is significantly affected by the decisions of most, if not all, of these boards and commissions. It has a deep-vested interest in the type of their exclusive jurisdiction over areas filled with problems which plague its members presently under discussion, since these areas—housing, employment, education, and family maintenance, to mention several—are all deeply flavored by the degrading and rage-producing vinegar of racism. Therefore, the fairness, responsiveness, and representation of these governmental bodies are essential concerns of our community.

Take, for example, the matter of consumer protection. If the black community is not to be victimized by unscrupulous businesses, the regulation, supervision, and remedial functions of a quasi-judicial body like the Federal Trade Commission must be truly effective in forcing disclosure and truthful advertisement, and regulating the quality of products placed before the consumer. But this effectiveness will depend largely on the commission's understanding of a sensitivity toward the black community. For example, the commission should have a special concern for quality and truthfulness in the manufacturing and sale of hair care products, some food products, clothing, used car dealers, and a host of other businesses which exploit blacks (and poor white and other ethnic groups) throughout this country.

The Federal Housing Administration, while not strictly a quasi-judicial body, does conduct administrative hearings of a type which border close upon the subject matter in question. Because of its tremendous impact on the black community, there is urgent need to gain access and demand meaningful responsiveness from this agency. Housing in this country, especially for the black community, is worse than desperate. Caught between the physical and psychological forces of astronomical and increasing rent costs, grossly inadequate and deteriorating fixtures and construction material, often nonexistent maintenance, teeming rat population, and now reported death and disease from lead-filled paint, those who are tenants in the inner city and rural areas as well are faced with an apparently hopeless situation. We must be concerned, we must become involved, for the great majority of these hopeless tenants are black, and the solution to many of their problems are grounded in the law, including proper administrative law. And it is in the latter that we, the black attorneys, are at a disadvantage because of a lack of awareness, knowledge, and, therefore, expertise.

It is not only the black tenant who suffers from unresponsive, insensitive, conflicting Federal Housing Administrative policy decisions. Witness the very recent debacle over whether that agency supported the construction of low-cost and middle-income housing in suburbia. Their position was reminiscent of the old shell game; now you see it, now you don't. It is, of course, gratifying that an ever increasing number of blacks are homeowners across this country. But many—far too many—find that their fulfilled dreams of homeownership are turned into financial nightmare, and ownership becomes a farce in the face of unconscionable mortgage and land contract obligations, shoddy workmanship and construction, and homes built with substandard materials—all wrapped in the brightly colored but deceptive package of ballooning prices.

In the face of the above realities, which are now being widely publicized and admitted by that agency, there is an outcry for change. But I, for one, believe that there will be no change, or at best ineffectual change, unless knowledgeable blacks assume the responsibility, obligation—no, duty—of being involved. For the Federal Housing Administration must be made more responsive so as to become a vehicle for lowering consumer risk, aiding in the regulating and monitoring of construction prices and standards, and, most important, advising our community of their legal rights as consumers and promoting the prosecution—criminal and civil—of those who perpetuate these ills and profit from the resultant human and social tragedies.

And consider the matter of employment. The 1964 Civil Rights Act was hailed as the basis for immediate elimination of racial discrimination in employment. The act created the Equal Employment Opportunity Commission as a quasi-judicial agency to aid in the implementation of the goals of the legislation. Yet after eight years of operation the EEOC is still faced by the ugly unchanging face of discrimination. Blacks continue to be barred from skilled trade and craft unions and are vastly underrepresented in the high-growth profit industries. They are still excluded from supervisory, technical, and managerial positions in our corporate structures. Employers still operate on the policy of black being "the last to be hired and first to be fired." And don't forget the unions, those citadels of workers' rights and welfare. Far too frequently union officials still are unresponsive and insensitive to the interests and rights of their black members.

On the state level the same conditions and problems are just as acute, damaging, and demoralizing. They differ only in terms of the number of people affected and the extent of the jurisdictional area.

Illustrative of the problems discussed above are state created quasi-judicial agencies in the field of workmen's compensation law which exist in every state of this nation. For the black community the social responsiveness required and which must be expected of these agencies regulating the law is most crucial. The extent of this crucial need for responsiveness in the various workmen's compensation agencies may be evidenced by the nature of the workmen's compensation practice in the State of Michigan.

Now I confess that in respect to federal agencies my statement was based upon material read and information received from various sources. But in respect to the workmen's compensation practice I speak from experience. I have spent seventeen years of my twenty years of practice exclusively in this field. For seven of those years I was a member of the Workmen's Compensation Department of the State of Michigan and September 2 of this year will have completed ten years as a practicing attorney before that department.

This service with the department and practice exposed me to circumstances which I feel certain are representative of the general trend of the law in this area in other comparable urban areas of this country. I knew, as in Michigan, in the great industrial and manufacturing centers "blacks" are relegated to unrewarding, repetitious, heavy, and inherently dangerous jobs, thereby disproportionately exposing themselves to disabling injury. And once that tragedy strikes, as it does so many times, the injured employee's and/or his family's right, future, and economic life rest in the hands of those attorneys, hearing referees and appeal board members constituting the system of quasi-jurisdiction of the workmen's compensation law of a state.

What role of involvement does the black attorney play in this field as well as in similar fields?

I am not one generally prone to the use of statistics, but let's review a few that I have been able to secure. On the federal level:

(1) ICC: now eleven commissioners—no black.
(2) FTC: five members—no black.
(3) FPC: five members—no black.
(4) SEC: five members—no black.
(5) FCC: seven members—one recently appointed black.
(6) EEOC five members—two black.
(7) NLRB: six members—one black.

I am sure that in light of the above facts and the effect the above agencies have upon the lives of our people, we are not just underrepresented. We are virtually unrepresented.

But let us return to the workmen's compensation practice, especially as it exists in Michigan. Well over 33,000 persons suffer compensable injuries every year. For any given day 50 percent of the claimants appearing before the referees in Detroit are black. What do we have in the way of black representation in our department? Two black attorneys. There is one more thing you should know that is of deep concern to me. There is no doubt in my mind that 25 percent of the claimants coming before the department are black. But do you know that up to two years ago I was the only black attorney in the entire state practicing exclusively in workmen's compensation? Donald Hobson, my partner, joined me in practice then and now has about 80 percent of his practice in that area. I can name *three* other black attorneys in Michigan who could reach this status in several years.

Now what is so important about this status that I express such a deep concern about? How significant is it when we evaluate it in terms of those other great concerns affecting black attorneys and the black community such as racism in the law schools, bar examinations, and practice before our courts of record? Do I mean we are to forget the plight of our black brother in criminal cases and that of tenants and the poor in their ceaseless economical battle to eke out a living, only to be thwarted and harassed by legalistic matters?

No, that is not my intention. My desire is to make you aware of an area of our lives that if we could effect some meaningful changes, those changes would eliminate or greatly reduce that fundamental basis that causes many of the problems in the criminal courts, in tenants' cases, and in cases involving unpaid debts.

Procedures, rulings, litigation, and decision of those quasi-judicial bodies named and unnamed are the root causes of the economic deprivation among our people, as inferior education is the root cause of social and cultural unrest. And we will remain in that economic state unless meaningful effective change occurs. And, further, if change does not occur, the list of claimants before the criminal court and debtor court will increase day by day.

We must become members of these boards and agencies; we must appear to practice before them and must practice before them effectively. Our people's very lives are in the balance, and to so many of them it is their last resort. Put simply, I am suggesting that the so-called sacrifice of time and effort necessary to gain access to quasi-judicial bodies can, does, and should have a twofold benefit: (1) It has the capacity to make those bodies, depending upon you, more responsible to the black community at large; and (2) it results in the attainment of an expertise in the black attorney which not only benefits the black community, but also goes far in benefiting the attorney. How do we secure access to this area of decision-making? Experience has taught me that the most accessible key to entrance into those quasi-judicial areas is politics. For you see, as we pointed out earlier, unlike judges of courts of record who are in most cases elected, officials and members of these agencies are appointed by a political figure, and the query you are asked when you seek entry more often is as follows: (1) What political party do you belong to, and (2) what have been your contributions to the party?

Here again, in my opinion, exists the black attorney's greatest handicap, for his involvement in politics, at least in Michigan, is nonexistent not only in form of active participation but financial contributions as well. A tragedy, too. For me, politics and law go together just like ham and eggs. Fortunately, however, the situation is not as critical as it sounds. For if the black attorney so desires, this door is wide open, and in the black community there are those who eagerly wait the type of independent leadership he can bring to this area.

The challenge is before us; we must take up the gauntlet and gain access to the quasi-judicial and administrative bodies which determine rights and affect the lives of so many black Americans. Unless we do, we condemn ourselves and the black community to "business as usual" on fundamental legal and human rights issues which go to the very core of the existence of each of us. We must act to promote the interest of our people as have other groups and factions of this society done to foster their particular interest. In many regards the fate of the black community is in our hands; therefore, we must act now. It could be already too late.

IV.

CONCLUSION

A great organization and a great jurist honored each other in New Orleans, Louisiana, on July 2, 1974. At its seventy-fifth annual convention, the National Associaton for the Advancement of Colored People (NAACP) awarded its Spingarn Medal to Judge Damon J. Keith, and he paid tribute to it as the preeminent paladin of the people, white as well as black. Judge Keith's remarks ranged over the broad area of problems and progress in the civil rights field, North and South, and called attention to the even broader concern about governmental abuse of power that threatens life and liberty in an unprecedented manner. From his student days at West Virginia State College and Howard University Law School to his juristic days in the U.S. District Court for the Eastern District of Michigan, Judge Keith has exemplified the principle that has guided the NAACP in its role as the perennial champion of civil rights. That principle, expressed in 1910 by W. E. B. DuBois in the first issue of *The Crisis* magazine, is "to stand for the rights of men, irrespective of color or race, for the highest ideals of American democracy." Judge Keith urged our rededication to it. His remarks, in tone and texture, provide an appropriate conclusion to this book.

NAACP: PALADIN OF THE PEOPLE

(Address Before the Seventy-fifth Annual NAACP Convention)

Damon J. Keith

IT IS ONE of the highlights of my life to be selected as a recipient of the revered Spingarn Medal of the National

Association for the Advancement of Colored People. All members of my family are life members of the NAACP. I speak to you as a former chairman of the Detroit Membership Campaign, a former officer and member of the Detroit Branch Board of Directors, and a former chairman of Detroit's Freedom Fund Dinner, a project which has contributed more than $1,000,000 to the work of this great organization.

My love and concern for the NAACP are deeply rooted in the life struggles of my family and community. I remember as a boy going with my father to the segregated St. Antoine YMCA in Detroit to listen to Walter White and Dr. W. E. B. DuBois. At that time they spoke as Roy Wilkins speaks now of the vital role that the NAACP has to play to free America of racism and racial segregation.

So I stand here tonight, therefore, acutely aware of the honored meaning and purpose of this award. It is a symbol of our common striving, our victories, our determination, and our firm belief in the ultimate triumph of the goals of freedom and equality which we seek.

With deep personal gratitude, I humbly accept this award.

Throughout its splendid history, the NAACP has been at the vanguard of the struggle for equal justice and opportunity for black people in this country. It has pressed forward unrelentingly and in the face of great obstacles to break the shackles of racial segregation. It has raised its voice of protest and defense on behalf of all of us who have never enjoyed the fruits of life and labor free of racial oppression. As a member of the bar and the federal judiciary, I also know that the NAACP has served with honor the cause of law and constitutional democracy in this land. In truth then, it must be recognized that the necessary work of the NAACP—of the thousands of faithful members, black and white, who have carried its mission—is not for black people alone, but for America and all Americans.

These reasons bring to one of my background and experience a sense of the special significance of this award. It is especially meaningful and doubly gratifying to receive the Spingarn Medal in the twentieth anniversary of the single most important event in this great organization's history.

On Monday, May 17, 1954, Chief Justice Earl Warren read a unanimous Supreme Court decision. This decision has been acclaimed as the most important act of government since the Emancipation Proclamation almost 100 years earlier. The Chief Justice phrased the issue before the Court in this manner: "Does segregation of children in public schools solely on the basis of race, even though the physical facilities and other 'tangible' factors may be equal, deprive the children of the minority group of equal educational opportunities?" The Court's answer to this question sounded the legal death knell to government enforced segregation in this country.

"We conclude," Chief Justice Warren wrote, "that in the field of public education the doctrine of 'separate but equal' has no place. Separate education facilities are inherently unequal." The Supreme Court, in these often quoted words, had decided that under the Fourteenth Amendment to the Constitution, black children were entitled to receive (the same and) equal treatment under the laws that had been previously accorded only white children. No longer, the decision promised, would black children be taught that they were created equal and at the same time be forced to live a life of second-class citizenship. We are indebted to that small group of dedicated men and women who formed the NAACP for the promise and hope of equality for black Americans that came with the *Brown* decision.

We are living in a period of great change and uncertainty, in a time, it is fair to say, which tries the souls of all of us. Not only have black Americans not attained the status of first-class citizens promised by the *Brown* decision twenty years ago, but in many areas there is evidence of a drifting away, even from the commitment to that goal. We are witness to an [*sic*] historic assault on the institutions of our democracy and on the Constitution upon which they are built. These are developments about which we all should be concerned, but they are not grounds for forsaking the struggle for equality among all Americans or for losing faith in the ideals of our Constitution. *We must move on. We must go forward.* It is only in battles like those which have always confronted this organization that the true weapons of freedom and justice are tested; and it is our responsibility to lift up those weapons against injustice and tyranny wherever they may exist. To do less would be to succumb to that injustice and to aid in the process of giving up our liberties in the name of a false freedom and security.

The Supreme Court in 1954 ruled that segregation in the public schools of Topeka, Kansas, was unconstitutional. It was a little-noticed appendage to that decision that segregation in the nation's capital was also ruled unconstitutional. This is important in understanding the pervasiveness of the cancer of racism which has afflicted our society. It is significant because the schools of the District of Columbia were segregated, *not because of a local school board, but because the federal government had decreed they should be segregated.* The Court's decision, on May 17, 1954, then, not only was necessary to outlaw segregation imposed by state government, but it was also necessary to outlaw that imposed by the federal government. What black Americans have had to overcome, therefore, was the most all-inclusive system of racial discrimination possible in a democracy.

Those who say now that blacks should pull themselves up by their bootstraps, as other ethnic groups have done, fail to appreciate the nature of the obstacles which continue to impede equal access to opportunity even today, twenty years after segregation was declared unconstitutional. Because the systematic discrimination against blacks in America was rooted so firmly in our institutions and because racism was at one time the official policy of American governments on all levels, there simply have been no bootstraps to pull on. No group in America has faced and overcome these kinds of obstacles. No ethnic group can point to its own experiences as examples for black Americans to emulate.

The Constitution teaches us that all men are entitled to

equal treatment under the laws. It has been because of the dedicated and tireless efforts of men and women who believed in the Constitution's teaching that many of the obstacles confronting blacks in this country have fallen. And it remains for those of us charged with upholding that Constitution and those who still believe in it to see to it that the struggle for equal protection of the laws continues until the need for that struggle ceases and it becomes but another chapter in the history of a strong and proud people.

We have witnessed over the past twenty years a realization that racial discrimination is not a phenomenon indigenous to the South. The civil rights movement in the 1960's and the coverage it received in the national media pointed out to people in Los Angeles, and New York, and Detroit that formerly accepted facts of life were the same practices being challenged in the South as racial discrimination. With this awareness, the struggle moved out of the living rooms of crowded urban tenements. With this awareness, the struggle somersaulted into the streets and into the courts of Northern cities, where it was protested that racial discrimination wherever it occurred and in whatever form was unfair and therefore illegal.

The complacency which had allowed an intolerable situation to last for too many years already was swept away in the wake of justice.

The Civil Rights Act of 1964, which was regarded by many as a means of ending discrimination in the South, became an important means used by Northern blacks to obtain employment in industries which prior to 1964 had either employed only token blacks or none at all. Shortly after the act was passed, it was conclusively decided by the Supreme Court in a case called *Griggs* v. *Duke Power* that private employers could not use tests and other screening devices that were not necessary to select employees if their result was to exclude blacks from employment. That decision, in my opinion even more than *Brown*, has proved most significant in combating racial discrimination.

Perhaps nowhere is the effect of past racial discrimination more evident than in cases where black people have been denied jobs based on artificial job requirements. After it became illegal for employers to refuse to hire blacks because of their race, devices proliferated which allowed employers to reach the same result under a more acceptable name. Thus, it became necessary for construction workers to have high school degrees; it became an indispensable requirement that truck drivers pass a standardized test which tested, not ability to drive a truck, but the ability simply to pass the test.

Where blacks were hired, they were put in low-paying jobs in separate departments with no future and no dignity. When this system was challenged, the employers merely removed the partitions. In their places, they instituted seniority systems which rewarded those who had gained longevity on the job with job security and which kept newly arrived blacks on a bottom rung with little hope for advancement and no increase in pay.

This process continued unabated and with each new job requirement, blacks found it more and more difficult to obtain employment. But there are those who protested that these were but "objective" requirements and that everyone had to meet them before he was hired. In effect, this was but a more sophisticated way of saying that blacks failed to satisfy the requirements because they were less capable than whites; it became the new argument in support of black inferiority.

Yet it remains the uncontroverted evidence that blacks failed to satisfy the requirements, not because they were inferior, but because each such requirement exploited the effects of past segregation and discrimination. In fact, it is fair to say that some of those effects are directly related to discriminatory practices which remain with us even now, notwithstanding that they were declared unconstitutional twenty years ago.

Thus, when black applicants fail to pass standardized tests which are geared to the education norms of schools which exclude them, how can we say that those tests are objective, or fair? When blacks are not able to meet the requirements for on-the-job experience in industries which would not hire them, how can we say that those requirements are objective? The fact is that no requirement for obtaining a job, which is rooted in experiences from which black Americans have been excluded, can be said to be objective and, therefore, fair to blacks. Where such unrealistic standards are set, they must be exposed for what they are and then discarded. To allow such obstacles to exist would only perpetuate the thinly veiled discriminatory devices and further delay the day when truly objective standards can be used to judge a man's ability.

The conclusion is inescapable: So long as black Americans are excluded from the mainstream of American life, it will be the duty of the courts to enforce the Constitution's guarantee of equal protection in ways which prevent the exclusion. Whatever legal remedy is necessary in order to achieve equal opportunity and to provide every child in America with a decent education, it will be the duty of courts to order it. As long as employers refuse to hire qualified blacks because of their color, it will be the duty of the courts to order that they be hired, and where such refusals in the past have resulted in injury, it should be their duty to provide a remedy. *Justice tolerates nothing less than this, and we, as American citizens, should accept nothing less.*

To you who must press forward in the demand for justice in the face of adversity, I can only offer what for me has been good advice:

> Ye shall not respect persons in judgment; but ye shall hear the small as well as the great; ye shall not be afraid on the face of man; for the judgment is God's; and the cause that is too hard for you, bring it unto me, and I will hear it.—Deuteronomy—First Chapter, Seventeenth Verse.

In closing, I would like to turn briefly to a subject which should give us all some cause for concern. Perhaps never before since the Civil War have our institutions of government been subjected to the stresses to which they are being subjected today. Our Constitution is being severely strained, and the power of governmental authority is being abused in a way that, if allowed to go unabated, will surely subvert our form of government and reduce our cherished traditions of freedom to meaningless words of history.

Whenever a democratic system is involved in an unpopular war or allows senseless bias against a group of its citizens to go unchecked, there will be protests and resistance on the part of some of the citizens. And on occasion, those believing strongly in their convictions will sometimes go to excesses to make their point. But our American form of government *was born to protest,* and the founders *of our nation sought to protect forever the right of the people to protest against what they felt was wrong.* When there are excesses, there are laws to protect the people, and there are processes, guaranteed by the Constitution, to protect the wrongdoer. Our judicial system, and therefore our liberties, depend on respect for both the law and the processes designed to protect the lawbreaker. Whenever there is a great erosion of either, our liberties are endangered.

Nothing, then, is more ominous than a powerful government which, out of fear that the national security is endangered, relaxes its respect for the constitutional guarantee of due process to those Americans suspected of crimes. We are not a society which depends on secrecy for its existence. On the contrary, we are a society which depends for its existence on the people's *right to know, open debate, and democratic representation in the councils of government.*

It could not be tolerated, therefore, in a court of law for the American government to refuse to release to an accused man materials which it had obtained through an unauthorized telephone wiretap.

And so I say to you here tonight, rededicate yourselves to the principles of the NAACP as expressed by Dr. W. E. B. DuBois in the first edition of *The Crisis* magazine in 1910: "to stand for the rights of men, irrespective of color or race, for the highest ideals of American democracy." Remembering too the stern advice of Frederick Douglass, when he spoke more than a hundred years ago about the philosophy of reform:

> The whole history of the progress of human liberty shows that all concessions yet made to her august claims, have been born of earnest struggle. The conflict has been exciting, agitating, all-absorbing, and for the time being putting all other tumults to silence. It must do this or it does nothing. *If there is no struggle, there is no progress.* Those who profess to favor freedom and yet deprecate agitation, are men who want crops without plowing up the ground, they want rain without thunder and lightning. They want the ocean without the awful roar of its many waters.

James Weldon Johnson said: "Facing the rising sun, of a new day begun, let us march on, till victory is won."

You and I and others of our fellow Americans are the bearers of this struggle. With strong hearts and free minds, let us press forward.

NOTES

A CRY FOR EQUAL JUSTICE

1. Robert L. Carter, "The Black Lawyer," *The Humanist*, Vol. XXIX, No. 5 (September-October, 1969), pp. 13-14.

2. Bruce McM. Wright, "A View from the Bench," a paper read at Metropolitan Applied Research Center, New York Nity, April 3, 1974. Judge Wright was the black lawyer involved in this episode.

3. John Oliver Killens, *Black Man's Burden* (New York: Simon and Schuster, 1970), p. 21.

4. This section is based entirely on Walter F. Murphy and C. Herman Pritchett, (eds.), *Courts, Judges and Politics: An Introduction to the Judicial Process* (New York: Random House, 1961).

5. *Ibid.*, p. 155.

6. Victor G. Rosenblum and A. Didrick Castberg, eds., *Cases on Constitutional Law: Political Roles of the Supreme Court* (Homewood, Illinois: The Dorsey Press, 1973), p. 207.

7. A. Leon Higginbotham, Jr., "Racism and the Early American Legal Process," *The Annals of the American Academy of Political and Social Science*, Vol. CCCCVII (May, 1973), p. 15. (hereafter *Annals*).

8. See A. Leon Higginbotham, Jr.'s review of Derrick A. Bell, Jr., *Race, Racism, and American Law* (Boston: Little, Brown & Co., 1973) in *University of Pennsylvania Law Review*, Vol. CXXII, No. 4 (April, 1974), pp. 1044 n-45 n.

9. Haywood Burns, "Racism and American Law," in Robert Lefcourt, ed. *Law Against The People: Essays to Demystify Law, Order and the Courts* (New York: Vintage Books, April, 1971), pp. 50-51.

10. Bell, *op. cit.*, pp. 1-2, 22-23, 57.

11. Higginbotham's review in *University of Pennsylvania Law Review*, pp. 1049-64.

12. Higginbotham, "Racism and the Early American Legal Process," *op. cit.*, pp. 2-17; quotation on p. 16.

13. Carter, *op. cit.*, pp. 12-14.

14. *Ibid.*, p. 13.

15. *Ibid.*, pp. 14-16; Charles Hamilton Houston, "The Need for Negro Lawyers," *Journal of Negro Education*, Vol. IV, No. 1 (January, 1935), p. 51; Bruce McM. Wright, "The Black Judicial Officer and the Black Bar," a

327

paper read at the meeting of the Judicial Council, National Bar Association, Miami Beach, Florida, August 2, 1972.

16. Walter J. Leonard, "The Development of the Black Bar," *Annals*, pp. 134-36.

17. Kenneth S. Tollett, "Black Lawyers, Their Education, and the Black Community," *Howard Law Journal*, Vol. XVII, No. 2 (Winter, 1972), pp. 328-29.

18. *Ibid.*, p. 329.

19. Leonard, *op. cit.*, p. 137, and his "George Lewis Ruffin: The First to Dream," *Harvard Law School Bulletin*, Vol. XXII, No. 3 (February, 1971), pp. 38-39.

20. Leonard, "The Development of the Black Bar," *op. cit.*, p. 137.

21. Tollett, *op. cit.*, pp. 329-31. See Appendix.

22. *Ibid.*, pp. 332-39; Edward B. Toles, "Fifty Years of Progress for Black Lawyers," *50th Anniversary Program* (Kansas City: National Bar Association, n.d.), p. 33.

23. Harry T. Edwards, "A New Role for the Black Law Graduate—A Reality of an Illusion?"*Michigan Law Review*, Vol. LXIX (August, 1971), pp. 1407-23.

24. Acel Moore, "Black Judges, Police—But Few Prosecutors," Philadelphia *Inquirer*, July 21, 1974.

25. "The Black Judge in America: A Statistical Profile," *Judicature*, Vol. LVII, No. 1 (June-July, 1973), pp. 18-20.

26. Regina A. Davis, *A Preliminary Report of the Experiences of the Minority Judiciary in the City of New York.* A Report Prepared for the Coalition of Concerned Black Americans (New York: The Coalition, August, 1974), p. 9.

27. Beverly Blair Cook, "Black Representation in the Third Branch," *The Black Law Journal*, Vol. I, No. 3 (Winter, 1971), pp. 260-79.

28. Beverly Blair Cook, "Black Representation In the Third Branch," a paper read at the meeting of the Judicial Council, National Bar Association, Memphis, Tennessee, April 21, 1972.

29. *National Bar Association Judicial Council Newsletter,* Vol. I, No. 2 (July, 1972), pp. 2,8.

30. Gilbert Ware, "Black Judges, White Justice," *New York Law Journal,* August 13, 1971; Gilbert Ware, ed., "Proceedings: Founding Convention of the Judicial Council of the National Bar Association," *Journal of Public Law,* Vol. XX, No. 2 (1971), pp. 371-442.

31. Interview with George W. Crockett, Jr., judge, Recorder's Court (Detroit), August 2, 1971.

32. Interview with Edward F. Bell, judge, Wayne County (Detroit) Circuit Court, August 3, 1971. His comments at the Symposium on the Black Lawyer in America Today are reported in "The Black Lawyer and the Judiciary," *Harvard Law Bulletin, op. cit.,* p. 31.

33. W. Haywood Burns, "The Role of the Black Bar in Black People's Struggle for Social Justice," in Christine Philpot Clark, ed., *Minority Opportunities in Law for Blacks, Puerto Ricans, & Chicanos* (New York: Law Journal Press, 1974), p. 190.

34. "National Bar Association Position Statement," *The National Bar Bulletin*, Vol. I, No. 4 (Spring-Summer, 1969), pp. 1-2.

35. Derrick A. Bell, Jr., *Brief of the National Conference of Black Lawyers Amicus Curiae in Support of Respondents in DeFunis* v. *Odegaard in the Supreme Court of the United States*, October Term, 1973, pp. 21-22.

36. Trenchant articles about the DeFunis case, written by Derrick A. Bell, Jr., and Walter Leonard, and transcripts of oral arguments before the Supreme Court and the opinion of the Supreme Court of the State of Washington appear in *The Black Law Journal*, Vol. III, No. 3 (1974). See also Gilbert Ware, "The Fallacy of Reverse Discrimination," *Encore American & Worldwide News*, (April, 1975), pp. 8, 10, 14.

37. "Lawyers Charge Bar Exam Racism," San Francisco *Chronicle*, August 1, 1973, p. 4, and also "The Report of the Philadelphia Bar Association Special Committee on Pennsylvania Bar Admission Procedures— Racial Discrimination in Administration of the Pennsylvania Bar Examination," *Temple Law Quarterly*, Vol. XLIV, No. 2 (Winter, 1971), pp. 141-258, and "Southern Lawyers: Blacks & The Bar," *Civil Liberties* (March, 1974), pp. 1-2.

38. Kellis E. Parker and Betty J. Stebman, "Legal Education for Blacks," *Annals*, p. 152.

39. Discussion with Lennox S. Hinds, national director of the National Conference of Black Lawyers, and Justice Robert N. C. Nix, Jr., chairman of the Judicial Council, National Bar Association, in Philadelphia, Pennsylvania, February 21, 1974. See *Attica: The Official Report of the New York State Special Commission on Attica* (New York: Bantam Books, September, 1972).

40. Burns, "The Role of the Black Bar," *op. cit.*, pp. 189-90; also NCBL, *The Problem—The Solution* (n.d.); NCBL 1973 Activities Report (December 5, 1973); Lennox S. Hinds, "A National Legal Network: Organizing for Change; Black Lawyers and the Criminal Justice System," *The Black Law Journal*, Vol. III, No. 1 (Spring 1973), pp. 96-102. A widespread assumption is that reform of the civilian system is sufficient to ensure equal justice. The assumption, however, is mistaken and dangerous. To be effective, reform must also cover the military system, which is also racist. Gilbert Ware, "Spider Webs & Racism in the Armed Forces," *The Urban League News* (April 1, 1973), p. 5; and *Report of the Task Force on the Administration of Military Justice in the Armed Forces*, Vol. I (Washington: Department of Defense, November 30, 1972).

41. "National Bar Association Position Statement," *op. cit.*, pp. 1-2.

42. Raymond Pace Alexander, "The National Bar Association—Its Aims

and Purposes," *National Bar Journal,* Vol. I, No. 1 (July, 1941), pp. 1-2.

43. These bar members included Judge Wendell E. Green, Judge Albert George, C. Francis Stradford, Jesse N. Baker, William H. Haynes, George C. Adams, Edward H. Wright, and Richard E. Westbrooks. See Toles, *op. cit.,* p. 23.

44. The other officers were Charles H. Calloway, vice-president, Wendell E. Green, secretary, and Charles P. Howard, assistant secretary. The other founders were S. Joe Brown, Gertrude E. Bush, James B. Morris, C. Francis Stradford, Jesse N. Baker, William H. Haynes, George C. Adams, and L. Amasa Knox. *Ibid.,* p. 24.

45. *Ibid.,* p. 25.

46. Alexander, *op. cit.,* p. 4.

47. Revius O. Ortique, Jr., "The National Bar Association—Not Just an Option," *Judicature,* Vol. LIII, No. 9 (April-May, 1970), p. 392.

48. Alexander, *op cit.,* pp. 5-15. The primary organizational resistance to racism has been provided by the National Association for the Advancement of Colored People, as is generally known and conceded. See, for example, William H. Hastie, "Toward an Equalitarian Legal Order, 1930-1950," *Annals,* pp. 18-31. But our focal point is the organized black bar.

49. "National Bar Day," *National Bar Journal,* Vol. I, No. 1 (July, 1941), pp. 89-90. Also Henry J. Richardson, "Report of the Legal Aid Division of the National Bar Association, Inc.," *ibid.,* pp. 130-41, and "Appointing Counsel to Defend Indigents," *National Bar Journal,* Vol. II, No. 1 (June, 1944), pp. 78-79, which reveal the NBA's early concern about a serious problem that is still with us, namely, providing for the adequate defense of the indigent.

50. Charles W. Anderson, Jr., "The South's Challenge to the Negro Lawyer," *National Bar Journal,* Vol. III, No. 1 (March, 1945), pp. 39-41.

51. Earl B. Dickerson, "Over the President's Desk," *National Bar Journal,* Vol. V, No. 3 (September, 1947), pp. 360-61.

52. Earl B. Dickerson, "Over the President's Desk," *National Bar Journal,* Vol. V, No. 4 (December, 1947), pp. 455-56.

53. Ortique, *op. cit.,* p. 392.

54. Bell, *Race, Racism and American Law, op. cit.,* p. xxxix; Tollett, *op. cit.,* p. 349.

55. Joseph C. Howard, "Why We Organize," *Journal of Public Law, op. cit.,* p. 382.

56. Interview with George W. Crockett, Jr., judge, Recorder's Court (Detroit), August 2, 1971.

57. Charlotte and Wolf Leslau, *African Proverbs* (Mount Vernon: The Peter Pauper Press, 1962), p. 23.

58. See Gilbert Ware, "More Than a Judge," *Encore American & Worldwide News* (February 3, 1975), pp. 15-16; also William K. Stevens, "Black Judges Termed Sympathetic to Accused," New York *Times,* Feb-

ruary 19, 1974; William Raspberry, "Judge . . . and Judgment," Washington *Post*, November 29, 1971, and "Judgment of the Jurist," Washington
Post, December 1, 1971; Michele Washington, "Black Judges in White
America," *The Black Law Journal*, Vol. I, No. 3 (Winter, 1971), pp. 241-245,
and Warner Smith, "George W. Crockett: The Opener," *ibid.*, pp. 247-59.

59. Frances E. W. Harper, "The Slave Auction," in Bradford Chambers
and Rebecca Moon, eds., *Right On! An Anthology of Black Literature* (New
York: New American Library, 1970), p. 42.

60. Higginbotham, "Racism and the Early American Legal Process," *op.
cit.*, p. 17.

61. *Ibid.*

62. Arna Bontemps and Langston Hughes, *The Book of Negro Folklore*
(New York: Dodd, Mead & Co., 1958), p. 291; see also in Jean Wagner, *Black
Poets of the United States: From Paul Lawrence Dunbar to Langston Hughes*
(Urbana: University of Illinois Press, 1973), p. 28. Also Gilbert Ware,
"Auction Block Justice," *Focus*, Vol. II, No. 9 (July, 1974), pp. 4-5. *Focus* is
published by the Joint Center for Political Studies, Washington, D.C.

I. RACE, JUSTICE, AND POLITICS

1. William K. Stevens, "Black Judges Termed Sympathetic to Accused,"
New York *Times*, February 19, 1974.

2. Richard Quinney, *The Social Reality of Crime* (Boston: Little, Brown
and Company, 1970), pp. 4, 11, 15-22; quotation on p. 18.

3. David Easton, *The Political System* (New York: Alfred A. Knopf,
1953); Glendon A. Schubert, *Judicial Policy-Making: The Political Role of the
Courts* (Glenview, Illinois: Scott, Foresman and Company, 1964); Sheldon
Goldman and Thomas P. Jahnige, *The Federal Courts as a Political System*
(New York: Harper & Row, 1971); Kenneth N. Vines and Herbert Jacob,
Studies in Judicial Politics (New Orleans: Tulane University, 1963); and
Jonathon D. Casper, *The Politics of Civil Liberties* (New York: Harper & Row,
Publishers, 1972).

4. Harold Laswell, *Politics: Who Gets What, When, and How* (New York:
McGraw-Hill, 1936).

5. Jerome Frank, *Courts on Trial: Myth and Reality in American Justice*
(Princeton: Princeton University Press, 1973), pp. 8-9.

6. Herbert Jacob, *Urban Justice: Law and Order in American Cities*
(Englewood Cliffs: Prentice-Hall, Inc. 1973), p. 3.

7. *Ibid.*, pp. 5-8. Also Schubert, *op. cit.*, pp. 7-17.

8. Herbert Jacob, *Justice in America: Courts, Lawyers and the Judicial
Process* (Boston: Little, Brown and Company, 1972), pp. 13-17.

9. Duane Lockard, *The Politics of State and Local Government* (New York:

The Macmillan Company, 1963), pp. 485-93. On the importance of lower courts in the judicial-political process, see Kenneth M. Dolbeare, *Trial Courts in Urban Politics* (New York: John Wiley & Sons, Inc., 1967).

10. Interview with Joseph C. Howard, judge, Supreme Bench of Baltimore City, August 4, 1971.

11. Interviews with Milton B. Allen, state's attorney of Baltimore City, January 27, 1974, and June 24, 1974. ,

12. Richard A. Watson and Rondal G. Downing, *The Politics of the Bench and the Bar: Judicial Selection Under the Missouri Nonpartisan Court Plan* (New York: John Wiley and Sons, Inc., 1969), pp. 2, 3, 349.

13. Jacob, *Justice in America, op. cit.,* pp. 110-111. Fifteen states have adopted the plan in whole or in part, and four others use it voluntarily.

14. Joel B. Grossman, "The Selection of Judges," in Herbert Jacob, ed., *Law, Politics, and the Federal Courts* (Boston: Little, Brown and Company, 1967), pp. 51-72.

15. *The National Bar Bulletin,* (October-December, 1971), p. 1.

16. *National Bar Association Judicial Council Newsletter,* Vol. I, No. 2 (July, 1972), p. 2, and Beverly Blair Cook, "Black Representation in the Third Branch," a paper read at the meeting of the Judicial Council, Memphis, Tennessee, April 21, 1972; and see Joel B. Grossman, *Lawyers and Judges: The ABA and the Politics of Judicial Selection* (New York: John Wiley and Sons, Inc., 1965).

17. Gayle Nelson, *National Roster of Black Elected Officials,* Vol. IV (Washington: Joint Center for Political Studies, April 1974), pp. v-xxvii. See also Chuck Stone, *Black Political Power in America,* rev. ed. (New York: A Delta Book, 1970).

18. Harold Baron, with Harriet Stulman, Richard Rothstein, and Rennard Davis, "Black Powerlessness in Chicago," in Edward S. Greenberg, Neal Milner, and David J. Olson, eds., *Black Politics: The Inevitability of Conflict* (New York: Holt, Rinehart and Winston, Inc., 1971), pp. 105-15.

19. Vernon Jarrett, "Take-over by Blacks Is Far Off," Philadelphia *Inquirer,* December 26, 1973, p. 11-A.

20. Francis Fox Piven and Richard A. Cloward, "Black Control of Cities," in Greenberg *et al., op. cit.,* pp. 118-30.

21. Edward F. Bell, "The Black Lawyer and The Judiciary," *Harvard Law School Bulletin,* Vol. XXII, No. 3 (February, 1971), p. 31.

22. Charles L. Sanders, "Detroit's Rebel Judge Crockett," *Ebony,* Vol. XXIV, No. 10 (August, 1969), pp. 114-115. Also James H. Dygert, "The Black Thoughts of Judge Crockett," *Esquire,* Vol. LIV, No. 6 (December, 1970), p. 120 ff.

23. George W. Crockett, Jr., "A Black Judge Speaks," *Judicature,* Vol. LIII, No. 9 (April-May, 1970), p. 363.

24. Warner Smith, "George W. Crockett: The Opener," *The Black Law Journal,* Vol. I, No. 3 (Winter, 1971), pp. 256-58; quotation on p. 257.

25. Sanders, *op. cit.*, pp. 116, 118.

26. Crockett, *op. cit.,* pp. 364-65. The Detroit People Against Racism agreed, saying that the press questioned "Crockett's legitimacy" when he used his power to protect black people's rights. "Hearing All About It," *Civil Rights Digest* (Summer, 1969), p. 28.

27. Sanders, *op. cit.,* p. 116.

28. Smith, *op. cit.,* pp. 256-57.

29. George W. Crockett, Jr., "The Role of the Black Judge," *Journal of Public Law,* Vol. XX, No. 2, (1971), pp. 397-400.

II. CRIMINAL JUSTICE AND BLACKS

1. Daniel J. Freed, "The Nonsystem of Criminal Justice," in James S. Campbell, Joseph R. Sahid, and David P. Stang, *Law and Order Reconsidered,* A Staff Report to the National Commission on the Causes and Prevention of Violence (Washington: U.S. Government Printing Office, 1969), pp. 265-75. For a perceptive overview of law and justice in America, see Duane Lockard, *The Perverted Priorities of American Politics* (New York: The Macmillan Company, 1971), pp. 168-225.

2. See Edwin M. Schur, *Our Criminal Society: The Social and Legal Sources of Crime in America* (Englewood Cliffs: Prentice-Hall, Inc., 1969), pp. 191-228.

3. The Conference of Mayors, the National League of Cities, and the National Urban Coalition are several of the critics of federal efforts to help the states and cities combat crime. See, for example, *Law and Disorder II: State Planning and Programming Under Title I of the Omnibus Crime Control and Safe Streets Act of 1968* (Washington: National Urban Coalition, 1970).

4. The President's Commission on Law Enforcement and the Administration of Justice, *Task Force Report: The Courts.* A Report Prepared by the Task Force on 3the Administration of Justice (Washington: U.S. Government Printing Office, 1967), p. 9. But this description of the sequence of criminal proceedings is drawn from Herbert Jacob, *Justice in America: Courts, Lawyers and the Judicial Process* (Boston: Little, Brown and Company, 1972), pp. 164-80, except as noted.

5. *Task Force Report: The Courts, op. cit.,* pp. 37-40. In March, 1970, there were 160,863 inmates in jail in America, and 83,079 had not been convicted of crimes. *Crime and the Law* (Washington: Congressional Quarterly, Inc., 1971), p. 12.

6. The negotiated guilty plea is considered in *Task Force Report: The Courts, op. cit.,* pp. 4-13, and in *The Challenge of Crime in a Free Society.* A Report by the President's Commission on Law Enforcement and the

Administration of Justice (Washington: U.S. Government Printing Office, February, 1967), pp. 134-37.

7. These administrative techniques are given thorough treatment in The National Advisory Commission on Criminal Justice Standards and Goals, *Courts*. A Report by the Task Force on Courts (Washington: U.S. Government Printing Office, 1973), Chapters 1-3.

8. *Ibid.*, pp. 13-14.

9. Marvin E. Frankel, *Criminal Sentences: Law Without Order* (New York: Hill and Wang, 1973). For recommended changes in sentencing procedures, see James Drew, "Judicial Discretion and the Sentencing Process," *Howard Law Journal*, Vol. XVII, No. 4 (1973), pp. 858-942.

10. A concise explanation of appellate action is given in Jacob, *op. cit.*, pp. 188-206.

11. Task Force on Corrections, *Task Force Report: Corrections*. A Report to the President's Commission on Law Enforcement and the Administration of Justice (Washington: U.S. Government Printing Office, 1967), pp. 1-4; National Advisory Commission on Criminal Justice Standards and Goals, *Corrections* (Washington: U.S. Government Printing Office, 1973); Edith Elizabeth Flynn, "Jails and Criminals Justice," in LLoyd O. Ohlin, ed., *Prisoners in America* (Englewood Cliffs: Prentice-Hall, Inc., 1973), pp. 49-88; *Soledad Brother: The Prison Letters of George Jackson* (New York: Bantam Books, Inc., 1970); *Attica: The Official Report of the New York State Special Commission on Attica* (New York: Bantam Books, Inc., 1972); and also Eldridge Cleaver, *Soul on Ice* (New York: Dell Publishing Co., Inc., 1970).

12. Eldridge Cleaver, "Post-Prison Writings and Speeches," in Virginia B. Ermer and John H. Strange, eds., *Blacks and Bureaucracy: Readings in the Problems and Politics of Change* (New York: Thomas Y. Crowell Company, 1972), pp. 30-31.

13. Jacob, *op. cit.*, pp. 178-179.

14. Lois G. Forer, *No One Will Lissen: How Our Legal System Brutalizes the Youthful Poor* (New York: Grosset & Dunlap, 1970), pp. 28-36. As for the rights of juveniles, see Beatrice Levidow "Overdue Process for Juveniles: For the Retroactive Restoration of Constitutional Rights," *Howard Law Journal*, Vol. XVII, No. 1 (1971), pp. 402-34. Also National Institute of Mental Health, *The Juvenile Court: A Status Report*. A Report Prepared by the Center for Studies of Crime and Delinquency (Washington: U.S. Government Printing Office, 1972); The President's Commission on Law Enforcement and the Administration of Justice, *Juvenile Delinquency and Youth Crime*. A Report Prepared by the Task Force on Juvenile Delinquency (Washington: U.S. Government Printing Office, 1967); Lisa A. Richette, *The Throwaway Children* (New York: Dell Publishing Co., Inc. 1969); LaMar T. Empey, *"Juvenile Justice Reform: Diversion, Due Process, and Deinstitutionalization,"* in Ohlin, *op. cit.*, pp. 13-48.

15. *The Challenge of Crime in a Free Society, op. cit.*, pp. 79-80.

16. *Corrections, op. cit.*, p. 249.

17. *The Challenge of Crime in a Free Society, op. cit.*, pp. 80-81.

18. *Ibid.*, p. 81.

19. *Corrections, op. cit.*, pp. 247-48.

20. Although they are not without flaws, self-surveys are improving our understanding of the actual crime extent. Schur, *op. cit.*, pp. 36-39; Quinney, *op. cit.*, pp. 217-22; Roger Hood and Richard Sparks, *Key Issues in Criminology,* (New York: McGraw-Hill Book Company, 1970), pp. 11-79.

21. Schur, *op. cit.*, pp. 45-46.

22. *Ibid.*, pp. 46-47.

23. Ramsey Clark, *Crime in America: Observations on Its Nature, Causes, Prevention and Control* (New York: Simon and Schuster, 1970), pp. 35-43; quotation on p. 42.

24. *Ibid.*, pp. 56-66.

25. *Ibid.*, pp. 66-67.

26. William Ryan, *Blaming the Victim* (New York: Vintage Books, 1972).

27. *Report of the National Advisory Commission on Civil Disorders* (New York: Bantam Books, 1968); Southern Regional Council, *Southern Justice: An Indictment* (Atlanta: The Council, n.d.); U.S. Commission on Civil Rights, *Justice* (Washington: U.S. Government Printing Office, 1961) (The commission's superb reports are too numerous even to mention but are required readings in this matter of equality.); Andrew Overby, "Discrimination Against Minority Groups," in Leon Radzinowicz and Marvin E. Wolfgang, eds., *The Criminal in the Arms of the Law,* Vol. II (New York: Basic Books, Inc., Publishers, 1971), pp. 569-81.

28. Haywood Burns, "Can A Black Man Get a Fair Trial in This Country?" *New York Times Magazine* (July 12, 1970). A young black lawyer told of a Gaston County, Florida, courtroom where above the clerk's desk Martin Luther King, Jr., appears in caricature, sitting in a rocking chair, holding a mint julep. The inscription: "Is this what Martin Luther Coon has in mind?" Imagine yourself to be black and entering that courtroom in any capacity at all. The remarks were made at the workshop "Racism in Criminal Court Proceedings," held at the annual meeting of the Judicial Council of the National Bar Association, Atlanta, George, August 5, 1971.

29. Donald L. Barlett and James B. Steele's series "Crime and Injustice" appeared in the Philadelphia *Inquirer* during the week of February 18, 1973. Their findings were published subsequently in a special supplement of that newspaper.

30. Burns, *op. cit.*

31. Len Lear, "Youth Study Center's Heating System on Full Blast 12 Months a Year for Last Five Years," Philadelphia *Tribune,* July 1, 1975, p. 1.

32. John Guinther's remarks were delivered to the Pennsylvania Joint

Council on the Criminal Justice System, Allentown, Pennsylvania, February 6, 1975. See his article, "A Child's Garden of Horrors," *Philadelphia Magazine*, Vol. LXVI, No. 3 (March, 1975), pp. 93, 140.

33. Lear, *op. cit.*, p. 1.

34. See Forer, *op. cit.*; Richette, *op. cit.*; and Marvin Wolfgang, Robert M. Siglio, and Thorsten Sellin, *Delinquency in a Birth Cohort* (Chicago: The University of Chicago Press, 1972), pp. 220-26.

III. CIVIL JUSTICE AND BLACKS

1. Jerome E. Carlin, Jan Howard, and Heldon L. Messinger, *Civil Justice and the Poor: Issues for Sociological Research*, (New York: Russell Sage Foundation, 1967), pp. 4-19.

2. Patricia M. Wald and Robert L. Wald, "Law and the Grievances of the Poor," in James S. Campbell, Joseph R. Sahid, and David P. Stang, *Law and Order Reconsidered*, a Staff Report to the National Commission on the Causes and Prevention of Violence (Washington: U.S. Government Printing Office, 1969), pp. 27-28.

3. *Ibid.*, pp. 28-29.

4. *Ibid.*, pp. 30-33.

5. Leonard Downie, Jr., *Justice Denied: The Case for Reform of the Courts* (Baltimore: Penguin Books, Inc., 1973), p. 91.

6. *Ibid.*, pp. 91-94.

7. Wald and Wald, *op. cit.*, pp. 33-34.

8. Robert P. Bass, quoted in Martin Mayer, *The Lawyers* (New York: Dell Publishing Co., Inc., July 1970), p. 261.

9. Wald and Wald, *op. cit.*, pp. 35-36.

10. *Ibid.*, pp. 37-38.

11. Carlin *et al.*, *op. cit.*, pp. 49-51; quotation on p. 51.

12. Mayer, *op. cit.*, pp. 272-76. Legal aid also was caught in the political storm that engulfed the anti-poverty program: John C. Donovan, *The Politics of Poverty*, 2d ed. (Indianapolis: The Bobbs-Merrill Company, Inc., 1973).

13. Carlin *et al.*, *op. cit.*, pp. 47-48.

14. *Ibid.*, p. 55.

15. Herbert Jacob, *Urban Justice: Law and Order in American Cities* (Englewood Cliffs: Prentice Hall, Inc., 1973), p. 39.

16. F. Raymond Marks, Kirk Leswing, and Barbara A. Fortinsky, *The Lawyer, The Public, and Professional Responsibility* (Chicago: American Bar Foundation, 1972), pp. 20, 41, 186-97.

17. Jacob, *op. cit.*, pp. 47-51.

18. Lewis Mayers, *The American Legal System: The Administration of Jus-*

tice in the United States by Judicial, Administrative, Military and Arbitral Tribunals, rev. ed. (New York: Harper & Row, Publishers, 1964), pp. 151-83.

19. This discussion of civil proceedings is based on Jacob, *op. cit.*, pp. 119-32.

20. *Report of the National Advisory Commission on Civil Disorders* (New York: Bantam Books, 1968), p. 274. Perhaps the best account of consumer exploitation is David Caplovitz, *The Poor Pay More* (New York: The Free Press, 1967), but see also Gerald Leinwand, ed. *The Consumer* (New York: Pocket Books, 1970). For a further consideration of the point about the intermingling of disorders, civil and criminal justice, and politics, see Gilbert Ware, "Spiro Agnew: Firebrand of the Word," *New South,* Vol. XXVI, No. 3 (Summer, 1971), pp. 30-48, and "Agnew's Corruption Founded in Racism," *Southern Voices,* Vol. I, No. 4 (October-November, 1974), pp. 34-36.

21. Downie, *op. cit.*, pp. 75-76.

22. Samuel F. Yette, *The Choice: The Issue of Black Survival in America* (New York: G. P. Putnam's Sons, 1971), pp. 190-91; quotation on p. 191.

23. Regarding governmental crimes against blacks, see Jethro K. Lieberman, *How the Government Breaks the Law* (New York: Stein and Day, 1972), pp. 126-38.

24. Dorothy B. James, *Poverty, Politics, and Change* (Englewood Cliffs: Prentice-Hall, Inc., 1972), pp. 9-13.

25. Alan Batchelder, "Poverty: The Special Case of the Negro," in Burton A. Weisbrod, ed., *The Economics of Poverty: An American Paradox* (Englewood Cliffs: Prentice-Hall, Inc., 1965), p. 101.

26. Austin Scott, "Black Job Picture Called 'Explosive,' " *Washington Post,* (June 2, 1974), pp. 1, 2.

27. Haywood Burns, "Can a Black Man Get a Fair Trial in This Country?," New York Times Magazine (July 12, 1970).

28. Wald and Wald, *op. cit.*, pp. 39-43.

29. Marks *et al., op. cit.*, p. 186.

30. William K. Stevens, "Black Judges Termed Sympathetic to Accused," New York *Times* (February 19, 1974).

31. Quoted in Downie, *op. cit.*, p. 74.

32. Sterling D. Spero and Abram L. Harris, *The Black Worker* (New York: Atheneum, 1969), pp. 3-15. See also Arthur M. Ross, "The Negro in the American Economy," in Arthur M. Ross and Herbert Hill, eds., *Employment, Race, and Poverty* (New York: Harcourt, Brace, World, Inc., 1967), pp. 3-9.

33. U.S. Commission on Civil Rights, *Statement on Affirmative Action for Equal Employment Opportunities* (Washington: U.S. Government Printing Office, 1973), p. 2.

34. Herbert Hill, "The New Judicial Perception of Employment Discrimination: Litigation Under Title VII of the Civil Rights Act of 1964," *University of Colorado Law Review,* Vol. XLIII, No. 3 (March, 1972), pp.

244-45. Unemployment figures reported by the government do not measure accurately the extent of black joblessness, for they do not take into account a group in which blacks undoubtedly are prominent—namely, the "invisible army of unemployed." This body, says Professor Charles C. Killingsworth, are people who are willing and able to work but were forced out of the labor market so long ago that discouragement prevents their searching for work and thus being included in the labor force. Tom Kahn, "The Economics of Inequality," in Louis A. Berman, Joyce L. Kornbluh, and J. A. Miller, eds., *Negroes and Jobs: A Book of Readings*, 2d printing (Ann Arbor: The University of Michigan Press, 1969), p. 19. Government officials admit the validity of Killingsworth's concept as it pertains to blacks. See Harry A. Ploski and Ernest Kaiser, *AFRO USA: A Reference Work on the Black Experience* (New York: Bellwether Publishing Company, Inc., 1971), p. 416.

35. A. H. Raskin, "The Unlucky 5.8%, Translated," New York *Times* (October 6, 1974).

36. Kahn, *op. cit.*, pp. 20-23; quotation on p. 21 (author's italics).

37. Yette, *op. cit.*, p. 18.

38. Hill, *op. cit.*, and see U.S. Commission on Civil Rights, *Federal Civil Rights Enforcement Effort* (Washington: U.S. Government Printing Office, 1970), pp. 55-423.

39. Hill, *op. cit.*, pp. 246-47, 251-54, 256-57.

40. Herbert Hill, "Preferential Hiring: Correcting the Demerit System," *Social Policy* (July-August, 1973), pp. 96-102.

41. Hill, "The New Judicial Perception of Employment Discrimination," *op. cit.*, pp. 262-64.

42. *Statement on Affirmative Action for Equal Employment Opportunities, op. cit.*, pp. 7-8.

43. Herbert Hill, "The Racial Practices of Organized Labor—The Age of Gompers and After," in Ross and Hill *op. cit.*, pp. 365-402. On racism in public employment civilian and non-civilian, see U. S. Commission on Civil Rights, *Employment* (Washington: U.S. Government Printing Office, 1961), and *For All The People . . . By All the People: A Report on Equal Opportunity In State and Local Government* (Washington: U.S. Government Printing Office, 1969).

44. Herbert Hill, "Racism and Organized Labor," *New School Bulletin* (reprint), Vol. XXVIII, No. 6 (February 8, 1971).

45. William B. Gould, "Black Workers Inside the House of Labor," *The Annals of the American Academy of Political and Social Science*, Vol. CCCCVII (May, 1973), pp. 78-90 (hereafter *Annals*).

46. *Statement on Affirmatives for Equal Employment Opportunities, op. cit.*, p. 3.

47. Bernard J. Frieden, "Housing and National Urban Goals: Old

Policies and New Realities," in James Q. Wilson, ed., *The Metropolitan Enigma: Inquiries into the Nature and Dimensions of America's "Urban Crisis"* (Washington: Chamber of Commerce of the United States, 1967), pp. 157-58.

48. Samuel Lubell, *The Hidden Crisis in American Politics* (New York: W. W. Norton & Co., Inc., 1970), p. 98.

49. Ashley A. Foard and Hilbert Fefferman, "Federal Urban Renewal Legislation," in James Q. Wilson, ed., *Urban Renewal: The Record and the Controversy* (Cambridge: M.I.T. Press, 1966), pp. 96-101. The Housing and Community Development Act of 1974 replaces categorical aid for urban renewal with block grants, giving local officials greater discretion in the use of federal funds. "Housing Bill: Opportunity and Challenge," *Focus*, Vol. II, No. 11 (September, 1974), p. 3.

50. William L. Slayton, "The Operation and Achievements of the Urban Renewal Program," in Wilson, *Urban Renewal, op. cit.*, p. 208, and for an explanation of the program, pp. 195-202.

51. Herbert J. Gans, "The Failure of Urban Renewal," in *ibid.*, pp. 539-46.

52. Wilton S. Sogg and Warren Wertheimer, "Legal and Governmental Issues in Urban Renewal," in *ibid.*, pp. 126-35.

53. Gans, *op. cit.*, p. 539-42; quotations on pp. 539, 541. Martin Anderson also comments on the "strong racial overtones" of urban renewal; see *The Federal Bulldozer: A Critical Analysis of Urban Renewal*, 1949-1962 (Cambridge: M.I.T. Press, 1964), pp. 7-8. Charles Abrams considers the virtues and vices of urban renewal in *The City is the Frontier*, (New York: Harper Colophon Books, 1967).

54. Gans, *op. cit.*, pp. 541-42, and *Report of the National Advisory Commission of Civil Disorders, op. cit.*, pp. 468-72.

55. Anthony Downs, *Urban Problems and Prospects* (Chicago: Markham Publishing Company, 1970), p. 116.

56. U.S. Commission on Civil Rights, *Understanding Fair Housing* (Washington: U.S. Government Printing Office, 1973), p. 18, and *Equal Opportunity in Suburbia* (Washington: The Commission, July, 1974); Simpson F. Lawson, *Above Property Rights,* a report prepared for the U.S. Commission on Civil Rights (Washington: U.S. Government Printing Office, 1973).

57. U.S. Commission on Civil Rights, *Housing* (Washington: U.S. Government Printing Office, 1961), pp. 2-3, 16, 23-25, and *Federal Civil Rights Enforcement Effort, op. cit.*, pp. 424-546.

58. Senator Abraham A. Ribicoff, "The Future of School Integration in the United States," *Journal of Law and Education*, Vol. I, No. 1 (February, 1972), pp. 9-10, 13. Also David E. Wagoner, "Where School Desegregation Isn't Happening," *The Education Digest,* Vol. XXXVII, No. 4 (December, 1971), pp. 21-24. For perspective on school segregation, see Albert P.

Blaustein and Clarence Clyde Ferguson, *Desegregation and the Law: The Meaning and Effect of the School Segregation Cases* (New Brunswick: Rutgers University Press, 1957); various reports by the U.S. Commission of Civil Rights, including *Education* (1961), *Racial Isolation in the Public Schools* (1967), *Public Education* (1963 and 1964), *Southern School Desegregation* (July, 1967); Jack Greenberg, *Race Relations and American Law* (New York: Columbia University Press, 1959); Virgil A. Clift, Archibald W. Anderson, and H. Gordon Hullfish, *Negro Education in America: Its Adequacy, Problems, and Needs* (New York: Harper & Brothers, 1962): Robbins L. Gates, *The Making of Massive Resistance: Virginia's Politics of Public School Desegregation, 1954-1956* (Chapel Hill: The University of North Carolina Press, 1962); Dean W. Determan and Gilbert Ware, "New Dimensions in Education: Title VI of the Civil Rights Act of 1964," *The Journal of Negro Education,* Vol. XXXC, No. 1. (Winter, 1966), pp. 5-10. The problem of racism in higher education merits the attention given to it by Nelson H. Harris, "Desegregation in Institutions of Higher Learning," in Clift *et al.*, eds., *op. cit.*, pp. 235-50; U.S. Commission on Civil Rights, *Equal Protection of the Laws in Public Higher Education* (Washington: U.S. Government Printing Office, 1961); Gilbert Ware and Dean W. Determan, "The Federal Dollar, The Negro College, and The Negro Student," *The Journal of Negro Education,* Vol. XXXV, No. 4 (Fall, 1966), pp. 459-68.

59.   Ribicoff, *op. cit.*, pp. 10, 14-19.

60.   U.S. Commission on Civil Rights, *The Diminishing Barrier: A Report on School Desegregation in Nine Communities* (Washington: U.S. Government Printing Office, 1972), pp. 1-2.

61.   Marian Wright Edelman, "Southern School Desegregation, 1954-1973: A Judicial-Political Overview," *Annals,* p. 35.

62.   Reubin O'D. Askew, "Busing Is Not the Issue," in *Inequality in Education* (Cambridge: The Harvard Center for Law and Education, March, 1972), pp. 3-4.

63.   "The Cities: Boston Rhetoric Is No Help" New York *Times* (October 13, 1974), p. F-2.; *Brown* v. *Board of Education of Topeka,* 347 U.S. 483 (1954).

64.   Edelman, *op. cit.*, pp. 31-41.

65.   U.S. Commission on Civil Rights, *Your Child and Busing* (Washington: The Commission, May, 1972), pp. 2-3. Schools are not the only facilities which are segregated largely because of housing patterns. Hospitals, libraries, parks, and stores are additional such facilities. Karl E. Taeuber and Alma F. Taeuber, *Negroes in Cities: Residential Segregation and Neighborhood Change* (New York: Atheneum, 1969), p. 1.

66.   William L. Taylor, "Metropolitan-Wide Desegregation," in *Inequality in Education, op. cit.*, pp. 45-47; quotations on pp. 46 and 47. Obscured by the turmoil about busing are the advantages of metropolitan desegregation—namely, that it may be easier to effectuate than single-district

desegregation, it holds promise for stable integration, it exceeds simple integration in educational merit, and it promotes school accountability and community participation. *Ibid.*, pp. 47-49.

    67.   *Davis* v. *School District of Pontiac, Inc.*, 309 F. Supp 734 (1970). See Robert J. Herbst, "The Legal Struggle to Integrate Schools in the North," *The Annals, op. cit.*, pp. 43-62.